Jack the Ripper

Peter Hodgson

PNEUMA SPRINGS PUBLISHING UK

First Published in 2011 by:
Pneuma Springs Publishing

Jack the Ripper

Pneuma Springs

British Library Cataloguing in Publication Data

Hodgson, Peter.
Jack the Ripper : through the mists of time.
1. Jack, the Ripper. 2. Jack, the Ripper--In literature.
3. Jack, the Ripper--In motion pictures. 4. Serial
murders--England--London--History--19th century.
5. London (England)--Social conditions--19th century.
I. Title
364.1'5232'092-dc22

ISBN-13: 9781907728259

Pneuma Springs Publishing
A Subsidiary of Pneuma Springs Ltd.
7 Groveherst Road, Dartford Kent, DA1 5JD.
E: admin@pneumasprings.co.uk
W: www.pneumasprings.co.uk

Jack the Ripper

Through the Mists of Time

Contents

ACKNOWLEDGMENTS (FIRST EDITION)

My gratitude is extended to the following people who have helped me, in one way or another, during the preparation of this book: Professor Sir Christopher Frayling of the Royal College of Art (who kindly allowed me the use of material from his BBC documentary *Timewatch*), Jonathan Evans of the Royal London Hospital, Nick Warren, FRCS, Dr Stuart Priestley, Roger Jackson, Steve Connolley, Stewart Evans, Paul Begg, Ross Strachan, Karl Deakin, Chris Garland, Tony Foley, Andy Aliffe, Robert Ramsden, Dave Wray, Paul Egginton of the British Broadcasting Corporation (for permission to use a still from the 1959 film *Jack the Ripper*), Tony Miller of the Whitechapel Mission (for permission to use the photograph of an 'East London street') and the staff at the Tower Hamlets Local History Archives Department. I am grateful to my wife, Michelle, for her relentless support.

I am grateful for permission to use extracts from Edwin T Woodhall's *Jack the Ripper or When London Walked in Terror* (reprinted by P&D Riley), and *The Last Sherlock Holmes Story* by Michael Dibdin, published by Jonathan Cape. *Reprinted by permission of The Random House Group Ltd.*

A special thank you goes to Warren Cooke for creating the evocative images of Annie Chapman and 'Jack the Ripper'.

Various Film companies have helped to immortalise the infamous Ripper and some of their films appear in this book. I am grateful to: Twentieth Century Fox, Columbia Pictures, Hammer Films, Ambassador Films, Warner Brothers Pictures, Mid-Century Film Productions, Euston Films Ltd, Rowdy Herrington Films, Zenith Productions, Tanglewood Entertainments and Universal Pictures.

I would like to acknowledge various authors whose work I have referred to and in many cases summarised: Mei Trow, John Wilding, Kevin O'Donnell, Shirley Harrison, Paul Begg, Martin Fido, Keith Skinner, Robin Odell, Melvin Harris, Stewart Evans, Paul Gainey, William Beadle, James Tully, Bob Hinton, Bernard Brown, Peter Turnbull, Graham Norton, A P Wolf, Pamela Ball, Peter Underwood, Trevor Marriott, Robert Ressler, John Douglas, Professor David Canter, Austin Mitchelson, Pamela West, Patricia Cornwell, Terrence Lore Smith, Lucius Shepard, R Chetwynd-Hayes, Robert Bloch, Marie Belloc Lowndes, Frederick Dannay, Manfred Lee, William Baring-Gould, Donald McCormick, Dr Dennis Halstead, Leonard Matters, William Stewart, Stephen Knight, Tom Robinson, Walter Dew, Sir Basil Thomson and F A Beaumont.

Finally, I should like to acknowledge Treasure Press whose chapter 'East End Slaughters' – from *Infamous Murders* – is discussed in this book.

FOREWORD TO THE FIRST EDITION

The unsolved crimes committed by the man who became known as 'Jack the Ripper' undoubtedly constitute one of the world's greatest conundrums. Can there ever be a final answer to the question, 'Who was he?' Well, numerous authors and people with more than just a passing interest in the case would answer, 'Yes, the mystery is solved. We know who murdered those unfortunate women in London's East End in 1888.' But to know that a fact is really true, you need to have indisputable evidence that proves 'truth', and with the case of The East End Murderer, The Whitechapel Fiend, Jack the Ripper - or whatever you wish to call him - there is no hard evidence that enables us to say, without the slightest reservation, that a particular person was responsible.

My interest in the murders goes back to when I was a mere lad of fifteen. I remember browsing through several books in the oversize section of the Harris library in Preston and coming across one book that contained a section on the Whitechapel murders. Apart from the chilling name we now associate with those distant crimes, I knew little else. As the years passed by I went from one book to another hoping to find the answer to this fascinating riddle. It was not to be. There was no answer in 1888 and there isn't now.

What is perhaps significant today is that to know the identity of the murderer would probably be something of an anticlimax; it doesn't matter 'who' because the fiction is far more potent than the fact. Having said that, the fog-laden stories with their hollow cries of 'Another 'orrible murder!' - along with the many explanations and theories - have seduced me into becoming an ardent enthusiast of this ongoing saga. Even as I write this introduction, the newspapers are priming readers with details of forthcoming films about the Ripper.

I will always be intrigued by the unanswered questions, and I must point out that I have the greatest respect for the authors and researchers who have diligently searched for that small item of 'lost' material that has brought us closer to another possible solution.

You may be surprised to learn that there is far more information available about the murderer's victims than the man himself. The Ripper murdered at least four women. Their appalling injuries are well documented, and the sites of the crime locations are visited every year by thousands of people from all parts of the globe. Apart from these facts, what can be said about the killer himself? Very little, I'm afraid, but a detailed study of his crimes - the mutilations in particular - have led me to the core of his grotesque fantasies.

This book highlights some of the greatest works, in both fact and fiction, of the Ripper phenomenon. It clearly shows how this deranged serial killer became transformed into an illusory character simply by virtue of his elementary medical know-how. Thanks to the films and the fiction, the real killer has metamorphosed into the 'other' Jack the Ripper. The latter, with his black bag and top hat, is a variant of a real human being, the likes of which are well known today: Peter Sutcliffe and Jeffrey Dahmer, to name just two.

During the writing of this book I was not concerned about having a new suspect because, inevitably, new suspects become old ones and the search continues for someone else; but I do have a *preferred* candidate who is mentioned towards the end of the book.

Finally, *Jack the Ripper – Through the Mists of Time* is a sort of breathing space; it is a moment in time when we can, and should, see what has happened to the Ripper machine. The story has been racing along at speed for over one hundred and twenty years. With all its fantasy, fiction and theories it has become like a rapidly spreading virus that mutates at every opportunity, giving rise to more concepts and beliefs.

The time has come to pull back the reins of this awesome myth and look at what the murderer might really have been like – and what we have made him.

Foreword to the Revised Edition

The spectre of Jack the Ripper haunts the streets of Whitechapel as much today as it did over one hundred and twenty years ago. I use the word 'spectre' because in many ways that's what the killer was, or rather what the newspapers of the day transformed him into. It was as if 'Jack' became invisible during that autumn of terror when his razor-sharp knife carved an everlasting impression in criminal history. In 2009 a Channel 5 documentary entitled *Jack the Ripper: Tabloid Killer – Revealed,* named Frederick Best as being the author of a letter sent to the Central News Agency in 1888 and signed 'Jack the Ripper.' Best worked for the *Star* as a freelance journalist. A sample of his writing was obtained for analysis, and a leading handwriting expert concluded the writing in both letters was by the same hand. Not only did this hoax boost sales of the *Star* edition, it gave the killer a chilling and unforgettable nickname. Reporting the terrible mutilations on the victims no doubt intensified public interest as well as creating fear and panic.

Today the same question is asked: Was the murderer an insane Jew, a sailor, an artist, a slaughterman, a black magician, or even a secret agent?

Interest in those ghastly crimes is sustained as Ripper-related programmes come to our screens, and viewing is occasionally punctuated by re-runs of Ripper movies that are sure to entertain us. In 2009 a new three-part drama called *Whitechapel* was shown on TV and became the most watched series for that year; and so Jack the Ripper's audience – if we can call it such – becomes bigger with every passing year.

My interest in the crimes is revitalised whenever a Ripper documentary is shown or a new theory is published. Writers and enthusiasts look in every corner hoping to find 'new' information that will give us a clearer insight into the period when the murders occurred. On rare occasions something remarkable turns up. In 2007 an item was listed on eBay and turned out to be one of the most important photographic discoveries on the Ripper case for a quarter of a century. The photograph was listed as showing a Whitechapel street in the 1890s. The banner heading included the words, 'Scene of Infamous Whitechapel Murders London.'

Fortunately, the only bidder was author Philip Hutchinson, a respected Ripper tour guide. His relentless research proved conclusively that the photo showed Dutfield's Yard where Ripper-victim Elizabeth Stride was murdered in 1888. The shot was taken circa 1900 and shows the exact spot where Stride was killed. The yard itself would have looked exactly the same as it did when the murder occurred. The image appeared for the first time in Hutchinson's remarkable book, *The Jack the Ripper Location Photographs.*

People like me find such photographs immensely interesting. We want to delve deeper into the Ripper's world; we scrutinise the faces of the people who lived in those 'dark' days and nights, and our emotions are stirred by images of the long-gone streets once inhabited by those poor, hapless ladies who will never be forgotten.

Since the first edition of this book was published in 2002 several new solutions to the mystery have gone into print, and the film *From Hell* gave fans of horror a psychic Inspector Abberline (played by Johnny Depp), who rises from the smoke of an opium den to track down an aristocratic, gentleman Ripper.

And so the Ripper machine races on, taking with it all that is plausible and factual, all that is glamorised and entertaining . . . all that is pure nonsense.

As previously written, this book does not offer a new theory to end all theories. My preferred candidate for the role of Jack the Ripper has never been a likely suspect, but in 2008 the Broadmoor files relating to this person were made available for public viewing. Did these files contain the key to solving the killer's identity once and for all? Well, I wasn't going to let such an opportunity pass by.

This volume has been updated and revised. During its preparation I have been able to make changes which, I hope, make it more worthy as a comment on a modern cultural myth.

Peter Hodgson 2011

ACKNOWLEDGMENTS (REVISED EDITION)

In this revised edition I would like to extend my gratitude to true crime bookseller Loretta Lay, and to the staff at the Berkshire Record Office.

I am grateful to Rachel Houlihan for her assistance and IT expertise, and to John Henderson of Euro London Films Ltd.

I would like to express my appreciation to Jonathan Evans, Archivist at the Royal London Hospital Archives and Museum, and to Paul O'Neill, one of the most able men of his generation.

Stuart A Hodgson deserves special thanks for his lifelike recreations of Mary Ann Nichols, Catharine Eddowes, and the lady of whom so little is known – Mary Jane Kelly.

QUICK REFERENCE

Dr Robert Anderson (Later, Sir)
On 31 August 1888 was appointed Assistant Commissioner of the Metropolitan Police CID. Retired in 1901 and was knighted.

Frederick Abberline
Scotland Yard detective inspector. Supervised enquiries on the ground during the Whitechapel murders investigation.

Wynne Edwin Baxter
Coroner who presided over the inquests of Mary Ann Nichols, Annie Chapman, Elizabeth Stride, Alice McKenzie and Frances Coles.

Dr William Frederick Blackwell
The first doctor to be summoned to the scene of the Stride murder. On his arrival (at 1.16 a.m.) he pronounced her dead.

Dr Thomas Bond
Police Surgeon to A Division (Westminster). Attended the murder scene of Mary Jane Kelly, and inspected the body of Alice McKenzie at the mortuary. He believed that McKenzie was a Ripper victim.

Dr Frederick Gordon Brown
City of London police surgeon. He attended the Catharine Eddowes' murder scene.

Inspector Joseph Chandler
The first senior police officer at the scene of Annie Chapman's murder.

Louis Diemschutz
Steward of the International Workingmen's Educational Club, 40 Berner Street. He discovered the body of Elizabeth Stride in Dutfield's Yard.

Joseph Lawende
At 1.35 a.m., 30 September 1888, Lawende observed a man and woman talking at the entrance to Church Passage which led to Mitre Square where Catharine Eddowes was murdered a few minutes later. His friends, Harry Harris and Joseph Levy, took no notice of the couple. At a later date Lawende was shown Eddowes' body at the mortuary. He identified her by the clothes she was wearing.

Dr Rees Ralph Llewellyn
Local Whitechapel doctor. Was summoned from his surgery at 4.00 a.m., 31 August 1888, to examine the body of Mary Ann Nichols who had been murdered in Buck's Row.

Police Constable Alfred Long
On the morning of 30 September 1888 at 2.55 a.m. Long discovered a torn piece of Catharine Eddowes' bloodstained apron on the ground in front of the staircase of 108–119 Wentworth Model Dwellings in Goulston Street. Written on the wall above the apron was the chalked message, 'The Juwes are the men that will not be blamed for nothing.'

George Lusk
President of the Whitechapel Vigilance Committee. On October 16 1888 he received a parcel containing half a human kidney and a letter. The kidney was allegedly taken from the body of Catharine Eddowes.

Dr Roderick MacDonald
Coroner at Mary Jane Kelly's inquest.

Sir Melville Macnaghten
Joined the Metropolitan Police Force as Assistant Chief Constable, CID, in 1889. Became Assistant Commissioner, CID, from 1903 to 1913. In 1894 he wrote a confidential report (referred to as the 'Macnaghten Memoranda') in which he named three people whom he believed were more likely to have been Jack the Ripper than Thomas Cutbush. The three people were Montague John Druitt, Aaron Kosminski and Michael Ostrog.

Dr George Bagster Phillips
The Divisional Police Surgeon for H Division (Whitechapel). He examined the bodies of Annie Chapman, Elizabeth Stride and Mary Jane Kelly all in situ. He attended the post-mortem of Catharine Eddowes.

Israel Schwartz
On 30 September 1888 at 12.45 a.m. Schwartz saw a man and woman arguing at the gateway to Dutfield's Yard in Berner Street. He witnessed the woman being thrown onto the pavement. After the murder of Elizabeth Stride (which occurred in theYard) Schwartz was taken to view the body at the mortuary and identified her as the woman he had seen arguing.

Dr George William Sequeira
The first doctor to arrive at Mitre Square where Catharine Eddowes was murdered. He pronounced her dead and awaited the arrival of Dr Frederick Gordon Brown.

Major Henry Smith
Acting Commissioner of the City of London Police. He took charge of the Eddowes' murder investigation.

Chief Inspector Donald Sutherland Swanson
Was in charge of the Whitechapel murders investigation from September 1 to October 6 1888. Thereafter he was desk officer under the leadership of Dr Robert Anderson. Swanson read every report - in fact anything pertaining to the case - and acquired an intimate knowledge of the murders.

Sir Charles Warren
Commissioner of the Metropolitan Police from 1886 to 1888. His resignation was accepted on the day of Mary Kelly's murder. The failure of the police to apprehend the Whitechapel murderer had nothing to do with his resignation.

1
Murder in Whitechapel

The police files on the Jack the Ripper case were officially closed in 1892, and it was the opinion of the Assistant Commissioner of the Metropolitan CID, Dr Robert Anderson, that the person responsible for the murders was dangerous only to a certain class of women who lived in and around Whitechapel in the East End of London. He also went on to say that the general public who lived in the area where the murders were committed were just as safe during the crime period as they had been before and after it. Anderson was of course referring to the prostitute class, women of the night who plied the age-old trade on the rough-and-ready streets of the East End. They must have been hardened women to indulge in such activities.

Venereal disease was rife amongst them; in fact, all sorts of diseases ran through the poor working-class population, and death itself hung like a shadow in every street. The rigours of East End life were intolerable to some and suicide was the only means of escape - suicide by cutting one's own wrist or by jumping into the river. Fifty-five per cent of the children died before they were five years old. The West End was more prosperous, healthier, but even so the figure for this region was about eighteen per cent. Little kids would go out on the streets thieving and begging - they knew hunger and poverty and ill health. If they were lucky enough to make it into their teenage years they invariably had to leave their homes to make room for an ever-increasing family. For the boys who did make it into men, and who were fortunate enough to find work, the wages were extremely low, the hours long and the conditions were often intolerable. The jobs requiring prolonged physical strength were usually taken on by workers from the cloth industries or by country folk from areas where farming had started to decline. The country workers were fitter and healthier people, some of whom became dockland labourers, railway men and corn and timber merchants. Less fortunate men and women could find themselves in a 'sweatshop', the latter being a place where 'sweated labour' took place - a term meaning long hours work for low wages. It was a difficult struggle, particularly for men with families to keep. You could earn up to thirty shillings a week if times were good, and that would involve working for fourteen hours a day, seven days a week, in a sweatshop. The work was mundane. Women could, for example, sew linings into trousers or stitch buttons onto pants, repair shirts and other garments. Other jobs included making matchboxes, shelling peas or sack-making. The pay was pitiable. Today it is difficult for us to imagine the living conditions in those times. Empty houses were non-existent; the East End was teeming with people.

Then there were the common lodging houses. In Whitechapel alone there were over two hundred of them and they provided accommodation for over eight thousand people. You could rent a reasonably comfortable room for four shillings a week (that's about twenty pence in today's money!), and if you didn't spend the rest of your money on ale, as many did, you had to watch out for the pickpockets and ruffians. But let's be sure about the situation in this area, an area which would become known all over the world as being the hunting ground for the most talked about serial killer. Mile End, Spitalfields and Whitechapel, all sections of the East End, harboured working-class people as well as the homeless. Crime, violence and prostitution were all clearly abundant amongst this underprivileged and mostly forgotten section of the metropolis. Yet many decent and honest people lived there too. There *was* happiness to be found on the streets. Women would sit at the front of their houses during the day enjoying a chat with their friends; children could play and enjoy themselves, and laughter occasionally rang out. For some though, the loss of a job would inevitably mean no money, no food and a merciless struggle for survival.

'Dossing' was a term frequently used and referred to the hiring of a bed for a night in one of the many common lodging houses. In such establishments both men and women would prepare food and wash their clothes. The sleeping quarters consisted of rows of beds on both sides of the same room and the price was four pence per bed per night. In some of the other lodging houses you could get a cheaper kip for the night. A rope was tied across a room and you had to lean against it and go to sleep - sounds impossible to me - but that's what they did back then. I have mentioned prostitution, which was taken up out of necessity rather than choice. Some women worked for very low wages and sold their bodies as well. Although this was the case in the East End, and no doubt many other depressed areas in towns around the country, most girls were brought up to be housewives, and were taught domestic skills. Ladies who had received a decent education found jobs as house servants, nurses, bookkeepers and clerks. Other than that there were the sweated trades of the textile industries. Many women worked as cigarette makers or laundresses and there were varying types of factory work, although men's wages were higher. Women were considered to be less reliable on account of them leaving work to get married. At the Bryant and May matchworks in East London, women worked ten hours a day for four shillings per week, and they had to pay fines for uncleanliness or breaking the rules of the work place. British social reformer and theosophist, Annie Besant, who was a member of the Fabian Society, drew attention to the conditions of the match girls and helped them in their struggle for more pay and fair play. However, low wages and long hours were part of the working system and the situation was taken very much for granted. Many women who took to prostitution for extra money did so reluctantly. In October 1888 there were an estimated 1,200 'unfortunates' in Whitechapel alone.

The Assistant Commissioner was probably correct in stating that only a 'certain class of women' was at risk during the period of murders. In Whitechapel you could get a 'knee-trembler' for four pence but the women were unclean and mostly ugly. They would perform in darkened doorways, backyards, alleys and courts. Even at the height of these atrocious murders, prostitutes were prepared to carry on with their business, in spite of knowing that they might meet this deranged and vicious murderer.

It would be fair to say that the police at the time were unfailing in their efforts to apprehend the murderer. It is indeed a great pity that they were not to be rewarded. Crime was commonplace in this part of London and the police had their work cut out for them. Some of the worst streets were Thrawl Street, Dorset Street and Flower and Dean Street - the very same streets that the Ripper knew well and where he could mingle without attracting attention. In these streets the police were treated with hostility. This only made their job more difficult in an increasingly populated small area of London. Irish immigrants came to settle there after the 1846 potato famine and 1881 onwards saw the influx of Jews from the pogroms of Russia and Russian Poland. Their numbers increased, and within a few years there was an estimated 60,000 Jews in East London. These new arrivals lived in small and well-defined areas; they were housed together in tenement blocks or new model dwellings which became more Jewish as time went on. After being persecuted for so long abroad many of them had scant regard for 'truth', and to this end they would say anything to enable them to get along. The Cockneys didn't like them, however, because, apart from being 'foreign' they were prepared to live together in large numbers and they would work for less pay - which of course made it more difficult for anybody else to get a job.

Now that we possess a little knowledge about Victorian life in the East End we can begin to look at the murders themselves. The question is, how many murders can be attributed to the man who became known as 'Jack the Ripper'? The general consensus today, amongst writers and crime historians, is that the number was four or five.

Sir Melville Macnaghten was the Chief Constable of the CID, Scotland Yard, from 1890 to 1903. He had joined the Metropolitan Police in 1889 and in 1894 he wrote a document which became known as the 'Macnaghten Memoranda'. Although he was not personally involved in the Ripper investigation he made certain statements about the Whitechapel murderer. He wrote that the murderer had five victims and five victims only. He listed their names and the dates when they died. They were:

1. Mary Ann Nichols, 31 August 1888.
2. Annie Chapman, 8 September 1888.
3. Elizabeth Stride, 30 September 1888.
4. Catharine Eddowes, 30 September 1888.
5. Mary Jane Kelly, 9 November 1888.

You will have noticed that Elizabeth Stride and Catharine Eddowes were both murdered on the same date. All five murders occurred in Spitalfields and Whitechapel in a ten-week period and in an area covering approximately one square mile. There were two other murders previous to that of Nichols which were thought to be the work of the Ripper due to the terrible injuries sustained by the victims.

On 2 April, Bank Holiday Monday, that same year, a 45-year-old prostitute by the name of Emma Elizabeth Smith was attacked in the early hours of the morning as she travelled home along Osborne Street. She had been followed by three men who seized the woman, beat her up and then robbed her. She managed to reach her home on George Street and from there she was taken to the London Hospital where she died three days later. A few months later, on Bank Holiday Monday, 6 August, 39-year-old Martha Tabram and her friend, Mary Connolly (nicknamed 'Pearly Poll'), went out in the evening for drinks and a good time. During the course of the evening they met up with two guardsmen and went drinking in various public houses along the Whitechapel High Street. Just before midnight the two women went their separate ways. Martha went off toward a street called George Yard with her client, whilst Pearly Poll took the other soldier to Angel Alley for a knee-trembler. At 4.50 a.m. a man named John Reeves discovered Martha's lifeless body on the first-floor landing of George Yard

Building: a block of dwellings in George Yard Street. She had been stabbed repeatedly – thirty-nine stab wounds in all. It has been generally accepted, for some years now, that the Whitechapel murderer had five victims. Emma Smith had been beaten and robbed by a bunch of thugs. And as for poor Martha Tabram – well, although it was a frenzied attack, it was dissimilar to the murders which occurred afterwards. Is it possible that she was the first victim of Jack the Ripper? Can anybody know for sure? Personally, I am not convinced she was.

The first victim of the Ripper to be considered here is 43-year-old Mary Ann Nichols, known as 'Polly' to her acquaintances. She was married at nineteen and had five children by her husband. In 1880 the relationship ended, probably due to her drinking habits, and she took to prostitution to make money. Mary Ann Nichols had been drinking on the night of 30 August. She spent her money. All she needed was four pence for her doss; just four pence would have saved her life, but she met the wrong client.

At 3.30 a.m. people were making off to work. One such person was Charles Cross, a carman (cart driver). He was walking down Buck's Row at 3.40 when he spotted a dark shape lying in front of a gateway which led into a stable yard. The only available light was from a gas lamp which stood at the far end of the street. Cross went over to investigate and saw that it was the body of a woman. He stooped forward to get a closer look when he heard footsteps coming along the pavement. It was another carman, a chap named Robert Paul who, like Cross, was on his way to work. Paul moved to one side, not wanting to get involved, but he was called over to have a look at the body. The men decided to find a policeman. Only minutes afterwards Police Constable John Neil, who was on his beat, came down Buck's Row when he noticed the body. Aided by his bull's-eye lantern it became immediately obvious that the woman had been murdered – her throat had been cut. She was lying lengthways along the street. Her bonnet was on the ground next to her. PC Neil stayed at the scene and was soon to be joined by PC John Thain, who had noticed Neil waving his lamp for assistance. Meanwhile, the two carmen had found a policeman at the corner of Hanbury Street and Baker's Row. He was PC Mizen. After listening to the two men he carried on to Buck's Row whilst Cross and Paul continued on their way to work. So, three policemen were at the crime scene within minutes of the body having been discovered. A doctor had to be summoned, and it was PC Thain who informed Dr Rees Ralph Llewellyn of the incident at Buck's Row. PC Mizen went for assistance and was soon to return with an 'ambulance'. In those days this was a trolley, somewhat similar to a gurney. The doctor pronounced the woman dead and the body was taken to Old

Montague Street Workhouse Infirmary. He noticed that there was only a small amount of blood in the gutter; most of it had been soaked up by the woman's clothing. Dr Llewellyn was in no doubt that she was killed at the location where she was found. Her throat had been cut and there were several abdominal incisions.

As the injuries were inflicted from left to right, the doctor concluded that the murderer may have been left-handed. There was no doubt at all that the knife used in the attack was fairly sharp and had a long blade. There had been no signs of a struggle during the attack and there were no blood stains on Polly Nichols' breasts or the front of her clothing. This is an important point because it tells us that Polly was lying down when her throat was cut; also it tells us that her heart had stopped beating, otherwise blood, which is under pressure due to the rhythm of the heart, would have spurted out onto her clothing. It is clear that the murderer strangled her first before commencing the knife assault. PC Neil had previously patrolled Buck's Row at 3.15 a.m. and seen nothing suspicious then. The arrival of Charles Cross at 3.40 indicates that Polly was murdered between these times.

The police questioned many inhabitants and workers in that locality but their inquiries failed to produce a viable lead.

The second murder took place on 8 September in the back yard of Number 29 Hanbury Street, Spitalfields - a lodging house which was only half a mile from the site of Polly Nichols' murder. The woman's name was Annie Chapman (known locally as 'Dark Annie'). She was forty-seven years old at the time of her death. Annie was married in 1869 and had three children. She had variously lived in Windsor and West London. She left her family behind in 1882 and this break-up may have been due to her drunken and immoral ways. However, her decline eventually took her to the East End, and from May onwards in 1888 she lived mainly at Crossingham's lodging house. It was managed by Timothy Donovan and stood opposite Miller's Court where the final Ripper victim lived.

At 1.30 a.m., or thereabouts, on 8 September, Annie was in the kitchen at Crossingham's lodgings. She was undernourished, feeling unwell, and had no money for her bed. Annie was asked to leave, and at 2 a.m. she was wandering around the locality probably hoping to pick up a punter, which she eventually did. Nobody knows what she did or where she went for the next three hours or so. In all probability Annie Chapman kept on the move until her luck was in - or so she thought.

She picked up a client just before 5.30 a.m. and judging by the events which were to follow, it is almost certain that this man was Jack the Ripper.

At 5.30 the same morning a lady called Elizabeth Long was on her way to Spitalfields market and her route took her down Hanbury Street, a street consisting of terraced lodging houses. Liz was certain of the time because of the chimes of a nearby clock. As she walked down the street she noticed a man and woman talking to each other just in front of Number 29. The man said to her, 'Will you?' to which she replied, 'Yes.' Dawn was just breaking and she managed to get a good look at the woman, whom she later identified as Annie Chapman. The man's face was turned away but Liz thought he looked about forty years old and was a little taller than the woman. She said he looked like a foreigner. He was wearing a dark coat and a deerstalker hat and according to Liz had a 'shabby genteel' appearance. She carried on walking but did not look back.

There were two doors at the front of the house and they were side by side; the door on the right was the entrance to the premises whilst the left side door led into a narrow indoor passage about twenty-five feet long which ran to the backyard. The streets became busier as it started to get lighter. It was Saturday and workers were preparing to go to market. John Richardson, the son of Amelia who lived and worked at Number 29, entered the backyard at 4.45 a.m. to check the cellar-door padlock. The front and back doors were always unlocked to facilitate the coming and going of lodgers. At the end of the narrow passage were a couple of stone steps leading down into the backyard. John checked the cellar door and then trimmed some leather off his work boots. It wasn't sunrise yet but there was just enough light for him to complete the task.

John Richardson was in the yard for a couple of minutes only, and as he found everything in order he went off to work. A carpenter named Albert Cadosh (who lived next door at Number 27), went into his backyard to use the lavatory at around the same time that Liz Long observed Annie with her client. Cadosh heard noises from the yard of Number 29, and shortly after he heard something fall against the fence which separated the backyards. He didn't pay any particular attention to the noises and went off to work. There is no doubt that young Mr Cadosh was literally only feet away from the Ripper as he began his onslaught. A man by the name of John Davies, who lived with his wife and sons at Number 29, discovered Annie's body at about 6 a.m. She was lying at the foot of the stone steps, parallel to the wooden fence that separated the two yards.

The sight which confronted poor Davies was so shocking that he ran straight out into the street for help. He came across two workmen who, after glancing at the corpse, went off to fetch help. Davies then went to Commercial Street Police Station before returning to Hanbury Street.

Inspector Joseph Chandler was the first officer to arrive at the scene. After viewing the body he sent for the Divisional Surgeon and for extra help. At 6.30 a.m. Dr George Bagster Phillips, the police surgeon, arrived. Shortly after his arrival he ordered the body to be taken to the mortuary. It was then that Phillips discovered the contents of Annie's pocket lying in a neat pile: a piece of course muslin, two combs and two farthings. This seemingly deliberate act was taken up by author Stephen Knight in his book *Jack the Ripper: The Final Solution,* which I shall be discussing later on.

Hundreds of folk had by now gathered in Hanbury Street. The inquest into Annie Chapman's death was held at the Working Lad's Institute and was conducted by Coroner Wynne Baxter, who had also presided over the inquest of Mary Nichols at the same establishment. Dr Phillips gave his testimony on 14 September and was recalled at a later date to give further evidence with respect to the mutilation of Annie's body. It is necessary here to give a brief summary of how she was killed and the nature of her injuries.

Annie was found lying on her back, with her knees pointing upwards. Her face and tongue were swollen and the tongue could be seen sticking out a little between her front teeth. The throat had been cut deeply with force; the incision went right round the neck. The abdomen had been opened up and the intestines had been lifted out of the body and placed over the shoulder. The uterus and parts of the bladder and vagina were missing and could not be found.

Annie Chapman was firstly strangled and her throat was cut as she lay on the ground. Dr Phillips thought that the weapon used was a sharp, narrow-bladed knife up to eight inches in length and possibly even longer. He thought that the murderer showed considerable anatomical knowledge. It was his opinion that the woman had been dead for at least two hours, which placed the time of her death at 4.30 a.m. The murder took place on the spot were the body was found. If the doctor's estimated time of death was correct, then the testimonies of John Richardson, Elizabeth Long and Albert Cadosh were questionable. In the end the police sided with Dr Phillips, although he did admit that he could have been wrong in his estimate owing to the fact that the air was cold and there was much loss of blood and body heat. I think we have to say that the good doctor was almost certainly wrong; Annie Chapman was murdered between 5.30 and 6 a.m.

A search of the backyard revealed certain clues, one of which was a wet leather apron found near a water tap and which was subsequently identified as belonging to John Richardson. The finding of the apron initially caused some concern as reports of a man nicknamed 'Leather Apron' had already been doing the rounds. After the Nichols' murder, prostitutes told police about a man who had been menacing their kind and had said to them, on various occasions, that he would rip them up.

On 10 September, Sergeant William Thick of H Division (the Metropolitan designated area which covered Whitechapel) arrested John Pizer, a 38-year-old boot finisher. Pizer, a Polish Jew, often wore a leather apron and used long, sharp knives for his trade. This man had an alibi for the night of the Polly Nichols murder. He was in Holloway, several miles away, and had spoken to a policeman about a glow in the sky which was emanating from a fire at London Docks. This took place in the early hours of 31 August, so he couldn't have been in two places at the same time. Sergeant Thick had known him for a long time and at Annie Chapman's inquest he testified that Pizer was known as 'Leather Apron'. John Pizer was cleared of any involvement in the murders.

What could have been a vital clue turned out to be a false lead. Part of an envelope was found with the letter M in a man's handwriting on one side, and on the reverse was the seal of the Sussex Regiment. Also found was a screwed up piece of paper containing two pills. Inspector Chandler's enquiries into stationery bearing the regimental seal failed to produce any significant leads.

The letter M on the envelope has been viewed as being a clue left by the killer himself and this will be discussed in the chapter named 'Jack's Diary?' Finally, there were markings on Annie's finger where she had worn two brass rings, and it was thought that her killer may have taken them. The rings, however, did not turn up. Inspector Frederick Abberline, of Scotland Yard, was informed of the murder in Hanbury Street. He was a most able detective and possessed intimate knowledge of the district where the murders had occurred. He was in charge of the men on the ground and there is little doubt that he was the best officer for that particular case. In 1888 he had served for fourteen years as Inspector for H Division.

On 10 September, two days after the murder of Annie Chapman, a Vigilance Committee was set up with the aim of assisting the police in their hunt for the killer. The elected president of the committee was George Lusk, who resided in the East End. Any tip-offs or information received from the public was passed on to the authorities. Sir Charles Warren, the Commissioner of the Met, was happy with the aims and practices set up by Lusk and his men.

We now come to what is frequently referred to as the 'double event'. Two murders in one night and both committed within a couple of hours. The murdered women were Elizabeth Stride and Catharine Eddowes. It is my belief that Stride was not a Ripper victim. However, most writers on the subject, and indeed the police at the time, believe she was. In order to present a complete picture of the murders it is essential that the circumstances surrounding this murder are included. Elizabeth Stride, née Gustafsdotter, was born on 27 November 1843 in Torslanda near Gothenburg in Sweden, and she came to London in 1866. She married John Thomas Stride in 1869 and it has been written that she had nine children by him. The marriage broke up in 1881. In 1885 she was living in Dorset Street with a man named Michael Kidney, but the relationship was a stormy one and Liz walked out on him several times. In September 1888 she was living in lodgings at 32 Flower and Dean Street, and had stayed there on previous occasions. Liz Stride was murdered in a small court in Berner Street, known as Dutfield's Yard. The court had two wooden gates to its entrance. The International Working Men's Educational Club stood to the right, and on the left was a row of terraced cottages. I have summarized the salient features of the events leading up to the murder of Elizabeth Stride. They are as follows:

11.45 p.m. to 12.00 a.m.

Matthew Packer (owner of a greengrocer's shop on Berner Street) told two private detectives that he sold half a pound of black grapes to a man who entered his shop in the company of a woman. A few days later he identified the body of Elizabeth Stride as being that woman. Unfortunately, Packer was a publicity seeker and the police regarded him as unreliable. He was not called as an inquest witness.

12.30 a.m.

PC William Smith, of the Met, was on his beat in Berner Street and saw Liz standing with a man opposite Dutfield's yard.

12.45 a.m.

Israel Schwartz, a Jewish immigrant, was passing down Berner Street and when he got to the wooden gates to the court he noticed a woman standing in the gateway. She was accosted by a man who spoke to her. He tried to pull her into the street but ended up throwing her onto the pavement. The woman screamed half-heartedly. Schwartz crossed over the street and observed another man who was lighting his pipe as he watched the incident. Liz's attacker called out 'Lipski' (a derogatory term used to insult Jews), apparently at the pipe man.

Schwartz walked on but soon ran off as he was under the impression that the 'pipe man' was following him. Schwartz later identified Liz as being the woman he had seen being ill-treated.

1 a.m. (approx)

Louis Diemschutz, Steward of the International WME Club, was returning from work on his pony and cart and turned into the gateway of Dutfield's Yard. As he did so the pony shied over to the left and Diemschutz noticed a heap on the ground. After prodding it with his whip he got down from his cart and lit a match to get a better look. He realised it was the body of a woman and ran directly into the club for assistance. He returned with two club members who discovered that the woman's throat had been slashed; the blood had trickled down her neck and into the gutter. Diemschutz and one of the club members ran off in search of a police officer.

It wasn't long before a small crowd started to gather near the gates to the court. Dr Blackwell was summoned and arrived at Berner Street at 1.16 a.m. He concluded that the woman had been dead about twenty minutes to half an hour. It is therefore reasonable to assume that Liz was murdered at about 12.55 a.m., bearing in mind she was alive at 12.45 a.m. In fact, Louis Diemschutz thought that the murder had just been committed as he drove in through the gates, and the attacker was hiding somewhere in the court itself.

Dr Blackwell performed the autopsy on the body while Dr Phillips took notes. Liz had suffered a clean cut to the throat; the cut was from left to right and was six inches in length. Death had resulted from loss of blood from the left carotid artery. At the inquest of Elizabeth Stride, Dr Phillips stated that the knife used to inflict the wound was not sharp and pointed but that it was round and one inch across. He also pointed out that the injuries were very much different to those of Chapman, in that Chapman's neck had been cut all round and down to the vertebral column.

The second murder of that dreadful night was to occur in gloomy Mitre Square, a mere ten minutes' walk from Berner Street. Mitre Square lay within the jurisdiction of the City of London Police Force, headed by Acting Commissioner Major Henry Smith. The woman who was savagely butchered in the early hours of 30 September was Catharine Eddowes. Cathy had told friends that she was married to Thomas Conway, a former soldier, in 1862. She had three children by him but in 1880 the couple split up and went their separate ways. Cathy was soon to meet another man, John Kelly, and she stayed with him up until her death. They shared lodgings at Flower and Dean Street. Cathy lived to be forty-six years old and was described as being a jolly soul, often heard singing. She was five feet five inches tall with dark hair and hazel eyes.

It was on the evening of 29 September that Cathy was arrested in Aldgate Street for making a disturbance. Two policemen took her to Bishopsgate Police Station where, due to her drunken state, she was placed in a cell until she had sobered up. At 1 a.m. she was reasonably stable enough to be allowed to go home and so she set off in the direction of Houndsditch and Mitre Square.

The next section of the story is of great importance because it furnishes us with a description of a man who could have been Jack the Ripper. At 1.35 a.m. three Jews were just leaving the Imperial Club, situated on Duke Street. Leading off Duke Street was a narrow passage (Church Passage), which ran directly into Mitre Square. The three men were Joseph Lawende, Harry Harris and Joseph Levy. As they left the club they saw a man and a woman talking quietly at the corner of Church Passage; there was certainly nothing notable or abnormal about the couple. Although the lighting was poor, Lawende could see enough detail to be able to furnish the police with a description of the man. His two companions did not pay particular attention to the man or the woman.

Cathy was wearing a black bonnet and black jacket that night, and I have to point out that Lawende did not see the woman's face as he passed by – she had her back towards him. At a later stage he identified Cathy Eddowes by her clothing only, so there remains the possibility that it was another couple. One must also bear in mind that Mitre Square was a secluded haunt for prostitutes. Although the attacker did not spend more than five minutes in the square, it was a very precarious location in which to be, from his point of view. Just opposite the scene of the crime stood Kearley and Tonge's warehouse where the watchman, George Morris, was working. The door to the warehouse was slightly open, but Morris heard nothing when the murder was taking place, which would have been between 1.35 and 1.45 a.m. At 1.40 a.m. PC James Harvey entered Church Passage, as it was part of his beat. He went to the end of the passage, without actually entering the square, and neither saw nor heard anything to attract his attention. The corner of the square where Cathy died was in near darkness, the closest lamp being about twenty yards away, and gas lamps in those days did not give out much light. It was 1.44 a.m. when PC Edward Watkins discovered the body. His beat usually took twelve to fourteen minutes to complete and he had previously entered Mitre Square at about 1.30 a.m. and seen nothing unusual with the aid of his lamp. The shocking sight of Cathy's mutilated body sent Watkins running over to the warehouse where he summoned George Morris to his aid. Morris ran off to get help whilst the anxious PC Watkins guarded the dead body.

Dr Sequeira, who lived close by, was alerted by one of the local policemen. He arrived at 1.55 a.m. and determined that the woman had been dead for not more than fifteen minutes. The City of London Police Surgeon, Dr Frederick Gordon Brown, arrived at 2 a.m. and conducted a more detailed examination of the body. Other police officers were to arrive at the scene, notably Major Henry Smith himself. The immediate area was searched by the police and anybody seen in the locality was questioned. At 2.55 a.m. PC Alfred Long was on his beat in Goulston Street, a few blocks away from Mitre Square, when he discovered what was the only clue ever left by the Ripper. It was a piece of Cathy Eddowes' apron lying at the foot of some stairs leading into 108–119 Wentworth Model Dwellings (cheap houses built for Jewish immigrants). The apron was bloodstained and had faecal matter upon it. It was compared to the torn apron worn by Cathy and the match was exact. Many authors and crime historians believe that Jack the Ripper had wiped his heavily bloodstained hands and probably his knife on this material as he made his way home, but there is another explanation as to why the Ripper tore a piece of apron from the murdered woman's clothing. PC Long had previously passed down Goulston Street at 2.20 a.m. and he stated that the apron was not there at that time. If this had been the case, then it would imply that Cathy's attacker had been hanging around in the vicinity for at least half an hour. This seems highly unlikely, but I believe there is a sound reason for this unusual behaviour. I shall discuss this aspect in a later chapter.

Above where the apron was found, PC Long also notice a chalked message which read: 'The Juwes are the men that will not be blamed for nothing'. This, now well-known message, has been a subject of discussion for many years. The word *Juwes* sparked off the imagination of one writer in the 1970s and his book had a big impact on the Ripper mystery. It is difficult to know how to interpret the words and it was uncertain at the time whether or not they had been written by the murderer. It was only after heated discussions that the words were finally erased. Sir Charles Warren gave the order; after all, Goulston Street was on his territory and not that of the City of London Police. It was part of a predominantly Jewish area, and with the recent events involving John Pizer there was a real possibility of riots or attacks on Jews.

Now back to Joseph Lawende. The police came across him during the course of their enquiries and the description he gave to them, of the man seen talking to Cathy Eddowes, was published in the *Police Gazette* in October 1888. Lawende's description described the man as... *age 30, height five feet seven or eight inches, complexion fair, medium build. He was wearing a pepper-and-salt coloured loose jacket* [*a fine mixture of dark and light colour*]. *He wore a grey cloth cap, the peak being of the same material, and a reddish neckerchief tied in a knot; he had the appearance of a sailor.*

At the inquest (conducted by Samuel Frederick Langham), Lawende told the coroner that he doubted he would recognise the man again. Catharine Eddowes' body was mutilated in a most diabolical fashion. Dr Brown's post-mortem report on her injuries is very detailed. I have included a very brief description of them. The wounds and cuts inflicted on poor Catharine were extensive. The throat had been cut deeply. There were no traces of blood on the surrounding bricks or pavement. The intestines were drawn out and placed over the right shoulder. There was much disfigurement of the face, including fine cuts to both eyelids and a cut on each side of the cheek which peeled up forming a triangular flap. The left kidney had been carefully removed, as was the uterus. Both the kidney and uterus were taken away by her killer. From the killer's point of view this was an extremely daring crime when one considers the police presence in the area, and the fact that he might have been remembered if he was the man seen talking to Cathy. It was his invincibility that made him so frightening; and moreover, a name was soon to be coined for him which not only captured the public imagination, but ensured that this killer would never be forgotten.

The imaginative and perennial name 'Jack the Ripper' first appeared in a letter sent to the Central News Agency and received there on 27 September 1888. It was written in red ink and dated 25 September. It read:

> Dear Boss,
>
> I keep on hearing the police have caught me but they wont fix me just yet. I have laughed when they look so clever and talk about being on the right track. That joke about Leather Apron gave me real fits. I am down on whores and I shant quit ripping them till I do get buckled. Grand work the last job was. I gave the lady no time to squeal. How can they catch me now. I love my work and want to start again. You will soon hear of me with my funny little games. I saved some of the proper red stuff in a ginger beer bottle over the last job to write with but it went thick like glue and I cant use it. Red ink is fit enough I

> hope ha ha. The next job I do I shall clip the ladys ears off and send to the police officers just for jolly wouldnt you. Keep this letter back till I do a bit more work, then give it out straight. My knife's so nice and sharp I want to get to work right away if I get a chance. Good luck.
>
> Yours truly
>
> Jack the Ripper

There was a second postscript which I have not included. The envelope in which the letter came was addressed to 'the 'Boss'. Was it written by the murderer? The letter is mocking and almost jovial in content. It was treated as a joke by the news editor but a second communication was received by the agency on 1 October. It was a postcard and undoubtedly in the same hand as the writer of the 'Dear Boss' letter. It Read:

> I wasnt codding dear old Boss when I gave you the tip, you ll hear about saucy Jackys work tomorrow double event this time number one squealed a bit couldnt finish straight off. had not time to get ears for police thanks for keeping last letter back till I got to work again.
>
> Jack the Ripper

After careful consideration, the letter and postcard were sent to the Metropolitan Police who, after studying them, were rather concerned about their content and, more importantly, who had written them. Copies of both letter and postcard were printed onto posters which were put on public display. The letters were also printed in various newspapers. The question of course was, 'Do you recognise this handwriting?' In hindsight, it would have facilitated the investigation had the correspondence not been published at all. The police were inundated with hoax letters from cranks - many of which were signed 'Jack the Ripper'.

As if the letters weren't enough, George Lusk received a cardboard box wrapped in brown paper on 16 October. In it was half a human kidney and a letter which Mr Lusk thought was from the Ripper himself. The letter began with 'Mr Lusk Sor' and ended, 'Catch me when you can Mishter Lusk'. It was as if the writer was trying to sound Irish. Lusk thought the matter over and on the advice of his committee friends, the kidney was taken for examination to Dr Openshaw, Curator of the Pathological Museum at the

London Hospital. Dr Openshaw told a *Star* newspaper reporter that in his opinion the specimen was indeed half a left human kidney, but he could not determine whether it was a man's or woman's, nor could he tell for what period of time it had been removed from the body, owing to the fact that it had been preserved in spirits. However, the doctor was misreported by the newspaper as saying that it was a 'ginny' kidney (meaning that it belonged to a heavy drinker), and that it came from a 45-year-old woman afflicted with Bright's disease. I shall return to what is now referred to as the 'Lusk Kidney' in a later chapter.

We now come to the final and perhaps most controversial victim of the Whitechapel murderer - Mary Jane Kelly. The details of Mary's earlier life cannot be definitely ascertained.

She was born in 1863 and by her own account she moved to Wales from Limerick when she was a small child. The story goes that she married a collier in 1879, but he died in a mining explosion a few years later. In 1884 Mary worked in a West End brothel from where she was taken to France by one of her clients. Apparently, not too happy abroad, she returned to London again and ended up in the East End. When she was not going steady with somebody she resorted to prostitution. Mary Kelly was about five feet seven inches tall. She was a well-built lass with blue eyes and dark blonde hair - all in all, an attractive girl. The real thread of her life can be picked up when she met Joseph Barnett in Commercial Street in 1887. Barnett, an Irish Cockney, was a labourer at Billingsgate market. There was an instant attraction between the two of them. He referred to her as 'Marie Jeanette.' They lived together in various lodgings in Spitalfields and Whitechapel and at the beginning of 1888 they rented a single room in Miller's Court off Dorset Street. The landlord was 37-year-old John McCarthy, who owned a grocer's shop at 27 Dorset Street, situated just at the corner of Miller's Court. Joseph and Mary's room was Number 13, a tiny, ill-furnished apartment which was situated on the right-hand side at the end of a narrow 20-foot passage which ran from Dorset Street, a street where many prostitutes lived.

Joe Barnett took care of Mary and frequently gave her money, although he was averse to her walking the streets and selling herself. On 30 October they had an argument and Joe walked out on her. He had previously been unemployed for some months and this may have put a strain on their relationship. He did continue to visit her after their break-up. On the afternoon of Thursday, 8 November, Mary spent some time with her friend, Maria Harvey, who was also a streetwalker. They went back to 13 Miller's

Court, and in the evening Joe called in to tell Mary that he had no money. At the time of his visit, Maria was still there, but she left shortly after Joe's arrival. He did not like other prostitutes staying with Mary. After a short while he went away. Between 8 p.m. and 11.45 p.m. that same evening, Mary's exact movements are unknown; it is thought that she went out plying her trade in nearby public houses. From the testimonies of certain witnesses we can summarise most events that occurred from 11.45 p.m. onwards:

11.45 p.m.

Mary Ann Cox, a prostitute who lived in Miller's Court, was making her way home when she saw Mary Kelly in the company of a man in Dorset Street. Cox followed them into Miller's Court. Mary was drunk and her companion was described as 35 years old, stout and with a blotchy face and carroty moustache. He was shabbily dressed and carried a pail of beer. The two Marys said goodnight to each other and went to their separate rooms. The man went inside with Mary and shortly afterwards Cox could hear Mary singing.

Midnight.

Mary Cox went back out onto the streets again and could still hear singing coming from Number 13.

1.00 a.m.

Cox returned to her room to warm her hands as it was a cold, rainy night. After a few minutes Cox went out again and Mary Kelly could be heard singing.

There was light emanating from her room. Elizabeth Prater, who lived in the room directly above Number 13, stood at the entrance to the court for twenty minutes. She was waiting for a man with whom she lived, but he did not turn up. She went into John McCarthy's shop and chatted with him. During this time she saw nobody entering or leaving the court. By this time the singing had stopped. At 1.30 a.m. she went up to her room. There was no sound coming from Mary Kelly's room. Elizabeth Prater then went to sleep.

2.00 a.m.

Unemployed labourer, George Hutchinson, who lived on Commercial Street, met Mary Kelly near Flower and Dean Street. He was an acquaintance of hers and she asked him for sixpence, to which he replied he had spent all his money. Mary left Hutchinson and she carried on for a short distance. Hutchinson noticed a man who was walking towards Mary. He spoke to her and they carried on walking together, passing Hutchinson who was standing beneath a lamp. Apparently, he managed to remember details of the man's appearance which he passed on to the police at a later stage. He followed the couple back to the entrance passage to Miller's Court. They stood talking for about three minutes and then entered the court. Intrigued by the appearance of this man, Hutchinson waited outside the court until 3 a.m. Nobody exited Miller's Court during his vigil.

2.30 a.m. (approx)

Sarah Lewis, a laundress, went to stay with a friend in Miller's Court. As she walked down Dorset Street she observed a man standing opposite the entrance to the court. He was looking up the court and seemed to be waiting or looking for someone. (It is possible that this man was George Hutchinson.)

3 a.m.

Mrs Cox returned to her lodgings. There was no sound or light coming from Mary's room.

3.30 to 4.00 a.m.

Mrs Prater was awakened by her kitten and remembers hearing the muffled cry of, 'Oh murder!' This seemed to come from nearby. Sarah Lewis said that she heard a cry which seemed to come from the direction of Number 13. Mrs Cox, however, could not sleep that morning and she stated that there was *no* cry of 'murder' during the night. She heard someone leave the court at 5.45 a.m.

8 to 8.30 a.m.

Mrs Caroline Maxwell stated that she spoke to Mary Kelly at the entrance to Miller's Court. Mary said that she had been for a drink at 'Ringer's'(the Britannia public house), but had since been sick.

8.45 a.m. (approx)

Mrs Maxwell saw Mary again, this time talking to a man outside Ringer's.

10.45 a.m.

Thomas Bowyer, who worked for John McCarthy, was sent to Number 13 to collect some rent money. It was the day of the Lord Mayor's Show and it was thought that Mr Bowyer might catch Mary at home before she went off to the procession. At this time Mary was dead. The door to her room was locked so Bowyer went around the corner to the broken window. He reached through the broken pane and moved the curtain to one side. He saw a heap of flesh on the bedside table and then his eyes fell upon the remains of a body upon the bed. Shocked by the gruesome and disturbing scene, he ran straight back to McCarthy with the terrible news.

The people who saw Mary Kelly's corpse in that little room off Dorset Street would never forget it. The existing photograph does not really convey the impact of the extensive mutilations which had been inflicted with unbelievable violence. Walter Dew (noted for his arrest of Dr Crippen) was a young detective officer actively engaged in the hunt for the Ripper. According to his memoirs he was one of the first police officers to view the mutilated corpse and found it to be a harrowing experience. Inspector Beck, of Commercial Street Police Station, was the first officer to arrive at the scene. He had received the news from John McCarthy and Thomas Bowyer. Dorset Street had to be cordoned off at both ends as news of the murder started filtering through the neighbourhood. Dr Phillips arrived at 11.15 a.m. but at this stage he could only view the body through the broken window. (It would have been immediately obvious to him that Mary was beyond help.) At 11.30 Inspector Abberline arrived, but was told by Dr Phillips not to enter the room until the arrival of the bloodhounds.

The bloodhounds did not reach Miller's Court; at 1.30 p.m. Superintendent Arnold, Head of H Division, arrived at the murder scene with the news that the order for their use had been revoked. The door to Number 13 was then duly forced by John McCarthy using a pickaxe. At approximately 4 p.m. Mary's body was taken to Shoreditch mortuary.

There was nothing in the way of clues to be found in the room. A few items were present: a candle stub, a pipe (belonging to Joe Barnett) and a ginger beer bottle. The ashes of the fire were still warm at 1.30 p.m. and contained the remains of women's clothing. Mary's clothes were neatly folded and had been placed over a chair at the foot of the bed. She was quite naked apart from a puffed sleeve blouse.

The post-mortem was carried out by Dr Phillips who was assisted by Dr Bond (the police surgeon from A Division), Dr Gordon Brown, Dr William Dukes and Dr Phillips' assistant. Dr Bond had not been present at the post-mortems of the previous victims, but after carefully studying medical notes relating to their injuries he wrote that the murderer had no scientific or anatomical knowledge. Mary Kelly was attacked in a most horrific and ferocious manner. Her face was mutilated beyond recognition. Both her breasts had been removed by more or less circular incisions. The abdomen had been opened up and the uterus and kidneys removed. The pericardium was open and the heart was absent. The missing heart was not found and I suspect that the murderer took it away with him. Dr Bond stated that rigor mortis had set in but increased during the examination, i.e. at 2 p.m. Aware that the exact time of death was difficult to pinpoint and that rigidity takes from 6 to 12 hours to set in (he wrote), he estimated the time of death to be 1 or 2 a.m. His deductions were based on the comparative coldness of the body at 2 p.m. and the fact that 'the recent remains of a meal' were found over the intestines and in the stomach. These conclusions are at great variance with Caroline Maxwell's testimony. Apparently, she spoke to Mary between 8 and 8.30 in the morning, (i.e. up to about seven hours after she was supposedly murdered).

The immediate cause of death was due to severance of the carotid artery. The cuts to the right thumb and back of the hand may have been sustained as Mary tried to defend herself, and the blood splashes on the wall to the right of the bed may have been caused by the throat being cut first as opposed to strangulation of the victim followed by severance of the throat. This would indicate a change in the modus operandi of the murderer, but this is not unusual. However, as she was so badly mutilated, it was impossible to say if strangulation had taken place and if the throat had been cut from left to right or vice versa.

The inquest took place on 12 November at Shoreditch Town Hall and was conducted by Roderick MacDonald. Past comment has been made on the fact that this inquest was over and done with in one day. The purpose of an inquest is to establish certain details which would include cause and time of death. These facts having been ascertained, the inquest was closed. Had it continued for another day or two, then George Hutchinson's testimony would have been heard in court, for on the evening of Monday 12 November he visited Commercial Street Police Station and made a statement. It contained a detailed description of the man he had seen with Mary on the night of the murder. Inspector Abberline questioned him thoroughly and believed his story to be true. Hutchinson gave a more detailed statement to the press. Part of it runs thus:

> The man was about five feet six inches, and 34 or 35 years of age, with dark complexion and dark moustache, turned up at the ends. He was wearing a long dark coat, trimmed with astrakhan, a white collar, with black necktie, in which was affixed a horseshoe pin. He wore a pair of dark 'spats' with light buttons over button boots and displayed from his waistcoat a massive gold chain. His watch chain had a big seal with a red stone hanging from it. He had a heavy moustache curled up and dark eyes and bushy eyebrows. He had no side whiskers and his chin was clean-shaven. He looked like a foreigner. He carried a small parcel in his hand about eight inches long, and it had a strap round it.

I find it incredible that so much detail about a man's attire could be observed in, what must have been, a very short space of time. In my opinion his statement should have been treated with great caution, especially as Hutchinson went to the police three days after the murder in Miller's Court had taken place.

As the months passed by the initial fear and panic began to subside. By spring there had been no further murders of that kind and the extra police and plain clothes patrols were stopped. It was a question of finance rather than their belief that the Ripper had gone away, died or had been locked in an asylum. We can never know for sure what actually happened to him.

News of a similar atrocity surfaced in July 1889, when a woman was found murdered in Castle Alley off Whitechapel High Street. She was Alice McKenzie (nicknamed 'Clay Pipe Alice'), and she was found to have two wounds in the left side of the neck, a shallow wound running from the left breast to the navel and several scratches from this wound towards the genitals. *The Times* newspaper never doubted that 'Jack' was at it again, but the nature of the wounds were markedly different to those found on Nichols, Chapman, Eddowes and Kelly. The Ripper was mentioned again in February 1891, when Frances Coles was murdered in Swallow Gardens. Her throat had been cut whilst she was lying on the ground but there were no abdominal mutilations. Thomas Sadler, a ship's fireman and a nasty piece of work, was charged with her murder. However, the evidence against him was weak and he was set free. Detectives were interested to know what Sadler was doing at the time of the Ripper murders and their investigations showed conclusively that he was away at sea. After 1891 there were no more murders that could be compared to those of Jack the Ripper.

As mentioned at the beginning of this chapter, the Metropolitan Police closed the file on the murders in 1892, the same time as Frederick Abberline retired from the force. Eleven years later he gave interviews for the *Pall Mall Gazette* in which he offered his opinion regarding a recently convicted murderer named Severin Klosowski (alias George Chapman). He believed that Klosowski was the Ripper. Walter Dew, writing in 1938, said that he could not express a definite opinion as to the identity of the murderer.

Dr Robert Anderson had overall charge of the investigation from 6 October 1888 up until 1892. In 1910 Anderson's memoirs had been published, and he had written that as a result of house-to-house enquiries the police came to the conclusion that the culprit was a low-class Jew. Readers were tantalised when he wrote, 'I should almost be tempted to disclose the identity of the murderer.' Chief Inspector Donald Swanson, who was in charge of the investigation from the beginning, passed all information he received to his superior, Dr Anderson. Swanson made pencil notes in his personal copy of Anderson's memoirs, *The Lighter Side of My Official Life*. When Swanson died some of his books and papers were handed down to his daughter, and upon her death they came into the possession of James Swanson, the Chief Inspector's grandson. One of the books was Anderson's memoirs containing the original pencil notes written by his grandfather. The notes (now referred to as the 'Swanson Marginalia') mention the name of Anderson's low-class Jew – 'Kosminski'. We shall learn more about Kosminski in a later chapter.

The Macnaghten Memoranda give details of three suspects whom the police had strong suspicions against. They were Mr M J Druitt, a doctor (in fact he was a lawyer); Kosminski, a Polish Jew who lived in the heart of the district; and Michael Ostrog, a Russian doctor and a convict who ended up in a lunatic asylum. Macnaghten wrote that Druitt was sexually insane and that 'private info' indicated that his own family believed him to have been the murderer. We do not know what the content of his private information was or from whom it was received.

Major Henry Smith wrote in his memoirs *From Constable to Commissioner* (1910) that there was no man living who knew as much about the murders as he did. The *True Crime* writer Hargrave Lee Adam (who died in 1946) wrote in his preface to the book *The Trial of George Chapman,* that Major Smith had told him the Ripper's identity was definitely known. If this was the case there must have been important reasons for keeping it secret.

It seems obvious to me that the senior officers involved in the hunt for the Ripper had their own ideas about his identity and it is this void, this space where the Ripper's name ought to have been, that has given rise to the many 'solutions' to the puzzle. The problem of Jack the Ripper's identity is indeterminable probably because, in truth, there was nobody who could be absolutely certain that their preferred suspect was the man they had so diligently searched for. The unforgettable trade name has perpetuated the mystery; but above all, the one thing about this Victorian murderer is the fact that he took tremendous risks, and if we can use the word 'luck' in relation to this series of gruesome crimes, then lucky he certainly was.

2

Black Bags and Top Hats

In glancing through a few of my books on Jack the Ripper, I noticed that the front covers of some of the more recent publications depict a top-hatted figure wearing a long, dark coat. This seems to be the standard image, the universal symbol of terror we now associate with the Ripper. The cover of the book, *Yours Truly from Hell,* written by Terrence Lore Smith for the centenary of the murders, shows a top-hatted silhouette with glowing eyes and a silver knife blade pointing upwards: the indestructible Ripper as a supernatural monster emerging from the fires of Hell. A 1966 version of the well-known novel, *The Lodger,* penned by Marie Belloc Lowndes, shows the eerie figure of a man with a top hat and clutching a brown bag as he walks down a misty street. He makes his first appearance on the doorstep of a house in Marylebone Road:

> On the top of the three steps which led up to the door, there stood the long, lanky figure of a man, clad in an Inverness cape and an old-fashioned top hat.

The top hat has become as much a part of Ripper mythology as the thick fogs of the alleyways of Whitechapel. Indeed, the most recurring theme in Ripper movies is the foggy street with an occasional hansom cab rattling by, a lone streetwalker ambling along and a bloodthirsty fiend hiding in the shadows wearing his hat and cape and holding his customary black bag. These are the main ingredients for yet another *'orrible murder*!

It has been written that Jack the Ripper initiated the age of the 'sex crime'. When we analyse his crimes and decipher the true meaning behind them it is easy to see why the Victorians found them to be incomprehensible. Successive crimes have been compared to the grisly murders belonging to that small time-frame in London's East End. In the 1980s and '90s the terms 'lust murder' and 'serial killer' began to emerge. What is frustrating for police forces around the world is the fact that serial killers strike at random; their victims are not known to them and consequently they are very difficult to track down. Sex crimes are more prevalent today than they were, say, sixty years ago. The term 'sex murder' is not easy to define and is not a term that you can look up in a book to see what it means. You might think that such a murder involves a sex act followed by the act of murder itself, but that is not always the case. Broadly speaking, serial killers are usually sexually motivated: they harbour distorted sexual emotions. In sex crimes there is not only a fusion of sex and violence, but a *confusion* between the two. This is usually acquired at an early age. The sexual psychopath then is able to attain sexual satisfaction from the violence of a murder. Jack the Ripper's 'sexual feelings' played an important part in his homicidal rampages.

The hidden and bizarre fantasies of a serial killer were simply not known about in the 1880s. It is only over the last twenty years or so that psychiatrists and criminologists have managed to gain some understanding of the motivation within these murderers. For the people of Whitechapel and Spitalfields this type of new crime instilled fear and anxiety. There was nothing available in those days which could provide answers to the questions surrounding those seemingly motiveless crimes, and even if there had been, crime detection was only in its infancy anyway. There were no sophisticated techniques like the ones we have today. A simple, rational explanation would have been enough to at least appease the emotions of the general public who lived in the area where these sex crimes occurred.

The idea that the murderer may have been a doctor, or at least someone with anatomical or medical knowledge, came about after the inquest into Annie Chapman's death. In his summing up on 26 September, 1888, Coroner Wynne Baxter said, 'The body has not been dissected, but the injuries have been made by someone who had considerable anatomical skill and knowledge. There are no meaningless cuts.' On the final day of the inquest the Coroner said that the murderer may not have been a lunatic. He then told the court that he had received information from the sub-curator of the Pathological Museum regarding an American who had asked the sub-curator to procure a number of specimens of the organ that was missing from the deceased. The American was willing to pay twenty pounds for each specimen, which he needed to use in conjunction with a publication he was working on.

Here we have a theory to explain why the murders might have been committed. It could have been a mad doctor who needed the organs for research purposes, or even somebody who was prepared to take enormous risks in the murder of prostitutes, so as to obtain the required organ in order to sell it. One can well imagine people from that era being persuaded to believe in such a scenario. It was a theme readily taken up by the newspapers of the day who were quick off the mark when they referred to Wynne Baxter's conclusions as a 'Burke and Hare' theory. Was there any truth in the theory? Apparently there was. The *British Medical Journal* ran an article to say that enquiries had been made at a medical school in the previous year. A foreign physician had been asking for certain body parts, but no sum of money had been offered.

So, even at this fairly early stage in the Whitechapel crime series, we have this idea coming through that a physician may somehow be implicated. These early seeds were to flower and blossom into the insane, 'mad doctor' theories which were to emerge in later years. In 1888 the gossip of the newspapers would have fuelled public imagination and the image of the Ripper as a doctor would begin to form, embellished by the addition of the little black bag. In those days black bags were commonplace items. Doctors carried them around and so did other citizens too.

Mrs Fanny Mortimer, a woman in her forties who lived at 36 Berner Street, was standing at her front door on the night that Liz Stride was murdered. Her house was only a few doors away from Dutfield's Yard, and she was at her front door at some time between 12.30 and 1 a.m. 30 September. Her original statement appeared in the *Daily News* and says that she saw a young man passing down the street who was carrying a black shiny bag. He came down the street from Commercial Road and Mrs Mortimer had seen nobody exit the yard before 1 a.m.

Ex-Chief Inspector Walter Dew wrote about this incident in his memoirs. Louis Diemschutz's name is incorrectly written, but this is understandable when one considers that Dew was writing his book fifty years later. This is what Walter Dew wrote:

> This woman was a Mrs Mortimer. After the main meeting at the clubhouse had broken up, some thirty or forty members who formed the choir remained behind to sing. Mrs Mortimer, as she had done on many previous occasions, came out to her gate the better to hear them. For ten minutes she remained there, seeing and hearing nothing which made her at all suspicious. Just as she was about to re-enter her cottage the woman heard the approach of a pony and cart. She knew this would be Lewis Dienschitz, the steward of the club. He went every Saturday to the market, returning about this hour of the early morning.

> At the same moment Mrs Mortimer observed something else, silent and sinister. A man, whom she judged to be about thirty, dressed in black, and carrying a small, shiny black bag, hurried furtively along the opposite side of the court. The woman was a little startled. The man's movements had been so quiet that she had not seen him until he was abreast of her. His head was turned away, as though he did not wish to be seen. A second later he had vanished round the corner leading to Commercial Road.

In fact the man carrying the black bag was Leon Goldstein, who went to the police the day after the Stride murder in order to vindicate himself. His bag contained nothing more than empty cigarette cases. His appearance at the police station was not widely publicised. On reading the extract from Walter Dew's memoirs, the man seen carrying the small black bag appears a suspicious character, and in all probability this story became inextricably linked to the murderer. Dew's writings are extremely interesting as they are based on his own knowledge from the days when it all happened. People were letting their imaginations run riot, conjuring up all kinds of fears about black magic and vampires. One of the strongest rumours at the time was that the culprit was a medical student or a doctor, but Dew's thoughts on the matter were clear. The mutilations carried out on the women were more likely to have been made by a maniac rather than a person who had a knowledge of surgery.

Would a doctor have been suspected of being the murderer simply because he was in the appropriate area carrying his black bag? The London Hospital was situated not far from the first murder scene at Buck's Row, and it would be interesting here to see what Dr Dennis Gratwick Halstead had to say about the murders. Dr Halstead was born in 1865 and began his medical career at the London Hospital in 1884. He was the author of *Doctor in the Nineties* (1959), which features an entire chapter on the Ripper murders and it makes fascinating reading. He wrote that the East End was a frightening place and the unknown killer became known as 'the terror of Whitechapel'. Few women dared to venture out alone after dark. The good doctor's work must have been trying at the best of times, particularly when one considers the types of patients that came his way. Sailors and dockhands of all nationalities used to frequent the brothels and opium dens situated in the dockland area and invariably the 'backwash of this seething tide of humanity' would end up in the receiving room at the hospital. There were drunkards in the last stages of alcoholism who thought nothing of assaulting the duty nurses, and prostitutes used to turn up covered in blood from their fights with gin bottles.

Halstead's opening paragraph on the murders tells us about the frantic efforts and house-to-house searches made by the police and the cross-questioning of hundreds of suspects. The mystery remained unsolved. Dr Halstead wrote that the murderer possessed anatomical knowledge and it was this belief that brought suspicion upon the medical profession itself, particularly the suspicions of the local police and plain-clothes detectives who were waiting in the back alleys ready to pounce. He makes an interesting point, though, in mentioning that the plain-clothes police were easy to spot and that it would not have been difficult for the Ripper to keep out of their way. If his writings were based totally on memory then he certainly deserved credit. Many inhabitants of Whitechapel looked capable of committing some sort of crime and the police thought they were making progress when they were looking for a man called 'Leather Apron'. It transpired that he was an unfortunate Polish Jew, Halstead wrote, and he was merely a boot-finisher by trade. He was released after questioning as was the case with many others. It was suggested that a butcher might have been responsible, his expertise having been gained through his butchering techniques. Slaughtermen too came under suspicion, but all clues and suspicions that were acted on came to a blank. Interestingly, the doctor wrote that it was a 'section of medical opinion' who dismissed the butcher or slaughterer theory in favour of the idea that the killer could have escaped detection and remained unknown amongst the criminal element because he was a member of the upper classes. The acute Dr Halstead pointed out how articles in *Punch* drew attention to the advertisement of murder mysteries on the stage and how they had an evil and corrupting influence on the people who were confronted with them - possibly even the murderer himself.

In the days following the inquest of Annie Chapman the medical staff at the London Hospital fell under suspicion and were often followed when walking through the neighbourhood. It seems that the locals avoided members of the medical profession. This fixation with black bags, doctors and surgeons, obviously gave rise to other theories that the killer may have been from the upper classes. The image that we have now of Jack the Ripper, wearing a top hat and carrying his black bag, is far removed from the reality of those murders in the autumn of 1888. The public and the press had their own ideas regarding the nature of the Ripper, and the possibility of a 'gentleman' murderer has given rise to many books and films which, even now, still hang on to this concept. In connection with the slaying of Mary

Kelly, Dr Halstead wrote:

> A great crowd immediately gathered outside Miller's Court, and there was consternation as the gory details became fully known. Once again the cry went up that the police and their blessed bloodhounds were on the wrong scent, but this time those who knew the woman Kelly were sure that they had recently seen her in the company of a sinister and handsome-looking stranger with a moustache, who carried a black bag around with him, and had been seen accosting four different women on the same evening on a previous occasion.

Dr Hasltead's chapter on the Whitechapel crimes is very interesting and well worth reading if you get the chance.

Daniel Farson was, amongst other things, a journalist and television presenter. He carried out his own research into the murders and his book, *Jack the Ripper*, was published in 1972. He managed to contact Mary Cox's niece, whose recollection of her aunt's story is illustrative. The information passed onto Mr Farson was that Mary Cox saw Kelly coming through the 'iron gate' with a gentleman who was a real toff. He was fine looking and wore an overcoat, cape and a high hat. He was carrying a Gladstone bag.

This seems to have been the impression of the murderer which caught the imagination of the public at the time: a gentleman, smart in appearance, dark moustache, hat, long dark coat and carrying small black bag. Of course this theme had its variations. In 1997 I managed to obtain a reprint of the book *Jack the Ripper or When London Walked in Terror*. It had been published sixty years earlier and was written by ex-Detective Sergeant Edwin T Woodhall. His introduction tells us that he was a detective turned author, and his book recounts some of the theories and stories which were put forward at the time of the murders. His recollections are interesting because there are parallels with the contents of his work and theories which were to appear in print decades later. Writing about the murder of Polly Nichols, he tells us some details about Constable Thain's beat. Thain caught sight of a tall man who, having been surprised at the approach of the policeman, crossed to the other side of the road:

> From the swift glimpse the constable caught some distance away, by the dimly lit rays of a street gas lamp, he appeared

> very white-faced with dark eyes and moustache. His age was hard to state, but judging by his build and the swift energetic way he moved - not an old man. However, the constable, used to the people's dress in this locality, did observe that the style and cut of the clothes seemed superior, and that he wore a rather big fashionable tweed cloth cap pulled well down over his eyes...

The key word in this paragraph is 'superior'. The constable did not get the chance to question the tall man as his attention was drawn to a man and his wife who were arguing in a nearby alley. 'Leather Apron' makes an appearance a little further on in the narrative. He is described as a 'big burly Russian Jew of an ignorant type'. As a suspect he was ruled out but another man was arrested not far from the crime scene (i.e. of Annie Chapman's murder). This man, we are told, had blood on his clothes and hands, but it turned out that he was a butcher who was employed at a nearby slaughterhouse. This raises a fairly important point and it is that slaughterers could walk about the streets with blood on their clothing without causing alarm to passers-by. This situation may well have facilitated the Ripper's movements on the nights of his murders. Woodhall himself believed that the murders were committed by someone who had medical training. Unfortunately, the book contains many errors and the author's recollections had obviously become confused. A dark-eyed stranger is briefly described in relation to the Mitre Square murder. The contradictory statement runs thus:

> The man seemed to have the peek of a cap pulled well down over his eyes, but the tailor noticed he was pale and had dark eyes and a moustache.

Anybody reading this book fifty years ago would have had no doubts at all concerning the killer's medical expertise. Regarding Mary Kelly's mutilations, he states, 'Every operation from a surgical point of view was found to be perfect.'

In Chapter Twelve of Woodhall's book we are introduced to the theory of the clairvoyant who helped the police in their investigations. The clairvoyant was Robert James Lees, and his alleged psychic identification of the Ripper has been the precursor to many theories concerning royalty and high-class gentlemen. This is the stuff of legend, and of all the solutions to the Ripper mystery, the royal conspiracy theories seem to have had the biggest impact. Edwin Woodhall claims the murderer was in fact tracked down by the use of clairvoyance and that the authorities knew who he was. In making his claim the author stated that he had the support of one of Britain's most powerful newspapers. In fact, the original story about Lees appeared in the Chicago *Sunday Times-Herald* in April 1895. It is a significant article in that it has spawned many erroneous ideas regarding the Ripper case.

The Lees story was apparently told by Dr Howard, who was a London physician, to William Greer Harrison of the Bohemian Club in San Francisco. Dr Howard sat in a court of enquiry concerning a brother physician who was proved to have been none other than Jack the Ripper. The supposed murderer was living in the West End of London and was a physician of high standing. Howard was sworn to secrecy but, under the influence of drink, he gave details of the story to a London clubman who was in Chicago at the time. Howard did not reveal the name of the murderer, but when the Ripper was eventually tracked down it was discovered he was a physician in good standing and with an extensive practice. He had been a student at Guy's Hospital and was an enthusiastic vivisectionist. The article stated that this man 'experienced the keenest delight in inflicting tortures upon defenceless animals' and only after a month of his marriage his wife discovered him holding a cat over the flame of a lamp, which he continued doing throughout the night until it died. The next day he was as lovable as ever. The article gave credit to Robert James Lees, the man who tracked down the Whitechapel fiend.

Lees was born in 1849 and his psychic powers became apparent when he was thirteen. In 1888 he lived in Peckham and was known for being a philanthropist and the author of several books on spiritualism. He gave private consultations as a medium and it was alleged that the late Prince Consort 'spoke' to people via Lees at a séance. It has been written that he became Queen Victoria's medium but the *Jack the Ripper A to Z* points out that biographers have failed to find any connection between the two.

Going back to the story of Lees and the Ripper, from the *Sunday Times-Herald,* we see that the clairvoyant was at the height of his powers during the first three murders. One day, whilst writing in his study, he had a feeling that another murder was about to be committed, and as hard as he tried he could not shake the feeling off. In his mind's eye he saw a man and a woman enter a narrow court.

Lees went to Scotland Yard with his story but they regarded him as a bit of a lunatic. However, the duty sergeant did take note of where the crime would be committed and the time when the couple entered the court. The following night a woman was seen with a man entering the court in question. The person who saw the couple thought the man was American because of the soft felt hat he had on. He looked like a gentleman. The body of a woman was discovered in the very spot which had been described by Mr Lees. Her throat had been cut from ear to ear and she had been horribly mutilated. Lees was shocked when he learned of the murder, and at the advice of a physician he took his family to the Continent. Whilst resting abroad he was free from his strange hallucinations.

During his absence there were four more murders and Lees decided to return to London. One day Lees and his wife were on an omnibus travelling down Edgware Road. A man had previously entered the vehicle and was wearing a dark suit of Scotch tweed over which was a light overcoat. The clairvoyant told his wife that the man was the Ripper, but she thought he was being foolish. The man got out at Oxford Street and was followed by Lees, who informed a police constable that his quarry was Jack the Ripper. Needless to say, the constable did not make an arrest. That very same night Lees had another vision in which he could clearly see the victim's face. He noticed that one of the ears had been cut off and the other one was attached only by a piece of skin. When the trance was over he rushed off to Scotland Yard and told an inspector what he had experienced. The officer was more inclined to take the story seriously after he learned about the severed ears. He took a postcard from his desk and showed it to Lees. The card was signed 'Jack the Ripper' and mentioned the ninth victim, whose ears were to be cut off. The inspector ordered 3,000 constables to wear plain clothes and these men, along with 1,500 detectives disguised as labourers, kept watch over the courts and alleys of Whitechapel. Still, the murderer came and went unchallenged, leaving behind his mutilated victim with the severed ears. Robert Lees was so upset by the atrocity that he left Britain and headed for the Continent again. Meanwhile, the Ripper continued his onslaught and reached a total of sixteen murders. After his return to England the clairvoyant had yet another vision but this time he decided to help the police in catching the murderer by using his 'magnetic influence'. One night the inspector and his aids followed closely behind Lees, who scoured the London streets on the scent of the elusive criminal. At 4 a.m. Lees halted at the gates of a West End mansion and pointed to an upper room, the window of which was illuminated by a faint light. The inspector looked at the mansion in disbelief as it was the residence of a celebrated physician. He told Lees that he would arrest the man, at the risk of jeopardising his own position, if he could describe the interior of the hall.

They waited until 7 a.m. and then entered the house. Lees' description of the interior hall was correct, apart from some minor details, and so they waited while one of the servants went to summon the doctor's wife. Upon questioning, the wife revealed that her husband had been absent from home on the nights of the murders and she did not believe that he was of sound mind. A thorough search of the house revealed a Scotch tweed suit, soft felt hat and a light overcoat. The physician was convinced of his guilt and asked to be killed at once. He was taken to a private insane asylum in Islington and a sham death and burial were undertaken to account for his disappearance. An empty coffin lies in the family vaults at Kensal Green. To the keepers at the asylum the illustrious patient is known as 'Thomas Mason'.

This account is more or less the gist of what appeared in the *Sunday Times-Herald.* The story itself originated in a club founded by Chicago journalists who delighted in creating tall stories. The 'Whitechapel Club' was the name given to this establishment. William Greer Harrison was a broker from San Francisco who felt the need to mingle with poets and writers but was thought of as being pretentious. What is certain is that Robert Lees did go to the police to offer his services in the hunt for the killer but he was regarded as being a fool and a madman. The Chicago newspaper story impressed at least one journalist in Britain who wrote his own piece for the *People* newspaper. The article appeared in the edition for 19 May 1895, and named Dr Benjamin Howard as being responsible for telling the story. Howard was out of the country when the story appeared, but on his return in January 1896, he wrote a furious letter to the editor of the *People,* in which he stated that there was nothing in the article concerning him which had the slightest foundation in fact.

Edwin Woodhall repeats the Chicago story in his 1937 book and towards the end of Chapter Twelve he wrote:

> Lengthy questioning of the doctor's wife brought to light the most amazing Jekyll and Hyde story ever heard. The man was one of London's most distinguished doctors – but he had a dual personality.

Woodhall's information was taken from a 1931 edition of the London *Daily Express,* and although the information had been lifted from the *Times-Herald,* it featured a small piece that was to further compound this fairy tale. The information, it said, had come from a secret document written by Lees which had been given to a friend and was to be released after Lees had died. His death occurred in January 1931 and the reappearance of the story was due to the curiosity of a crime reporter named Cyril Morton. Undoubtedly, Mr Morton was under the impression that Lees knew the identity of the Ripper. He had visited the daughter of Robert Lees but no information was forthcoming regarding her late father's involvement with the Ripper affair. Whilst at her home, Morton noticed a copy of the original 1895 story and shortly after his visit he managed to secure a copy for his own purposes. Morton's write-up for the *Daily Express* was basically the same as the 1895 original but there was no reference to its American sources. What made the rehash of this tale perhaps a little more persuasive was the addition of the 'secret document'. Thus the affair of the clairvoyant and Jack the Ripper swings into action in the 1930s with a newspaper article and a book written by an ex-detective sergeant. Robert Lees surfaced again in 1970 when Cynthia Legh wrote an article for *Light,* the Journal of the College of Psychic Studies. She first met Lees in 1912, after which he became a frequent visitor at her home in Cheshire. Her report says that the Queen had sent for him on several occasions and that she valued his exceptional gifts. Various spirit guides helped Lees with his writings, and on one occasion the guide spoke to him after a murder had been committed in Whitechapel and told him to go to the Queen, which he did. The Queen herself gave Robert James Lees enough authority to enable him to help the police with their enquiries. The incident about Lees taking the police to a doctor's house in London is again mentioned, also the fact that the Queen asked Lees and his family to leave London for five years in order to quell any rumours which may have reached the doctor's wife. The clairvoyant received a pension while he was away from London.

Here we can see how the royal connection is brought back to the boil. After Cynthia Legh's story was printed another theory appeared - this time in *The Criminologist* for November, 1970. The piece was entitled 'Jack the Ripper - A Solution', and was written by T E A Stowell, CBE, MD. The suspect's name was not mentioned; he was referred to simply as 'S', who was an heir to power and wealth. In August 1960, writer and crime historian Colin Wilson had a series of essays published in the London *Evening Standard* about the Ripper murders. Wilson used the details of the murders as a background for his first novel *Ritual in the Dark* (1960).

One of the readers of the *Evening Standard* was Dr Thomas Stowell. He was intrigued by Wilson's writings on the murders and so he wrote to the author saying that Wilson knew more about the murders than he was willing to admit. The two met at the Athenaeum and during the course of their meal Stowell got to the point of their meeting. In one of his articles Colin Wilson wrote that a man had been observed close to the scene of one of the Ripper murders and he had been described as looking like a 'gentleman'. Wilson pointed out that the description was merely an account given by a witness at the time of the atrocities. It was that fact alone which Stowell found interesting, and he went on to say that his instincts had been confirmed. He added that the Ripper was the Duke of Clarence. His 1970 article had given enough detail for one to be able to deduce that 'S' was Prince Albert Victor, Duke of Clarence, son of the Prince of Wales (later Edward V11). Stowell thought the Prince was suffering from syphilis and was being treated by Sir William Gull, Physician in Ordinary to Queen Victoria. As we have seen, there was speculation at the time of the murders that medical skill was shown in the removal of various organs. It is not difficult to see how Sir William Gull was to be implicated in the Ripper saga by theorists and myth makers. Sir William Gull was supposedly seen in Whitechapel on the night of a Ripper murder, and Stowell surmised that the purpose of his presence was to certify the murderer as being insane, so as to be kept under restraint. Dr Stowell received much attention after the publication of his article, so much so that he was invited to appear on BBC television for an interview with Kenneth Allsop. Stowell decided to go along with it but during the interview he declined to name his suspect. Six days later he wrote to *The Times* denying that 'S' was the Duke of Clarence. Before the letter appeared in the newspaper Dr Stowell died and his papers relating to the theory were destroyed by his family.

The medical theme, which has evolved as a way of partly explaining the murders, has been fairly prominent in books and films about the Whitechapel murders. This, coupled with theories involving gentlemen and doctors and even certain members of the royal family, has given us an everlasting impression of a top-hatted figure kitted out with his obligatory black bag and long, dark coat, stalking his victims through the fog-laden back alleys of London's East End. It's almost like a drama that would have been acted out in the theatres; almost like a Jekyll and Hyde production. Almost, but not quite, pure fiction.

Australian-born Leonard Matters wrote a full-length book on the Ripper mystery. It was published in 1929 and the author asks the question, 'Was the murderer a surgeon?' To which he answers, 'Almost positively, yes'. It would have been impossible for a man who was ignorant of physiology and anatomy to have carried out mutilations which were so precise and consistent. I was fortunate enough to obtain a copy of Matters' book, *The Mystery of Jack the Ripper,* in 1982, after I had written to a book-finding service listing my requirements. If I remember rightly, the book cost me £12. The author had spent some years in Buenos Aires as a newspaper editor, and in the introduction to his book he says that he came upon a confession which could, if true, dissipate much of the mystery surrounding Jack the Ripper.

Over half way through the book we are introduced to the report of the man with the black bag. They were commonly seen in the big cities during that time period, but as Matters points out, they went out of fashion at the time of the Whitechapel murders due to their connection with the murderer. Anyone seen carrying such a bag, by day or by night, would be set upon by angry crowds. A certain person entered the King Street Police Station and told the desk sergeant that he had lost his black bag. Not only did he speak about the murders, so we are told, he also offered to cut off the sergeant's head. He was placed in a cell and a police doctor declared that he was a homicidal lunatic. Apparently, he was believed to have been the person who was seen talking to Catharine Eddowes shortly before she was killed. He admitted that he had studied to be a medical man but became an engineer instead. He ended up in a lunatic asylum. We learn about the real 'Jack' in Matter's chapter on 'The Satanic Dr Stanley'. This man was a brilliant surgeon; he had connections with Harley Street professionals and was talked about and admired by students of the various London hospitals. He had been married, but his wife died when their son was only a few years old. From that time onwards Stanley retired from public life wishing to be left alone. He believed his son would follow in his footsteps and become one of the world's greatest surgeons. Dr Stanley told one of his colleagues that the lad would be famous and 'he will be hailed as a saviour of humanity.' All the doctor's hopes were hinged on the success of his son, but at the beginning of 1888 the son, a young man by then, died.

The author wrote that the only fictitious aspect of the Dr Stanley story was his name. He admitted that he could not find any proof to substantiate his claims and his search of the records of the General Medical Council of Great Britain failed to reveal the existence of a Dr Stanley in 1888. He goes on:

> The story of Dr Stanley so far as I have related it, is definitely based on the recital of an anonymous surgeon in Buenos Aires who claimed to have been a student in London under the doctor, and to have been present when he died in the Argentine capital ten years or more ago.

Let's continue with the story. The son's name was Herbert Stanley and in 1886 he met a young girl in a café. Her name was Marie Jeanette. Stanley was drunk as he and his university chums were celebrating their Boat Race victory. Marie was one of the best-looking girls he had ever seen. They went out together for a short while and then went to Paris for a week. This signalled the end. Herbert left Marie forever when he discovered that she had a disease. When his fellow students found out, Herbert was kicked out of college. Dr Stanley was determined to help his son and to this end he engaged the help of the best medical men in the world. They fought for months to save the son's life. The son died, but not before he had divulged the name of the girl who had ultimately been the cause of his death – Marie Jeanette Kelly. Dr Stanley stood beside the body of his son and said, 'I will find the woman. When I find her, I will kill her; by God, I will!'

Eventually, he did. Leaving his home one night in Portman Square he made his way to Wardour Street where Kelly was living in lodgings. The girl had moved out, but the present occupant told Stanley that Marie had gone to live in the East End. The task to find her proved difficult, especially in Whitechapel and Spitalfields, were thousands of streetwalkers lived. So, Stanley questions the unfortunates regarding Kelly's whereabouts. To cover his tracks he murders them using his long dagger and his surgical knife. His search brings him into contact with Martha Tabram, Polly Nichols and the rest. Catharine Eddowes gives her name as Kate Kelly, but she cannot have been an acquaintance of his son because she is old and ugly. All is not lost; she knew a 'Mary Kelly' who lived in Dorset Street. Needless to say, the satanic Dr Stanley finds Mary Kelly and satisfies his revengeful feelings. The task is done, and to quote from the Matters' book, 'And when next day they found the body of the woman, cut to pieces as he had sworn, her heart was on the pillow by her head!'

Ten years later Dr Stanley ends up in a hospital – the 'X' Hospital in Buenos Aires where he dies of cancer. Before he dies Dr Stanley summons one of his students from the early days who is now a doctor himself. The doctor arrives and duly hears Stanley's confession that he is Jack the Ripper. Soon after – Stanley is dead.

We must ask ourselves: Have these stories of doctors and gentlemen with their black bags and top hats really influenced our way of thinking about that particular criminal from the autumn of 1888? This question was the basis of a theme for a television programme which was shown on BBC 2 in September 1988. It was a documentary for a series called *Timewatch* and this particular episode, shown on the centenary of the murders, was called *Shadow of the Ripper.* It was written and presented by Sir Christopher Frayling, Rector of London's Royal College of Art, where he is also Professor of Cultural History. He has written many books and articles on aspects of cultural history and has studied the origins of famous novels like *Dracula, Dr Jekyll and Mr Hyde* and *The Hound of the Baskervilles.* His television contribution to the Ripper mystery is an important comment on how the murders were transformed into a Victorian melodrama by plays, books and films, and also how the newspapers of the time altered the public's conception of the murderer. Sir Christopher Frayling tells us that the real story of Jack the Ripper is not a 'whodunnit', but a story of newspaper men and the kind of person we think the killer must have been. He rightly points out that the West End newspapers had turned the gruesome murders in Whitechapel and the surrounding areas into a major media event.

William Thomas Stead was the editor of the *Pall Mall Gazette* and apart from experimenting with a more conspicuous style of newspaper format, known as the 'New Journalism', he used the Whitechapel murders as part of a campaign against the Metropolitan Police and particularly Sir Charles Warren. The Met were already a target for the radical press on account of, amongst other things, the heavy-handed tactics that were used to restrain 20,000 demonstrators who attempted to enter Trafalgar Square on 13 November 1887. One person was killed and hundreds were injured during the clashes between the police, who had a back-up of Grenadier Guards, and the demonstrators. The incident was later referred to as 'Bloody Sunday'. The W T Stead-versus-Warren saga became a 'larger than life variety turn', as Frayling puts it, and the stories soon found their places in the Victorian penny dreadful magazines like *The Illustrated Police News,* with their lurid drawings. What was to emerge from this growing amount of press coverage was the idea of the Ripper being a 'gentleman' or 'decadent aristocrat'. This came about when W T Stead quoted the Marquis de Sade with reference to what the murderer might be like as a person.

The idea of Jack the Ripper as a gentleman may also have arisen from the issues surrounding prostitution and in particular in relation to Stead's newspaper article about the abuse of children for the sexual gratification of upper-class gentlemen. Music halls and theatres, although places for fun and entertainment, may have provided 'entertainment' of a different kind. Some people thought they were brothels dressed up to look seemingly innocent. In the upper rooms of such places gentlemen took their women for sexual favours. Stead attacked these places; he wanted them to get rid of the 'sex' that was being projected by the dancers on stage, and he also attacked the West End toffs who indulged themselves in the bawdy atmosphere of cigars, wine and easy women.

From these types of settings emerged the myth of 'Jack' as a gentleman or as a Prince. From the campaigns against immorality within the higher classes came the belief that the murderer must have been a West End toff or a decadent aristocrat, a sort of Jekyll and Hyde character who lived in the West End by day, the East End by night. So, the Ripper was the Duke of

Clarence and Avondale, or Montague Druitt who was a barrister and member of the MCC. W T Stead and his followers were partly successful in their campaigns, because Wilton's music hall was transformed into a mission in 1888 and, as Frayling tells us, it was this very attention to the music halls and to vice in high places that moulded the image of Jack the Ripper for all time.

As previously mentioned, various details relating to the death of Annie Chapman gave rise to the belief that the murderer may have possessed medical knowledge or skill. The imagery of the sadistic and cruel doctor was available at that time in novels and anti-vivisectionist literature.

Women were taken into hospital theatres and underwent major surgery in front of an audience of medical students, and the allegations were saying that the operations were unnecessary and merely an aid to the students' education. The liberal press latched on to this notion of needless cruelty in theatres, and so 'Gentleman Jack' became 'Dr Jack'.

The more conservative opinions of the press like *Punch* drew readers' attention away from the sensational Ripper stories and, as well as pointing out the need for more policemen on the beat, it attacked the liberal press for obstructing the police authorities in their investigations. The East End was described as an abyss, full of strange inhabitants from other cultures and teaming with Jews from Eastern Europe. Out of the long, tedious years of unemployment there came a new breed of people who were becoming more politically outspoken. Socialists, anarchists and militants were apparent in the late 1880s and their views were expressed in various 'alternative' newspapers. The need for social reform brought General Booth and the Salvationists to the East End, along with all sorts of charity organisations. One newspaper jokingly suggested that the murderer might be a mad social reformer who had designs on calling attention to the plight of the people. Others gave credence to the theory that the Ripper could have been a slum dweller or a Jew, and so anybody who didn't fit in became a target for the vigilantes.

In summing up, Sir Christopher Frayling says that in our attempts to unmask the identity of the murderer we are fulfilling a desire to show that the Ripper belongs to a set of people we mistrust; whether this comes from cinema or comics or music halls, he represents a space into which we put all the people we don't like – and we call them 'Jack the Ripper'.

This well-balanced and informative documentary also features crime historian, writer and broadcaster Martin Fido, who explains the details of the murders to a group of pilgrims.

3

From a Jack to a Queen

By far the most prominent theory to emerge as an explanation for the murders committed by Jack the Ripper was expounded by Stephen Knight. Knight was a journalist for the *East London Advertiser*, for which he carried out his own research for an article on the Whitechapel murders. His book, *Jack the Ripper: The Final Solution* (1976), was a worldwide success. The book was described as brilliant, outstanding and plausible. I can remember reading it everyday on the train from Preston to Poulton-le-Fylde. The year was 1976 and I was halfway through my studies for a Certificate in Education at Poulton Teacher Training College. The book *is* extremely interesting and at the time of reading it I believed that the answer, at last, had been found.

It is now known that Knight's theory was incorrect because it was based on an untrue story told to him by a man named Joseph Sickert who died in 2003, but its impact was tremendous and the idea of a royal conspiracy still lingers today in the minds of many believers. The story of the country's greatest conspiracy is fascinating and it should be viewed as an important contribution in respect of understanding the mythology surrounding Jack the Ripper.

A book appeared in 1997, *The Jack the Ripper Whitechapel Murders*, by Kevin O'Donnell. It is based on the researches of a married couple, Andy and Sue Parlour. Andy Parlour is actually related to Mary Ann Nichols, the first victim in the Ripper crime series. In order to understand the account given by the Parlours it is necessary to go back to Stephen Knight's royal conspiracy theory to see how it interrelates with O'Donnell's later publication.

Jack the Ripper was not one man stalking his victims through the streets and alleys of the East End - he was three men! There were two killers and one accomplice; their intended victim was Mary Kelly. Stephen Knight was granted special access to the Scotland Yard files on the Ripper murders (open to the public in 1976), and to 'secret Home Office papers' connected with the murders. Both sources provided him with important information which was used to support his claims. We have already seen how, in 1970, Dr Thomas Stowell's article for the *Criminologist* revived interest in the Ripper case. In 1973 a new documentary series was made for BBC television. It was simply called *Jack the Ripper* and was presented by two fictitious TV detectives, Detective Chief Superintendents Barlow and Watt. It was supposed to be the final word on the Ripper, and although the six separate programmes were factual there was no definite proof for the Ripper's identity.

The final programme was tantalising for it featured a short sequence of a man called Joseph Sickert, whose story was investigated by Stephen Knight. Sickert's story exploded into the world of Ripperology and added a new dimension to the myths and falsehoods that have helped keep the mystery firmly fixed in the mind of the public. Before Sickert was aware of the proposal for a TV series based on the murders, he received a phone call from Stephen Knight. Knight became aware of Sickert through his friendship with Paul Bonner, the producer of the *Jack the Ripper* series. Joseph Sickert was told that the BBC were interested in his story, a story which apparently had been leaked to Paul Bonner and Elwyn Jones (journalist, TV producer and founder of the TV series *Z-Cars* and *Softly, Softly*) via a senior Scotland Yard man.

Knight was granted an interview with Sickert and the trail took him to an address in Islington. It turned out to be an artist's studio belonging to a Mr Harry Jonas. Sickert was also there and the two of them subjected the young journalist to an extensive bout of cross-examination aimed at discovering the source of his information. He learned that Sickert's story was a personal one and would not be allowed to be broadcast on TV should the facts become known. Knight returned to Islington a few days later and found the atmosphere to be far less tense than before. Slowly, the truth about the Jack the Ripper murders began to emerge and the pertinent facts of the case went back to events that took place in Cleveland Street, London.

It was there that Walter Sickert, Joseph's father, kept an artist's studio. A young girl known as Annie Elizabeth Crook (a Catholic girl) worked in a nearby tobacconist's/confectioner's shop. Her assistant was none other than Mary Kelly (referred to as 'Marie' Kelly in Knight's book). Prince Albert Victor, Duke of Clarence (known as 'Eddy' to his family and close friends), met Annie Crook at this very shop on one of his visits to the area. The story goes that Eddy fell in love with Annie Crook and a secret Catholic wedding took place in St Saviour's private chapel, the clandestine ceremony having been witnessed by Mary Kelly. The couple had a child, Alice Margaret, but the marriage ended after the police raided Cleveland Street in 1888. Annie was sent to various institutions and the child was left with Mary to be looked after. Mary was in a dangerous predicament; she had witnessed an illegal marriage and now had possession of a royal child. She took the baby away from Cleveland Street and they stayed at a convent in the East End.

Joseph Sickert was eventually persuaded to go public with his fantastic story, and in 1973 he made an appearance in the final episode of *Jack the Ripper* in which he gave a brief outline of his story. Stephen Knight was interested in the complete story. Joseph Sickert ('Hobo' to his friends), agreed to give Knight an interview. He had decided that it was only fair for the people of the East End to know the truth.

As a boy, Joseph recalled having a feeling that something sinister had been a part of his mother's life. His father Walter, who was an Impressionist painter, told his son the truth about the Ripper. Joseph was only fourteen at the time. The germ of this whole affair was to be found in the life of Prince Albert Victor Christian Edward. When he was twenty years of age his mother, Princess Alexandra, became concerned about his personal development and decided that it would do him good to get away from his routine way of life and confined environment. His father, Albert Edward, Prince of Wales, had very little to do with his son's upbringing. Alexandra wrote a letter to Walter Sickert and asked him to take the lad under his wing, but the undertaking was to be kept secret. If the knowledge had reached the ears of Queen Victoria there would have been hell to pay. The Prince would visit Sickert secretly, exiting his royal carriage at a certain place on the way and continuing the journey in an ordinary carriage driven by a ruthless man named John Netley. Prince Eddy posed as Sickert's younger brother Albert; he enjoyed his freedom and the experience of meeting new and varied people. His association with Sickert deepened and they became very close friends. They stayed at rented rooms at 15 Cleveland Street, and opposite stood Number 22 where Annie Elizabeth Crook worked. She was an illiterate girl but Eddy was attracted by her charm and by her resemblance to his own mother. At first, Annie was not aware of his true identity.

As previously mentioned, Annie had a child to the Prince. The affair between the two was a deeply kept secret. Annie lived in the basement of Number 6 Cleveland Street, and was joined by Mary Kelly who was paid by Sickert to look after the baby. A Catholic wedding ceremony took place with Sickert and Kelly as witnesses. Walter Sickert visited France on numerous occasions, and in Eddy's absence he also took Annie and the little girl. In the summer of 1886 Mary went to France with Annie and the child, and this probably ties in with her fondness of the name 'Marie Jeanette'.

Eddy's real identity did not remain a secret for long and once the truth was out it became impossible to stop the gossip and the wagging tongues. When the secret marriage of Prince Albert Victor to a commoner, a Catholic girl, became knowledge possessed by the Prime Minister and the Queen herself, it was decided that the matter had to be dealt with: the whole affair had to be brought to a definite end. Initially, Queen Victoria was furious, but after a while she decided that although the lad had been careless and unwise in his adventures, a severe reprimand would be enough to settle the matter once and for all.

Prime Minister Salisbury took a different view. In his eyes the Prince's actions could be the cause for great unrest amongst the people. Salisbury was convinced that the Prince's seedy, amorous relationship with a simple Catholic girl could lead to a revolution. The class difference between the East End (poor), and the West End (rich), was only too obvious; moreover, Victoria was referred to as the 'Famine Queen' by the Irish. There had been scandal involving her son Edward, and now there was Eddy and his unfortunate encounter with Annie Crook. If this became common knowledge, then surely it must mean the end of the monarchy. This sordid episode was of the greatest concern to the Prime Minister.

A raid on Cleveland Street was arranged and it was inadvertently witnessed by Walter Sickert. Eddy was removed from his premises in Cleveland Street and bungled into a hansom cab. Similarly, Annie Crook was removed from her basement apartment and forced, struggling, into a separate cab. From that moment onwards there was no future for Annie Elizabeth Crook - she suffered the hardships of the workhouses and was sent from one institution to another. It was imperative that she could not be traced. Eventually, Annie went insane; she died in 1920. Mary Kelly escaped with the royal child and somehow managed to return her to Sickert. He passed the child over to some relatives to be looked after but in 1895 he asked for the girl to be returned into his care. He took her to Dieppe where she stayed for several years.

These facts were passed on from Walter to his son, Joseph, but the story didn't end there - it had only just begun. Mary Kelly had witnessed an illegal marriage between a member of the Royal Family and a Catholic girl. She knew about their child, Alice Margaret, and she would have been aware of the inherent danger to the royal family if such information were to become public. Kelly thought the matter over and she confided with some friends, the outcome of which was a plan to extort money from the government itself. The blackmail scheme somehow managed to reach the ears of Salisbury, whose reaction was to maintain absolute secrecy over the affair. This could only be achieved by silencing the blackmailers.

The man chosen for the mission was Sir William Withey Gull, Physician in Ordinary to Queen Victoria. He was a loyal servant, and according to Knight he was not averse to rendering troublesome people harmless when it was deemed necessary.

Walter Sickert maintained that neither the government nor the royal family were involved with the plan to silence Mary Kelly and her associates. The whole thing was carried out in secret by the Masons. Both Salisbury and Gull were Freemasons of high standing and were prepared to go to extreme lengths to protect the Crown. Out of the Masonic plan to silence prostitutes came a character who would never be caught, because he did not exist - Jack the Ripper.

This was the tale as told by Joseph Sickert to Stephen Knight. The journalist's initial feelings were that the facts related to in Sickert's story were highly unlikely, but after further talks with him, and after a visit to Cleveland Street and the murder sites, he became more convinced that there might be some truth in it after all. One must consider the situation as it was in 1888 to realise the impact that Kelly's knowledge could have had. The Prime Minister was deeply worried and concerned for the well-being of the monarchy and the government. If Kelly's story was picked up by the republicans and socialists, and if the fate of Annie Crook became known, then all these facts could have provided extra ammunition for the revolutionaries.

In August 1888, an attempt at blackmail was made. Joseph Sickert did not reveal the name of the person who received the demand, but apparently it was for a meagre sum of money. The names of the blackmailers became known to Salisbury. They were Mary Kelly, Mary Ann Nichols, Annie Chapman and Elizabeth Stride. Sir William Gull was probably the best man for the job of silencing them. He was one of the country's most eminent Freemasons and had played a key role in the Cleveland Street operation. Joseph Sickert had always been convinced that Freemasonry was the 'behind-the-scenes' dictator within the government. With solid determination, Gull concocted a plan to ensure a total end to the blackmailing plot. It was thought unwise to capture and incarcerate the four women, as this would undoubtedly have caused them to reveal what they knew. One woman's story would have been ignored, but four women all telling the same story could have aroused suspicion. If they couldn't be left at large then the only other option was to kill them.

The women were to be silenced according to Masonic ritual. Sir William needed to survey the area where Kelly and the others lived and the man chosen to help him with this task was John Netley, who had already proved his worth by driving Eddy to Cleveland Street where he socialised with Walter Sickert. Sir Robert Anderson was the other high-ranking Freemason involved in the operation to silence the four women. He was a member of the same lodge as Gull and Salisbury. The whole operation was to be completed within a month, but something went wrong: Catharine Eddowes was mistaken for Kelly and because of the widespread panic that had gripped the East End, Kelly's murder was postponed for over a month. She was finally disposed of on 9 November, the day of the Lord Mayor's Show when the majority of policemen were performing duties connected with that event.

Walter Sickert said that the victims were located and then given a lift in the carriage. John Netley was the driver and Sir William Gull was the man inside the carriage who would carry out unspeakable horrors against the victim. The murders took place inside the carriage and the bodies were dumped at the places where they were discovered. Mary Kelly was murdered indoors because she had her own room, and Stride had to be murdered in Dutfield's Yard because she was too drunk to be coaxed into entering the carriage. Netley had followed Stride into Berner Street and after a confrontation he threw her to the ground and then killed her. Sir Robert Anderson kept watch from the other side of Berner Street. The murder completed, Netley and Anderson made their way back to the carriage and the trio set off towards Aldgate where Cathy Eddowes was about to be released from Bishopsgate Police Station. (Eddowes had given her name as Mary Ann Kelly at the police station.) Eddowes suffered the gruesome fate imposed by the Freemasons; it was a terrible mistake. The real Mary Kelly was eventually tracked down and her life ended in her own tiny room.

It can now be understood how Nichols, Chapman and Eddowes were murdered so swiftly and why there was so little blood at the crime scene. Most of the blood would have remained in the carriage where the Masonic slaughter had taken place. Walter Sickert was forced into keeping quiet about the blackmail threat and the subsequent deaths of the five prostitutes. He was allowed to remain in England and was reminded once in a while to keep his silence. Lord Salisbury himself paid Sickert £500 for one of his paintings; obviously payment in return for his silence. He accepted the money and kept the matter to himself until the day came when he saw fit to confide in his son, Joseph.

As previously mentioned, Alice Margaret was looked after in Dieppe; but whilst living in England two attempts were made on her life by the misguided John Netley. He tried to run her over using his cab. After the second attempt to murder Alice, Netley was pursued by onlookers and ran off towards Westminster Bridge where he promptly threw himself into the Thames and drowned. When Alice grew up she married a man named Gorman, who turned out to be impotent. She still regarded Sickert as her guardian and kept in close contact with him. Sexually frustrated, she became Sickert's mistress and in 1925 she bore him a son, Joseph. His name appears in the *Jack the Ripper A to Z* under the name 'Sickert, Joseph Gorman'. Walter Sickert died in 1942 and Alice Margaret in 1950. Certain clues pertaining to the Ripper murders are present in Walter Sickert's paintings. (This emanated from an unconscious desire to tell his story.) For example, his painting entitled 'Ennui' shows a man and a woman. On the wall in the background is a painting of Queen Victoria with a bird near to her head. Walter Sickert told his son that this bird is a gull.

Stephen Knight states that a cover-up was organised from the highest levels, and important facts in the Jack the Ripper affair were suppressed. This is why any theory concerning the murderer's identity always falls down: theories involving a midwife, Jewish slaughterman, mad social reformer or a deranged surgeon. They cannot be right simply because all the relevant facts are not available. Knight divides the cover-up operations into sections. Very briefly, this is what he wrote:

a) Important evidence was suppressed at the inquests into the Ripper's victims.
b) In 1889 Eddy was involved with a homosexual brothel in Cleveland Street. A scandal broke out but Eddy's connection with the brothel was suppressed, not because he was bisexual, but to maintain the cover-up of his involvement with Annie Crook.
c) A scapegoat was set up so that, if need be, the Ripper's capture could be announced, or at least there would be a prime candidate waiting to be discovered in later years by investigators.
d) Documents containing the true facts about the Whitechapel murders were destroyed.

In support of part a) Knight includes part of the dialogue between Coroner Wynne Baxter and Dr Phillips at the inquest of Annie Chapman. In answer to a question about the length of time taken to perform the incisions (i.e. on Chapman's body), Dr Phillips added that he thought it was a great pity that his evidence should be made public. At the coroner's request the women and children exited the room but Phillips remained obstinate and felt that in giving details of the injuries to the public, the ends of justice would be thwarted. Coroner Baxter persisted with his request for all the evidence to be given, and in the end Dr Phillips reluctantly agreed to give the results of his post-mortem examination. He was well aware of court procedure and it was the first time, at least in the Whitechapel district, that a doctor had asked for permission *not* to give evidence. This fact shows that he did not want to reveal certain aspects of his evidence. The reason for this was because the nature of Chapman's injuries were suggestive in that they relate to a particular *group* of people.

The inquest on Mary Kelly was conducted by Dr Roderick MacDonald, and Knight stated that this inquest was 'illegally wrested' from Coroner Baxter and then conducted in an illegal manner. The inquest does seem to have been completed in a very short time by MacDonald and it is true to say that he failed to add his signature to the certificate of findings. It must be added that Mary Kelly's body was confined to a mortuary which came under MacDonald's jurisdiction, as MacDonald rightly said, '...jurisdiction lies where the body lies, not where it was found.' Coroner MacDonald wanted to conceal evidence, we are told, and this is why the diligent Wynne Baxter did not get a crack of the whip. It also explains why the Scotland Yard file on the Kelly murder case is considerably smaller than the files on the other victims. As we have seen, the inquest was completed within one day and this meant that Hutchinson's statement could not be heard in court. Some theorists believe that Hutchinson is the only person to give a clear description of the man responsible for the Whitechapel murders.

Although the investigation led to hundreds of men being questioned, Sir Melville Macnaghten listed only three plausible suspects. Knight says that he listed two unknown Russians (one of these in fact was a Polish Jew), and a Mr M J Druitt. The 'Macnaghten Memoranda' was penned in 1894, six years after the crimes, and Stephen Knight made a valid point: Druitt died in December 1888 by committing suicide, so why should he be associated with the murders six years later? The reason for the sudden emergence of this mysterious suspect is that Macnaghten, a Freemason himself, invented a case against Druitt so that he could be presented as a likely suspect in the event of any serious investigation taking place. Walter Sickert described

Druitt as being a scapegoat, although he did not know how he was involved in the master plan, the cover-up as it were, that had been callously executed to protect the government and the monarchy.

Researching Freemasonry was a difficult task for Knight, but it was possible for him to gain some insight into their activities. Masonry originated in England in the Middle Ages and is one of the world's oldest and largest fraternal organisations. Members take part in elaborate and secret rituals dedicated to the promotion of brotherhood and morality. Knight quotes from *Freemasonry Exposed* (1826), by William Morgan, which explains that the oath, as taken by the Royal Arch Mason, does not *exempt* murder and treason. This means that under that particular oath all crimes can be perpetrated.

Sir Charles Warren was a leading Freemason, and in the light of information gathered together by Stephen Knight for his book, it is conceivable that Warren was given the post of Commissioner so as to assist in the cover-up. To be able to understand Masonic rituals and the associated clues connected to the Ripper crimes we need to be aware of a set of documents which once belonged to one of the highest and respected leaders in Freemasonry in France. They were apparently stolen from him at the turn of the century and subsequently translated. The documents became known as 'Protocols'. As pointed out in Knight's *Final Solution,* it would be ridiculous to say that these documents show Freemasonry to be an evil thing; Masons are law-abiding citizens. However, those in the lowest orders of Masonry are ignorant of the absolute allegiance of higher degree members and the terrible demands that befall them. The Protocols make it clear that absolute power is the ambition of Freemasons in the highest degrees, and human life must not be allowed to get in the way. With this in mind the question was asked: Could the murder of five unfortunates have been undertaken to illustrate the power of Freemasonry the world over?

When Knight studied the way in which the murders were executed he saw connections with Freemasonry. Part of the penalty for revealing Masonic secrets (for Masons in the lowest degree) was to have their throats cut from left to right. This was the case with the murdered women. The women were strangled first, so what was the point of cutting their throats? It shows that the cutting of the throat was a necessary part of the Masonic ritual. Knight draws our attention to further ghastly correlations between the mutilations inflicted on Chapman and Eddowes and the rituals imposed by the Masons. Part of Dr Phillips evidence on the posthumous mutilation of Annie Chapman revealed:

> The abdomen had been entirely laid open; the intestines severed from their mesenteric attachment had been lifted out of the body and placed on the shoulder of the corpse.

Dr Federick Gordon Brown gave evidence at the inquest on Catharine Eddowes. Part of her injuries were:

> The intestines were drawn out to a large extent and placed over the right shoulder.

Dr Brown was of the opinion that the intestines had been placed on the shoulder 'by design'. These injuries were Masonic in nature and are almost identical to the traditional murder of the apprentice Masons who were named Jubela, Jubelo and Jubelum. They were punished for the murder of the Grand Master Hiram Abiff by having their hearts and vitals taken out and thrown over their *left* shoulders. Polly Nichols had indeed been torn open and her legs had been extended in a formal fashion as if having been placed at the location were she was found. One might point to the fact that Eddowes' intestines were placed on her right shoulder and not her left, but Knight says that Mitre Square was the most vulnerable of the murder sites and the speed with which the body had to be deposited probably caused the mistake. The inverted 'V' carved into each cheek of Catharine Eddowes could be peeled up to form a triangular flap, and the sacred sign of Masonry is *two triangles.* The appalling injuries inflicted on Mary Kelly are strikingly similar to a ritualistic Masonic murder as depicted in William Hogarth's engraving entitled 'The Reward of Cruelty'. Hogarth, an eighteenth-century British painter and engraver, was also a Mason. Here are the main comparisons of the engraving to Kelly's mutilations:

> The victim in the engraving is formally laid out on a dissecting table and is completely naked. *Mary Kelly was found lying on her back and was entirely naked.* (Actually she was wearing a chemise.)
>
> Hogarth's victim is about to suffer facial mutilation and one of the Masons is cutting at the eye. *Mary Kelly sustained abominable facial mutilation.* The destruction of the eye in the engraving corresponds to the slits made to Eddowes' eyelids.
>
> The engraving shows that the abdomen has been opened up and the intestines are being pulled out. *Kelly's abdomen had been completely emptied of its viscera.*

Going back to the scene of the Chapman murder, we learned that various items had been *carefully* placed at her feet and that her two brass rings were missing. The act of placing Annie's belongings at her feet is a form of Masonic symbolism. The sacred metal of the Masons is brass; Hiram Abiff was a worker in brass. Dr Phillips was trying to aid the cover-up, as seen in his attempt to conceal evidence in court and also by removing the clue of the brass rings. Fascinating stuff? Well consider this. The name 'Mitre Square' has Masonic connections and was specially picked as a place to dump one of the murdered women. *Mitre* and *square* are the basic tools of the Freemasons. Stephen Knight shows us that two of the Masonic Lodges had some of their meetings in public houses situated in Hanbury Street.

The most conclusive proof that the murders were Masonic in origin is to be found in the Goulston Street message where part of Cathy Eddowes' apron was found by PC Long. The discovery of the writing (the 'Juwes' message) was enough to alert Sir Charles Warren, who personally visited the scene of the writing. As we have seen, what might have been an important clue was actually erased by the order of Sir Charles himself, who would not even allow a photograph of it to be taken. This strange message contained a clue that, once again, pointed the finger at Freemasonry. The word 'Juwes' is not a misspelling of the word 'Jews', for the Juwes were three apprentice Masons who murdered Hiram Abiff. Can there be any doubt at all that a Masonic cover-up had taken place? The four Masons who ruthlessly carried out the plan were Gull, Warren, Anderson and Salisbury; but one wonders how Walter Sickert, the painter and mentor of Prince Eddy, came to possess such detailed information. When Knight was considering the possibility of Gull's participation in the murders, he would have been aware of the fact that he was in his seventies at the time and he had suffered a stroke in the previous year. According to Dr Thomas Stowell, Sir William had a *slight* stroke in 1887; and a tribute to Gull, written after his death in 1890, tells us that after he was seized by paralysis (in the grounds of his home in Scotland), he was able to walk back to his house with assistance. Perhaps his stroke was not that severe after all. Furthermore, Robert James Lees used his clairvoyant powers to track down a respected West End physician, and although Gull is not mentioned by name there are enough clues in the 1895 *Sunday Times-Herald* article to suggest that Gull is the man in question.

Towards the end of his book, *Jack the Ripper: The Final Solution*, Stephen Knight wrote that Walter Sickert had told the truth, the whole truth, and nothing but the truth with regard to the Whitechapel murders. However, he could find no evidence at all to connect Sir Robert Anderson with the events just described. Anderson was appointed Assistant Commissioner of the Met on the day of Mary Nichols' murder, and on the day of Chapman's murder he went to Switzerland on sick leave and did not return until after the murders of Stride and Eddowes. It occurred to Knight that Walter Sickert had not told his son the whole truth. Walter's knowledge was very detailed; how could he have known so much? One of his paintings shows a man eating some black grapes ('Lazarus Breaks his Fast'), and this is an intentional clue because Gull gave poisonous grapes to his victims to render them unconscious. This is another example showing Sickert's in-depth knowledge, and it is not surprising to know that Knight concluded that Sickert, not Anderson, shared the carriage with Gull on the nights of the murders. Interestingly enough, Donald McCormick's *The Identity of Jack the Ripper* mentions a suggestion that Walter Sickert the painter was responsible for the murders. There is no other way for him to have possessed such intimate details of the conspiracy plan and how the crimes were carried out. Years ago, when I first read Knight's book, I was truly convinced that the mystery had been solved.

I feel that the story as told by Joseph Sickert has been given great credence over the years. As other theories have arisen, in particular with connection to the 'finding' of the Ripper Diary and the emergence of 'Dr' Francis Tumblety, the story of Prince Eddy and Annie Crook is largely forgotten, but, as we shall see, much of the mythology surrounding that story has been transposed into other similar themes. Sickert's tale is intriguing, no doubt, but from it we have learned little about Jack the Ripper; we learn much about ourselves.

In 1992 Dr David Abrahamsen's book, *Murder and Madness: The Secret Life of Jack the Ripper,* was published in America. The British publication describes Abrahamsen as a forensic scientist and says that he was an expert witness in the investigation of Lee Harvey Oswald and American serial murderer David Berkowitz.

Abrahamsen asks why the crimes were committed, because the answer to this question would enable one to eliminate many previous suspects. He states that the Ripper had a compulsion to kill and that murder for him was a way of gaining self-worth. The possibility that more than one person may have been involved in the crimes occurred to Abrahamsen after studying Annie Chapman's murder. He suggested that the killer spent extra time, more than he had planned, in the dissection of Chapman and therefore it is likely that he became worried about being captured. The Ripper's concern may have been caused by the sound of someone approaching, or perhaps by the fact that dawn was breaking. Now, if he had someone standing guard whilst he was engaged in murder, that would give him the chance he needed to complete the disembowelment. Further on in his book we come to the events surrounding Elizabeth Stride and Israel Schwartz. Schwartz observed Stride in the midst of an altercation with a man, and on crossing to the other side of the street he saw another man who was lighting his pipe. This business with the pipe smoker is emphasised by Dr Abrahamsen and becomes an important part of his theory. The fact that Stride was not mutilated is a further indication that there was an accomplice present at the crime scene.

Certain suspects are mentioned in passing: Alexander Pedachenko (a Russian secret agent), Dr Thomas Neill Cream and Prince Albert Victor Edward, who was the eldest son of the Prince of Wales and heir to the throne. Again, attention is drawn to Dr Thomas Stowell's article for the *Criminologist* and this forms the platform from which Abrahamsen brings in his two suspects - Prince Eddy and his Cambridge tutor, J K Stephen. His expertise as a forensic psychiatrist enables him to evaluate the emotional element in the Ripper murders and to penetrate into the psyche of Jack the Ripper. He says that the 'Juwes' message was written with the intention of focusing suspicion onto the Jews, and this explains why the message was erased. It also gave the killer a greater chance of escaping detection. The identities of the real murderers emerged as he delved deeper and deeper into the mystery. His true inspiration came from a book by A C Benson, *The Leaves of the Tree: Studies in Biography*. Benson's book presents an insight into the lifestyle of J K Stephen. Dr Abrahamsen wrote that Stephen was fond of boys and liked to play with them. He learned from Benson's account that Stephen had temper tantrums and used bad language when he was a teenager. This is a fairly accurate indicator of a disturbed personality. Stephen does not appear to have spent much time with his mother and this may have been the cause of his hostility towards women in general. Abrahamsen gives us some insight into Stephen's misogyny and his sexual friendship with younger boys. Stephen's poems patently reflect his dislike for women and in one poem in particular he wrote that he would not mind if 'she were done away with, killed, or ploughed.' From this hatred of women Abrahamsen speculates that the Ripper may have performed anal intercourse with some of his victims. This idea was reinforced because homosexuals practise this form of intercourse and there is little doubt that Stephen was homosexual.

Further along the trail we have confirmation of Stephen's presence at the scene of the Stride murder. Israel Schwartz saw J K Stephen lighting his pipe; he was extremely fond of his pipe and wrote a poem called 'The Grand

Old Pipe'. But how does Eddy become involved in all this? Both Stephen and Eddy were guilty of the murders. They shared life together as both friends and lovers and because J K hated all women - and prostitutes in particular - it would have been an easy matter for him to persuade Eddy to join him in the elimination of the Whitechapel whores. Dr Abrahamsen's theory hinges very much on J K Stephen's state of mind and his homosexual relationship with Eddy. The book gives detailed information on Stephen's medical history and an overview of the Prince's life and his family.

In his book, *Jack the Ripper Revealed* (1993), author John Wilding says that there was a considerable amount of evidence pointing to a cover-up having taken place, and this could only have happened if the murderer was an important person. Wilding set out to prove that the Jack the Ripper affair was connected to a certain royal personage. There is evidence that the police perverted the course of justice, a prime example being the Cleveland Street Scandal when the police raided a homosexual brothel there in 1889. Prince Albert Victor was supposedly at the brothel, along with other members of the aristocracy, but his involvement with Cleveland Street was hushed up by the authorities.

Eddy, we are told, did not have the psychological make-up to have been the murderer and, apart from this, he suffered from partial deafness. Therefore, there is even less chance of him being the killer, based on the premiss that good hearing was needed to detect the sound of an approaching policeman or member of the public. John Wilding worked closely with Stephen Knight during the writing of his *Final Solution,* and his own theories run on similar lines. However, he points out that it would have been dangerous for Mary Kelly to have taken Eddy's child to the East End where she could easily have been captured by her adversaries. Another valid point is that Mary would not have revealed the secret with her cronies because, being constantly drunk, they would merely have propagated her blackmail scheme, putting her in a very precarious situation.

Mary did indeed attempt to extort money from the Establishment but for different reasons than those elicited in Knight's theory. According to Wilding, it was Eddy's father, the Prince of Wales, who had caused the problem. It had arisen as a result of his sexual encounters. Furthermore, it has been shown throughout history that assignations between royalty and ordinary common folk have occurred. Eddy's father, Albert Edward, was nicknamed 'Bertie' and he harboured a strong passion for loose women. The question is asked: Was it possible that a link existed between Bertie and

Mary Kelly? She supposedly worked in a West End brothel before descending into the East End quagmire, and her refined but adventurous personality might have appealed to Bertie. Wilding speculates that the two may not have met each other in the West End and his researches uncovered a remarkable fact: Bertie, along with some of his wild friends, rented a flat in the East End, not far from where Mary Kelly plied her trade. It is highly likely that Bertie and his friends came across Kelly on one of their jaunts into Whitechapel and we may suppose that the Prince and the prostitute spent time together alone. That being the case, sexual intercourse would have taken place. This was a bad move on Bertie's part because Kelly was a Catholic girl and she could have become pregnant.

I think you can see where the story is leading to. John Wilding's theory is interesting and quite detailed. It would take up too many pages in this book to cover the main points properly. He collates information which shows that Montague Druitt and J K Stephen knew each other and explains why they executed the murder campaign. The five prostitutes were murdered in order to prevent a scandal arising from Mary Kelly's affair with Bertie (the affair resulted in Kelly's pregnancy). For me the pièce de résistance of Wilding's theory were his translations of the 'Juwes' message and certain Ripper letters received by the police. J K Stephen loved to play word games and Wilding was convinced that the Goulston Street writing had been written in coded form, invented by Stephen and used to taunt the police. *The Juwes are the men that will not be blamed for nothing* is an anagram; when translated it becomes, *F G Abberline. Now hate M J Druitt. He sent the woman to hell.* All very ingenious!

Kevin O'Donnell's *The Jack the Ripper Whitechapel Murders,* takes a fresh look at the murders. It is based on the researches undertaken by Andy and Sue Parlour, whose interest in the case originates from the fact that Andy was brought up in the East End and is related to Polly Nichols. He remembers his father making a reference to Edward VII and the murder of five women. O'Donnell's book succinctly covers Stephen Knight's theory and says that the mutilations inflicted on the women could be connected with Masonic lore. Also, the Parlours learned from a friend of theirs (a Mason) that the mutilations showed signs of Masonry. The Parlours speculate that Montague Druitt's suicide (by drowning himself in the Thames) is decidedly odd because he had been carrying a *return* train ticket and he was a good swimmer. It looks like Druitt was planning to return home, yet his body was discovered in the Thames and was weighted down by chunks of *masonry* in his pocket.

John Wilding's theory is given an airing and O'Donnell admits that although the anagrams are interesting, it is difficult to know if they really prove anything. The early traditions of a doctor/physician are shown to be of some value when considering the Ripper and his connection with royalty. Going back to the tale about Robert Lees and Sir William Gull, O'Donnell points out that there certainly was an asylum in Islington, and a pauper named Thomas Mason died there in 1896, at the same age that Gull would have been had he lived on. The Parlours remain convinced that the Ripper is a part of Masonic history; they have been told that the crimes of Jack the Ripper were connected to a royal physician and the Brotherhood. Needless to say, the Freemasons involved were sworn to secrecy.

Kevin O'Donnell and the Parlours visited Sir William Gull's grave at a church in Thorpe-le-Soken in Essex. A previous story relates to how Gull's grave was (and still is) big enough for more than two people. The physician is supposed to be buried there alongside his wife, but when the Parlours and O'Donnell marked the outline of the plot they realised that it was larger than a plot for five people! Some of the oral traditions were passed on to Andy and Sue when they lived in the village. Pearl Lonsdale lived there all her life and recounted a story about Gull. Apparently, he was a part of the murders and was protecting Bertie who had landed himself in trouble with one of the women (presumably Mary Kelly). There are lots of tales about Sir William Gull, including one from an elderly resident of the village who remembers the locals telling him that there were three coffins in Gull's grave. One was full of rocks.

Mary Jane Kelly was killed as an afterthought, according to the Parlours, and the Ripper murdered Eddowes by mistake. As we have seen, Eddowes used the name 'Kelly'. Mitre Square is a 'Masonic' name and Andy Parlour discovered something very revealing. If you take a map and join the four murder sites (i.e. Nichols, Chapman, Stride and Eddowes), and use the Mitre Square location as the apex, you will find that the shape of an arrow becomes apparent. It points towards the Houses of Parliament. The locations of the four murder sites are exactly half a mile from each other. This business with the arrow is intriguing is it not? It might, of course, be a coincidence; or on the other hand it might have been purposely engineered to serve as a latent clue that higher powers were responsible for the murders.

We have seen, in this brief examination of some of the 'royal conspiracy theories', for want of a better phrase, how the various players in the drama

(Gull, Eddy, Bertie, Druitt, Stephen, Sickert) have been accused in one form or another. Going back to my days at Poulton College I remember the Head of the Religious Studies and Philosophy Department saying that if you look hard enough you can probably gather enough information to show that witches flew around on broomsticks. I am sure that this could apply to the most implausible scenarios. We have never read that Queen Victoria was Jack the Ripper, have we? This idea, ludicrous as it may sound, could be the ultimate conclusion for the royal Ripper theorists. Somebody may have considered this possibility already and there could be some information to suggest that Victoria herself was involved; I wouldn't be at all surprised. At the end of the day we must ask ourselves: Can rumour, conjecture, coincidence, scandal and oral tradition really be that powerful? Personally, I think they can.

4

Jack in Fiction

The world of fictional writing has clouded the reality of those events from the autumn of 1888, and there is no doubting that fiction, as written for TV films and dramas, is often taken as being the truth. Apart from numerous newspaper and magazine articles that have surfaced over the years, there have been plays, musicals, short stories and novels – literally thousands of items from around the world focusing on the best-known, unknown killer ever. In the 1970s I bought a copy of Alexander Kelly's *Jack the Ripper: A Bibliography and Review of the Literature.* The chapter named 'Fiction and Drama' lists a wide variety of books, short stories and plays containing a Ripper theme, and since then there have been hundreds more.

Marie Belloc Lowndes was born in 1868 and during her life she wrote some sixty books. One of those books was *The Lodger* (1913), and it was to become a classic story in Ripper literature. It has inspired authors and film makers who have helped to sustain the mystery and interest in those distant murders. *The Lodger* plods along at an even pace and is centred around a married couple and their lodger. It is thoughtfully written, with perfect timing of the events which take place, so that a psychological tension starts to develop when the activities of the lodger become questionable.

Robert and Ellen Bunting live on Marylebone Road. Robert, an ex-butler, is referred to as 'Bunting' throughout the novel. The story opens with the Buntings sitting together at home feeling very much down and out and with little money to their name. Poor old Bunting has had to give up smoking. A 'real' character enters the story at an early stage. He is Joe Chandler, a detective and former friend of Robert Bunting. At the opening of the story there have already been four murders but there is no mention of the name 'Jack the Ripper'; he is referred to as 'The Avenger' throughout the book. A lodger arrives at the Bunting's home at just the right time, paying them enough money to keep up their rent payments and saving Ellen from the embarrassment of having to face the pawnshop. The lodger is described as a gentleman, wearing a top hat and carrying a brown leather bag. The leather bag is an important component in the story because its contents could reveal something about the lodger's character, but nobody manages to see inside it.

He gives his name as 'Mr Sleuth' and pays Ellen ten sovereigns in return for the normal services, peace and quiet and the proviso that she is to refrain from taking in any other lodgers. Strange. Mr Sleuth is offered the top room and also gets permission to use the stove for his experiments, having explained that he is a man of science. As the days pass by, Sleuth's character is slowly revealed. This vegetarian man is nocturnal and likes to read out loud from the Bible. He doesn't like the pictures of the Victorian belles that hang on the walls of his room and turns them the other way.

The lodger keeps himself to himself and is unaware of the coming and going of Joe Chandler. Joe keeps the Buntings updated on the investigation into the 'Avenger' murders. All is well, for a while at any rate, until Ellen notices that their lodger seems to be going out in the early hours of the morning from 2 a.m. until 5 a.m. Also, one of his suits goes missing *after* one of his early morning absences. Just as the tension starts to simmer in this novel, Daisy (Bunting's daughter to his first wife) comes back home after staying with Ellen's old aunt; (one wonders how this will affect Mr Sleuth). To a large degree the book concentrates on Ellen's suspicions about her religious guest. It's a culmination of those little things which prey on Ellen's doubts and add to her internal fears: the late night departures, the disappearance of the suit and now Sleuth's leather shoes, which have rubber soles. Her curiosity reaches such a pitch that she decides to search his room whilst he is out buying a new suit. She reaches his room only to discover that his bag is not there but his money is left on show. Ellen is not prepared to admit (even to herself) that Sleuth harbours a dark secret. She becomes protective towards him rather than hostile. Halfway through the novel Joe Chandler becomes acquainted with Daisy, but Ellen fears that he will discover something that she does not want to face up to; she would rather not know the truth. The foggy nights add to the eerie and suspenseful atmosphere and it becomes inevitable that Mrs Bunting will suspect her lodger of being the 'Avenger'. Despite her fears she remains silent, but another murder committed close by serves to tighten the grip on her. Her nerves start to tremble.

There is no mention of prostitutes at all: the victims are merely referred to as having been drunk, and this in itself seems to be the trigger for the murderer. The tension is steadily built up and becomes almost unbearable for Ellen when, after a double murder, the newspapers print a picture of an impression of a rubber-soled shoe. On the pretext of going to see the doctor, Ellen attends the inquest of the latest victim in the hope that she will hear something from a witness that will either confirm or relieve her hidden fears.

One witness, a Mr Cannot, says he passed a strange looking character in the early hours as he passed through Regent's Park. He described the man as looking educated and he seemed to be repeating poetry. He was carrying a leather bag. On her way home, through the misty streets, Ellen hears the newspaper boys shouting, 'Avenger inquest! Do you know him?' Suddenly she is gripped by terror.

A day or two later, Bunting stands in for a waiter who can't make it to a birthday party. It is on the very same night that Joe Chandler predicts a possible Avenger murder. On the evening in question, Ellen hears the lodger creeping out of the house at a quarter to twelve and he is obviously wearing his rubber-soled shoes. A few hours later, Bunting is returning from the party when he notices the tall, thin figure of Mr Sleuth on the opposite side of the street. Sleuth is accompanied by the ex-butler and as they approach the door to the house, Bunting steps forward to open it. As the lodger steps into the hallway, his cape brushes against Bunting's hand and he feels that it is wet and sticky. A later examination shows it to be blood. The final showdown occurs when Ellen and Daisy agree to visit Tussauds Waxworks with Mr Sleuth. By this time both Robert and Ellen share grave suspicions about their silent and religious guest. What will the outcome be? *The Lodger* has been described as a 'masterpiece of mounting horror' and the story has been converted for TV on several occasions. I shall be looking at one of the screen versions in the next chapter. *The Lodger* was reprinted in 1996 by Oxford University Press and it is likely to be around for many years to come.

As the Ripper centenary was approaching, several new books surfaced in America and England. One addition, to the now massive world of fictional 'Jack', was written by that master of the macabre, Robert Bloch. He was the author of *Psycho* and this story was made into one of the darkest and terrifying screen chillers ever by Alfred Hitchcock. He had already dabbled in the fictional world of Jack the Ripper when in 1926 he directed *The Lodger* – a silent film version with screen idol Ivor Novello as the main character.

Robert Bloch's book, *The Night of the Ripper* (1986), was first published in Great Britain. It is a skilful blend of fact and (mainly) fiction. The story very much reads like a whodunnit and both fictional characters and 'real life' people from the actual investigation itself appear throughout the novel.

It is centred around Fred Abberline, Mark Robinson (a young American doctor at the London Hospital), and a young nurse called Eva Sloane. Eva becomes the object of Robinson's desires – for a short while at any rate – so there is a love angle to the tale. The opening date for Bloch's story is 5 August 1888. Eva is on her way home from a music hall when she sees a man in a deerstalker cap, well-dressed and wearing a moustache. He resembles Queen Victoria's grandson, the Duke of Clarence. Bloch sets the scene: the Angel and Crown public house, the fog, the whores and the slaughterhouses… all the right ingredients for an 1888 Whitechapel.

Early in the story the reader's attention is drawn to Mark Robinson (who followed Martha Tabram on the night she was murdered) and Dr Hume. Hume seems to be an odd character because he likes using a scalpel and, just for good measure, there is Dr Trebor, a consultant who carries (yes, you've guessed it), a brown surgical bag. Abberline starts his investigation at the London Hospital where all the characters are based. He is convinced that a scalpel is the murder weapon, so perhaps the hospital is the best place to begin the investigation. We learn that Robinson is repulsed at the sight of blood (odd for a doctor), so he falls out of the list of suspects. Not surprisingly, he asks Eva out to dinner, but she has a fiancé (who is he?); and is it just a coincidence that he has a moustache and a peaked cap?

Doctors Hume and Trebor are questioned after the Nichols murder in Buck's Row, which is only a short distance from the London Hospital. The ever-vigilant George Lusk gets a mention (his suspect is 'Leather Apron'), and so does Forbes Winslow, who Abberline regards as the worst crank of them all. (L S Forbes Winslow was a real person. He was a qualified doctor and offered to help catch the Ripper. Indeed, at the time of the murders he told the police that given enough men, he could capture the Whitechapel murderer. He was critical of the police and their methods and believed that they lacked the imagination to catch such a clever criminal.)

Later in the story, Mark warns Eva that her fiancé could be the killer because of his appearance. Eva replies that many men would fit the description of the murderer, including Robinson. The answer seems to be near at hand when Eva is walking down the Whitechapel Road one evening. She notices a waxworks exhibition portraying the Ripper's victims, and then bumps into Dr Jeremy Hume. Reluctantly, she allows Hume to take her into the waxworks where an elderly chap shows them the crude models of Tabram, Nichols and Chapman. Hume seems to possess complete knowledge of Chapman's injuries, knowledge that shows there is a link between the mutilations and the Ripper's sexual desire. He even suggests that Eva was sexually aroused when she witnessed operations. Eva turns away and runs out of that awful place.

Meanwhile, Mark Robinson winds up in a public house where he meets Annie Fitzgerald. She thinks she knows the identity of the man whom Robinson is seeking – but she doesn't reveal his name. Unfortunately, Annie dies under the Ripper's knife at a place just off Berner Street. Robinson, in search of Annie for further information, happens to be at the crime scene and so is Dr Trebor. Is Trebor the Ripper? It is odd that he should be there at the right time, but news comes in from Mitre Square where another female has just been killed. Major Henry Smith becomes involved in the hunt for 'Jack' and proceeds to the location of the Goulston Street message along with Inspector MacWilliams. (Inspector James McWilliam was Head of the City Police in 1888.) They wait for the arrival of Sir Charles Warren who, in keeping with the true events, orders the 'Juwes' message to be rubbed out. Smith is not pleased.

At the hospital library Dr Trebor introduces Robinson to Dr A C Doyle, who explains how his Edinburgh tutor, Joseph Bell, gave him ideas for developing the character Sherlock Holmes. Doyle is certain that Holmes would have been well on his way to finding a solution to the mystery and he offers an explanation for the Ripper's invincibility. The culprit dresses himself as a woman to facilitate his escape and uses his bag to store his knife, cap and false moustache.

Inspector Abberline is knee-deep in the investigation by now and is summoned by the Home Secretary, Henry Matthews. Matthews has received a communication from the Queen implying that the murders may be connected to people in high places. The author seems to be involving all the popular suspects, including J K Stephen and John Netley. Abberline is requested to make discreet and unofficial inquiries at a male brothel in Cleveland Street. His investigation takes him to the Royal Lyceum Theatre where, backstage, he meets Richard Mansfield (the actor who appeared in the stage production of *Dr Jekyll and Mr Hyde*), George Bernard Shaw and Oscar Wilde. The inspector questions Wilde about Prince Eddy and J K Stephen. At home, Abberline reflects on the progress of the inquiry and begins to wonder if a cover-up is at work after all.

The story twists and turns and takes the reader down many avenues, so much so that an attempt to solve it oneself would ultimately have to be an act of guesswork, as there is no progressive logic in the plot. The turning point in Bloch's story comes when Inspector Abberline receives a letter from a Dr J F Williams of St Saviour's Infirmary. The letter states that three Ripper victims – Chapman, Nichols and Kelly – were treated at the infirmary before they died and it was *another* doctor who helped attend them. Abberline and Robinson are now hot on the trail of Jack the Ripper. They visit Dr Williams at St Saviour's and discover that some of the Ripper's victims were treated by a volunteer: a Russian by the name of Alexander Pedachenko who worked at a hairdressing shop on Westmoreland Road. His name had cropped up along with other suspects like Ostrog, Konovalov and Klosowski, but since Abberline had been busy investigating the theories of Robert Lees, Pedachenko was overlooked. Was Pedachenko the man known as Jack the Ripper? And, if so, how could he possibly be involved with Eddy and Lees' psychic visions? The answer is ingenious and, I have to say, there is a similarity to the conclusion in his acclaimed *Psycho*.

Robert Bloch's fictional work on Jack the Ripper actually began in 1943 with the publication of his short story, *Yours Truly, Jack the Ripper*. It features two characters: Dr John Carmody (a psychiatrist and a Ripper researcher of long standing), and member of the British Embassy, Sir Guy Hollis. The setting is Chicago in 1943. Hollis visits the psychiatrist and describes how he has detected a trail of unsolved Ripper-type murders which have occurred in New York, Africa and Europe, finally ending in Chicago. The psychiatrist points out that if the original murderer was thirty years old in 1888, he would be eighty-five years old in 1943. According to Sir Guy, the murders represent a blood sacrifice to the dark gods in return for which the Ripper is granted eternal youth. Carmody's friends are just the right kind of people that Jack would associate with: the Bohemians and the lunatic fringe. Eventually, Sir Guy Hollis and John Carmody take to the streets in search of the immortal fiend and they find themselves in an area with a similar layout to the original courts and alleys where his victims were found. After several gins in a seedy backstreet bar, they venture back into the cold night air. Hollis reveals that his own mother was slain by the murderer in 1888. He was right all along - the Ripper was alive and living in Chicago. Who will the next victim be? In an instant all is revealed as John Carmody pushes his drunken companion into a dark recess and pulls a knife from his coat pocket. A surprise ending indeed from that master of horror, Robert Bloch.

Amongst the books published to mark the centenary of the unsolved murders of 1888, one in particular was an outstanding contribution to 'Ripperature' - *Yours Truly, Jack the Ripper*, by Pamela West. Her book is extremely well researched, each chapter being punctuated by days and dates leading up to the first murder and ending in 1892. The cover shows a large eye with the image of a top-hatted silhouette across it. Presumably this represents the final scene as imposed on the victim's retina just prior to her death. This novel is written in the first person; it is in diary format and the intended writer is Inspector John West. (John West was made Acting Superintendent during the temporary absence of Superintendent Arnold. He was in charge of H Division whilst investigations into the murders of Nichols and Chapman were in progress.)

Pamela West's knowledge of the Whitechapel crimes, and her attention to detail, come together to form a truly authentic mood throughout the story. The atmosphere is intensified by the inclusion of all sorts of denizens and suspects - the doss-house drabs, the hawkers, Jews, socialists and the medical men - they are all there. There are few changes to what actually happened in that Autumn of 1888; even small details are included, like the use of the backyard toilets. A small point maybe, but essential in recreating those times from the nineteenth century. Several other 'real' characters appear in the story: Inspector Abberline, Sergeant William Thick (referred to as Willy 'Upright') and Inspector Joseph Helson, who was involved in the investigation from the outset.

Almost halfway through the plot John Pizer - the 'Leather Apron' suspect - is released from Leman Street Police Station and is not happy about his wrongful arrest. (In reality, John Pizer successfully sued various newspapers because of their libellous accusations.) Inspector Helson believes that their man must be local - how else could he know his way around those alleys and courts? Inspector West points to the fact that the local prostitutes know the alleys and courts better than anybody else and they know the police beats too. West is keeping his options open and he is only too aware of the present mixture of ethnic groups in the area. There was a large population of Jews in the area, not to mention the Russians, Indians and Malays. The question of motive leads the inspector to the Great Synagogue on Duke Street, where he meets up with Rabbi Adler. Inspector Helson prompted the investigation to go in this direction because the murders might be a blood sacrifice or a form of purification. After discussions, the Rabbi assures West that if the suspect is Jewish then he has surely turned his back on God and is more likely to be found at the socialist headquarters in Berner Street. The Rabbi also speaks about the shochet. This term was applied to a ritual Jewish slaughterman who knew exactly how to use a knife: food for thought. The inspector takes up on this because surely if one of these slaughterers went mad, he would have the weapon at his disposal and know how to use it. He is told that the shochets' knives are single-edged and do not have a point. The Rabbi further states that there is nothing more deplorable to a Jew than the mutilation of a dead body - be it a Jew or Gentile. Apart from this, the Old Testament says that a harlot should be killed by stoning or strangulation and not by having her throat cut.

Perhaps this narrows down the field of suspects for the detective, but there are many other different types of suspects to choose from. It could even be a sane person who is trying to draw attention to the slums of the

East End: an extremist social reformer. On 20 September it was a full moon and the diligent police inspector had made himself some rubber soles for his boots in the hope of increasing his chances of catching this silent madman – this ghost. Not only that; if the moon can affect the tide, might it not also affect a man's mind? Every avenue is explored. During the course of the investigation Inspector West is fortunate enough to bump into Mary Kelly and the gentle strains of a love story become apparent. Pamela West uses Kelly as a focal point towards the end of the story.

Back to the drawing board, and certain patterns start to emerge. The victims had their tongues cut out and the murderer used a scarlet scarf to strangle them with. What is disconcerting is that he seems to be cognisant with the policemen's routes. The next important date is 29 September and this brings us in contact with the tragic events surrounding Liz Stride. After buying a bag of cachous she wanders off, only to meet up with the Ripper. He is described as wearing dark clothes, of a good quality, and he carries a parcel under his arm. In this novel the Ripper engages in sex with his victims. He leads Liz into a small, dimly lit court and before killing her he takes her from behind.

Jack the Ripper then moves on towards Mitre Square just as Kate Eddowes is being released from a police station. It's not long before the two meet up and Kate decides on Mitre Square for the location of her client's knee-trembler. Pamela West's Ripper seems to like bums and asks if he can pinch Kate's bum in return for a scarf. He fixes the scarf around her neck and tells her to lift her petticoats so he can see her bottom. He also takes her from behind.

Apart from the bodily mutilations, Kate's face is horribly disfigured, giving her a 'Pierrot-like appearance'. (That the author should remark on the facial mutilations is commendable. It is a point that I shall be discussing later in this book.) Sir Charles Warren makes an appearance in Goulston Street and the 'Juwes' message is promptly erased. The inspector views the erasure of the message as an act of stupidity but he is under oath not even to write about it – the oath being that he must obey his superiors and uphold the law. I wondered at this stage if the reader was being drawn into the 'Freemasonic murder' scenario. Even the *Pall Mall Gazette* refers to a clue having been destroyed by Warren. A strange and baffling case it is for West, but one evening, as he turns the pages of *Beeton's Christmas Annual*, he reads a quote from Sherlock Holmes. 'Strange details, far from making a case more difficult, make it less so…'

The solution to the mystery begins to unfold after a visit to the London Hospital. Here, Dr Openshaw draws attention to a book on the subject of ancient religious customs and it contains little drawings of a human outline in various, specific configurations that are referred to as 'mantic signs'. It occurs to West that the bodies of the victims had been arranged in a similar fashion. He takes the book with him and shows it to Superintendent Arnold, who explains that the bodies were disturbed by the police in the course of their investigations; thus, the so-called 'arrangement of the bodies' is purely coincidental. But West is not sure about this explanation and, in his mind, he begins to question the behaviour of his superiors. Was it a coincidence that Anderson, Baxter, Abberline and Warren were all Freemasons? Later on, after reading passages from *War and Peace*, the truth about the grisly affair begins to take shape, and at last the most important question can be answered: *Why had the killer placed the intestines over the victim's shoulder?* The answer was that the murderer was committing his crimes according to Masonic ritual and, in addition, he was being protected by his lodge brothers, who were none other than West's superiors.

During a chance meeting with Mary Kelly, Inspector West asks her to start a new life with him, but alas she is contented with her lot. West warns the lass to watch out for herself and they part company. It is the last time he sees her alive. Following the terrible murder of Kelly, West is visited by a man named George Hutchinson who turns out to be an important witness. He saw a man with Mary Kelly shortly before she was murdered. He describes the man as having a Jewish appearance, but he was very well-dressed and had a gold Jubilee medal attached to a ribbon hanging from his chest. Silver and bronze Jubilee medals were common enough; indeed, West himself had been awarded a Policeman's Jubilee medal; but only members of the royal family had the gold ones! Although one can detect shades of the Stephen Knight theme towards the end of this book, it still stands as a highly original, compelling and sinister novel. I found it a delight to read.

Jack the Ripper is back – to celebrate the centenary of his gruesome crimes! This was the idea for Terrence Lore Smith's *Yours Truly, From Hell* (1988). It is a scary and gripping novel in which the author cleverly uses flashbacks from London's contemporary city streets to the fogs of Victorian Whitechapel. The story starts with Jim Lees (recognize the name?) who is a retired general and has been experiencing the most weird dreams of swirling mist, narrow alleys, a man with flat, silver-grey eyes and streetwalkers who are murdered. One dream in particular gives him cause for concern, for in it he sees a newspaper dated 31 August 1888. Other images in his dream seem to mirror certain events that have occurred in England on 31 August 1988, concerning one Polly Nichols. She is found murdered in Hyde Park. A constable was just too late to save her, but as he approached the mutilated body he saw the Ripper leaping into a carriage; the cab driver had silver eyes that shone in the dark. Although Polly was wearing modern clothes, detectives found a Victorian bonnet at her feet.

Sir Malcolm Stuart, the Deputy Commissioner, takes charge of the case. Stuart and the Home Secretary, Lord Desmonde, discuss the possibility that the murderer may attempt to re-enact the crimes of Jack the Ripper, and the next possible murder would have to occur on 8 September. The Hyde Park victim was obviously selected because of her name, but from where did the killer and his accomplice hire out the carriage used for their escape - and the Victorian clothes they were seen wearing? Detective Sergeant Clive follows up the clue of the carriage and this takes him to Tottenham Court studios where a selection of hansoms and carriages are kept for use in the film industry. To his dismay, he learns that none have been hired out recently.

Jim Lees and his wife Ann travel to England from Colorado Springs. Jim's dreams of the Victorian crimes are beginning to feature contemporary scenes, and he fears that a new wave of Ripper homicides may be committed, especially as it is one hundred years on from the original Whitechapel murders. No time is wasted. When in London, Lees visits Sir Malcolm and tells him about his dreams, and one dream in particular in which he is confronted by a modern-day cab driver with silvery eyes. The Deputy Commissioner had already learned about Lees' psychic intuition from a telephone conversation with Major-General Patrick Cochran of the US Army. Maybe Lees could be of some value. However, Stuart had already given orders to have the taxi firms checked out for drivers with unusual eyes.

Further into the story, Sir Malcolm receives a letter 'from Hell' and it is signed 'Jack the Ripper'. Not wanting to throw away any possible leads in the investigation, Sir Malcolm sends the letter and envelope to the forensic department for analysis. Meanwhile, news comes in regarding the investigation of the bonnet recovered from the Hyde Park murder. The bonnet was originally sold by Hanby and Sons, milliners, in 1888 and the shop was situated in Court Street, not far from Buck's Row. A meeting takes place with the Commissioner and Chief Inspector Dick Hughes. They discuss the autopsy reports for the Nichols murders of 1888 and 1988 and to their astonishment they discover that the injuries in both cases are identical.

The search for old 'silver eyes' is still in progress and this part of the enquiry takes Constable Colson to a taxi firm off Fulham Road where he is given the name of a driver who seems to fit the bill - Lucian T Nicholas. The trail leads Colson to an address in Brixton, but upon his arrival at the said address he is murdered. Shortly after this event, Jim Lees starts to have nightmarish dreams and it looks as though another Ripper murder is imminent. Annie Mackey, an erotic dancer and prostitute, is heading back to England from Marseilles. She is known as 'Dark Annie'. Back at the office and Lees, Cochran (who now features in the story) and Sir Malcolm wait for Polly Nichols' bonnet to be brought from the lab. Lees recognises it immediately from one of his dreams, but the hat is not as new as it was when found a few days earlier. Tests show that it had indeed been manufactured in the nineteenth century. What could cause it to fade so quickly?

8 September arrives. The police, in greater numbers than before, are vigilant and Jack the Ripper prepares for his next murder. He is described as wearing a top hat and silk cape. As the crucial hour approaches, a constable who is on foot patrol close to the scene of the next murder, experiences a strange tingling sensation. Glancing at his reflection in a shop window he is astounded to see that his uniform has changed to that of a Victorian policeman. In an instant his uniform changes back to normal again. Stuart receives a call from Jim Lees saying that he has 'seen' the second murder and the victim is to be found in a boat on the river Thames. 'Dark Annie' Mackey had indeed been brutally butchered. Who is this supernatural Ripper who prays to his master for swiftness, cunning and savagery?

As the novel progresses the reader is introduced to several new and important characters: General Sir Arthur Kelly, Venessa Cilone (Stuart's girlfriend and Kelly's niece), and Jillian Kelly (Venessa's cousin). The Kellys attend a dinner party hosted by Sir Malcolm and they travel there in a taxi – driven by the mysterious 'silver eyes'.

A young painter and insomniac named Kevin Boyle suddenly crops up as the events unfold. He lives in Spitalfields and during his nightly wanderings he experiences strange smells and, as well as encountering Victorian buildings that glow in the dark, he sees people dressed in the clothes of that era. Further on, Detective Sergeant Clive discovers Colson's putrefying body and retrieves a photograph of Lucian Nicholas from inside Colson's pocket. This photo is subsequently printed in the newspapers. The story gathers momentum as Clive attempts to trace the origin of the paper used in the letter 'from Hell', and finds himself at Twombley Cottage in Felpham, the home of an expert in manuscripts. Clive learns that the letter is written on Yellow-Moon notepaper, first manufactured in 1853 for Benjamin Disraeli. The last sales were on Christmas Eve in 1888.

Meanwhile, the Thames barge in which Annie Mackey was murdered is beginning to decay and the search goes on for Lucian Nicholas. Fortunately, Nicholas is seen on the Whitechapel underground station and Stuart sends in extra men. But who will the next victims be? The women chosen for the 'double event' murders are Felicia Bowen, a model and part-time call-girl, and Lisle Young, a failed actress turned alcoholic. Felicia played the part of Liz Stride in a horror film called *Blood of the Ripper*, whilst Lisle played Cath Eddowes in a horror flick entitled *The Latin Ripper*.

The novel becomes more exciting as the drama reaches its climax. Two Rippers are at work throughout the story: the original 'Jack', who is referred to as 'm' Lord' by Mary Kelly in the closing sequence; and the contemporary 'Jack' who has been specially chosen for the gruesome task. *Yours Truly, From Hell* is a brilliant story with a tremendous twist at the end. Jillian Kelly isn't all that she seems and Sir Malcolm Stuart saves the day.

The year 1988 saw a centenary collection of nineteen tales of terror in the form of a book titled *Jack the Ripper*. It is a Futura Publication, edited by Susan Casper and Gardner Dozois, and contains spine-chilling stories by such masters as Robert Bloch and Charles L Grant. One of my favourite stories from this collection is *Jack's Decline*, by Lucius Shepard.

The murderer is confined (possibly in an asylum), but after years of therapy and medical treatment he realises that little can be done to rid him of his terrible impulses from long ago; yet he is sickened by his own murderous tendencies. His own family, fearing that their secret might become public knowledge, have him sent from England to a hunting lodge in the north-east of Poland. He is issued with a German passport and given a new identity. From now on he is Gerhard Steigler and his new location provides him with the pleasures of the woodlands and countryside. From a hilltop he can see a small village where he knows there are women. The thoughts of their 'sex', and his knife, cause him to tremble uncontrollably for several days. For most of the time though he studies the German language, then literature, and finally he turns to gardening.

In 1915 he reaches the age of fifty-six and he is attended to by a new doctor who, through the use of hypnosis, reveals that his murderous deeds were caused by certain childhood traumas. One day, Gerhard places a friendly hand on the doctor's shoulder but the doctor pulls back and the look of horror and repulsion in his eyes is plain to see. Gerhard had been betrayed; the doctor's apparent hospitality had been an act all along.

The years roll on and Herr Steigler reaches his seventy-fifth birthday, but by this time there are no doctors to look after him; he is left only with his aches and pains and leather restraints. Even at this stage in his life he wonders if the demon inside him will be satiated. A few years later an old priest comes with news of a Nazi invasion and he tells Gerhard stories of Hitler and his friends. The priest departs and a month later the old man finds himself all alone, until the arrival of seven German officers who ask if they can billet at the lodge. At this stage one wonders what can possibly happen next but things begin to shape up with the arrival of five Jewish women, who are under guard. They are described as being young and lovely. That very same night the Ripper can hardly stop himself from taking up the knife and he searches the dark corridors of the lodge. The following day the female prisoners are locked up inside the lodge and the soldiers have to go elsewhere for a while.

Steigler can barely resist the temptation to slip down into the basement and have a long, lingering look at them. This he does. The women press themselves against the bars as he approaches; he notices their ripped dresses and he can plainly see their breasts and bellies. No harm will befall the ladies *if* they help him, but they must do as he says. This is Gerhard's only chance to obtain final release from the clutches of his demon.

A little later the German soldiers return to a sumptuous meal followed by copious amounts of wine, but the wine is laced with the Ripper's drugs - the drugs prescribed for his condition of insanity. Soon enough the soldiers are rendered harmless, except for the Captain, who receives a knife thrust in his back. The Captain falls back and his carotid artery is slashed by 'Red Jack'. Steigler frees the women, but now they must free him. He hands some written instructions to one woman (the butcher's daughter), and then removes his clothing to reveal a pattern of lines on his body indicating where he must be cut.

There is hesitation at first but Gerhard faces the ordeal and lies on the bed to receive the agonizing incisions inflicted by the butcher's daughter. He asks for his head to be raised so that he can see the evil entity crawling from the massive cavity in his stomach. Alas, he sees nothing! A fitting end for Jack the Ripper...

I have selected another story from the same volume, called *A Good Night's Work*. It was penned by Sarah Clemens and is an unusual story written in the first person, the apparent writer being Liz Stride, or rather the ghost of Liz Stride. She is trudging the East End's alleys and streets in her wet clothes and stops by a hole in the road where repairs are being made. It seems that her companions are lying there somewhere under the ground. Maybe that's where Liz wants to be. At last she is accosted by a potential client whose insults are not ignored. His clothes were of a good quality once but now they are as faded as the wet clothes that cling to Liz. He is carrying a small bag and goes off happily to a dark corner where he can finish the job. Things don't go too well for Jack in this surprising little story. After cutting her throat he waits and watches. There is no blood! The Ripper knows that he is insane but now his imagination is taking over completely. This is his chance, as Elizabeth Stride tells him, to do the job properly - not like the last time. (No pony and cart to interrupt his work.) Liz's old mates get their final revenge in this short story. They send Liz back from the grave and in the end she returns to them, happy once more, via the hole in the road, whilst the Thames waits for Jack and his little bag.

Another great writer of horror fiction took up the pen to write a remarkable story called 'The Gatecrasher'. The author was R Chetwynd-Hayes and this tale appeared along with several other titles in Michael Parry's book *Jack the Knife* (1975). In this story a group of people hold a séance in an attempt to make contact with the other side. One of the sitters, Edward Charlton, is not amused when his friends start fooling around. It appeared that they had gone to sleep with their eyes open. Indeed they had 'seen' or felt something odd, and they leave Edward on fairly bad terms. Edward is left alone in his flat. The night comes and goes with not a single minute of sleep. The following night he falls asleep in his chair only to wake up in an ice-cold room. He has a visitor. A long dark face stares at him from a mirror which hangs over his fireplace. Edward is summoned by the spirit and soon he finds himself treading the streets of Soho in the small hours. A girl appears from a shop doorway, and an offer of £30 is enough to entice her back to his place. Whoever she is, she dies horribly as Charlton, aided by the dark and sinister apparition, plunges his knife into her again and again. The following day, Edward is shocked by the sickening amount of blood in his room. But where is the body?

Another murder occurs. It is a younger girl this time, and finally the evil spirit from inside the mirror is almost satiated - almost! Charlton is called upon to complete the circle and give the spirit a chance to walk abroad. Jack the Ripper is now fully materialised and Charlton obliges by pulling himself forward onto the Ripper's knife. The years pass by and tenants come and go, but the mirror keeps its position above the fireplace. One evening the new tenants decide to hold a séance and this time the face of Charlton appears in the mirror. It looks as if the evil crusade will go on. 'The Gatecrasher' appeared with three other stories by the same author in the horror film *From*

Beyond the Grave (1973). Actor David Warner played the role of the modern-day Ripper.

It was inevitable that the Ripper murders would form the basis of a musical stage production. *Jack the Ripper*, the musical play, was written in 1976 by Ron Pember and Denis De Marne. The stage production first saw light in June 1974 (before its publication in book form), and took place at the Player's Theatre in London. The play is set amongst the surroundings of the East End and a music hall. It is a musical reconstruction of the Whitechapel murders featuring the canonical five victims, as well as Martha Tabram. It sways between fact and fiction but the killer's identity is not fully revealed.

In 1986 *The Harlot's Curse* – a play which centres itself around the life and times of Mary Kelly – graced the stage at the Old Synagogue in Princelet Street, London. The play was directed by Rodney Archer and Powell Jones; it concentrates on the upbringing of Mary in a high-class brothel referred to as the 'grand house'. It is a harrowing reconstruction of her life through a series of violent images and is accompanied by song and poetry. *The Times* commented, '...nursery rhymes played during an orgy create for once a genuinely chilling effect'. The play also highlights the sexual and social conditions from which the Ripper emerged, rather than the mystery of his identity, and in 1988 it won the £15,000 prize in London Weekend Television's Plays on Stage Award.

Author Paul West has been described as one of America's most original fiction writers. He wrote the acclaimed *Rat Man of Paris* and *Lord Byron's Doctor*, but what is relevant to this chapter is *The Women of Whitechapel and Jack the Ripper*, published in America in 1991. It is a long narrative and, according to the inside cover, is based on up-to-date research and written with dazzling imagination. West concentrates on the lives of the Ripper's victims, who are afforded sympathetic treatment in their harsh world of poverty and sex. The plot though is based heavily on Stephen Knight's not so up-to-date theory as propounded in his *Jack the Ripper: The Final Solution*, and once again Sir William Gull's carriage of death sets forth to track down Mary Kelly and her friends amidst the squalid gaslit streets of Whitechapel.

One of the first fictional works based on the murders was published in New York in 1889 and was entitled *The Whitechapel Murders, or An American Detective in London*. It was written by Frank Pinkerton and is a classic example of how those unsolved murders of 1888 were soon to be converted into fiction for the general public.

It would be impossible to include all the fictional works on Jack the Ripper in this volume; it would probably take a lifetime to track the books down, and even so, new material is constantly being produced. I have set aside a separate chapter to discuss some of the works on Sherlock Holmes and the Whitechapel mystery.

If 'Jack' is immortal now, it is only because he was immortal then. Shortly after the murder of Mary Kelly, crimson coloured booklets were sold to the East End inhabitants for a penny, this situation being comparable with today's Hammer Horror magazines featuring Frankenstein and Dracula.

The murderer possesses supernatural powers and has become almost like the great Holmes, but at the opposite end of the spectrum in the guise of super-monster. We want to cling onto the myth of Jack the Ripper; we don't see him as a sick little man sitting on the edge of his bed with his head bowed forward. He is truly immortal and can fly through the air and disappear at will. He is a black magician, a poet or a clergyman gone mad. He is a doctor or a surgeon. He can be anything you want him to be and now he laughs at the moon holding a knife which drips with the blood of his victims. And what is my favourite JTR story? It may not even have been written yet!

5
Jack in Films

> 'The police are searching for a criminal. In reality there are no criminals, there are only people doing what they must do because they are who they are. So perhaps the police are searching for someone who doesn't exist.'
>
> Jack Palance, *Man in the Attic*, 1953

There has never been a film that truly reflects the horror of the Ripper's crimes. This aspect is usually left to the imagination of the film viewer. Nowadays most of us have seen or heard about 'slasher' movies: *Friday 13th, Scream, I Know What You Did Last Summer*. In this type of film we witness the relentless pursuit of each victim until their moment of death. The murderer is usually a superficial character, someone like Freddie or Michael Myers. There is no real reason why he must commit his crimes – nor does there have to be. The idea of the plot merely serves to scare the viewer and the most frightening scenes often occur when you are expecting something to happen. It would be true to say that timing is of the essence here.

Audiences are thrilled by the slasher scenarios, which run parallel to modern-day films portraying the crimes of real and fictitious serial killers. There is a fascination with people who carry out serial murders; not only are the crimes horrific, they inevitably demand an answer to the question 'why?' The film *Citizen X* looks at the crimes of Andrei Chikatilo and at the psychology of the murderer. What was the meaning behind the killings and what were the reasons for this man's sickening behaviour? In the film *Silence of the Lambs*, the FBI use their profiling techniques to create a portrait of the type of person responsible for the crimes. This film was inspired by the macabre deeds of Edward Gein. He was a recluse who, in the 1950s, was living in the farming community of Plainfield, Wisconsin. Gein has been described as a necrophiliac serial killer and his fascination with the skin of corpses was one of the reasons for his visits to a Wisconsin graveyard from which he stole bodies. The skin was removed and he used it to cover his own body. This shocking practice led some people to speculate that he was trying to become like his dead mother. Gein's atrocities inspired the character of Norman Bates for Robert Bloch's chilling novel, *Psycho.*

Jack the Ripper is probably the ultimate symbol of terror. The name has surfaced again and again not only in books and magazines but on radio and television. This 'other' Jack the Ripper, as I prefer to call him, can be moulded for different parts in films whether they be horror or science fiction. American audiences have witnessed the variants in programmes such as *Vegas, Fantasy Island, Star Trek* and *Night Gallery,* and in Britain the Ripper theme was featured in an episode of the 1980s series *Jemima Shore Investigates,* featuring Patricia Hodge as a spare-time private investigator. The unforgettable soubriquet has been spoken in countless films and TV series, for example: *Till Death Us Do Part, Steptoe and Son, Only When I Laugh* and the memorable 1970s period drama, *Upstairs Downstairs.*

Many people enjoy the screen versions of the Whitechapel murders not only because they are based on fact - very loosely in some cases - but rather for the atmosphere of the London fogs, the gas lamps and the sounds of the horse-drawn vehicles. The Ripper stands alone; there is nobody else to compare him with, and the image of this sadistic Victorian killer with his top hat and black bag adds to the mystique of the character, while at the same time steering us away from the true events of 1888. In most Ripper films there is a medical or royal connection (sometimes a mixture of both), and television dramas can be very persuasive. Films featuring the Ripper go back to the silent era, and the Germans were the first to transform him into celluloid. Paul Leni's *Waxworks* (*Das Wachsfigurenkabinett*) was released in 1924 and is centred around three wax figures. One of them was the Whitechapel fiend who, in a caption, is referred to as 'Spring Heeled Jack'.

The first film version of *The Lodger,* by Marie Belloc Lowndes, appeared in England in 1927. It was directed by a young Alfred Hitchcock and featured the popular Ivor Novello as the main actor. Novello successfully played the part as a suspect for the murders and this atmospheric production gave Hitchcock a chance to dabble with his interest in murder and the dark recesses of the human mind. At first, the film distributors had their doubts but a few months later it received much applause and became a hit.

In 1944, 20th Century Fox gave us their version of the Lowndes story. Canadian actor Laird Cregar plays the sinister and imposing Mr Slade. He gives an impressive performance in this picture, which has been described by some as the best film ever made about Bloody Jack. The cast players were aptly chosen. The delightful Merle Oberon stars as music-hall dancer Kitty, and Cedrick Hardwicke is the head of the house where the lodger is staying. George Sanders is the sharp-minded inspector from Scotland Yard who is developing new criminology techniques. Mr Slade comes across as a relentless and at times pathetic character, whose self-appointed task is to avenge the death of his brother. In the end he attempts to murder Kitty but he is pursued through a theatre by the police and Sanders. They eventually trap him and the maniacal and heavily panting Cregar jumps through a window and into the Thames below. *The Lodger* is a super chiller with its depiction of a Scotland Yard manhunt for London's Jack the Ripper. Director John Brahm made another movie, called *Hangover Square,* which saw Sanders and Cregar in similar parts. The Canadian actor was thirty-one at the time and had a great desire to become a matinee idol. When preparing for his role in *Hangover Square,* Cregar went on a crash diet. Two months after the film was released, he died from a heart attack.

The troubled Mr Slade was played by actor Jack Palance in the 1953 film, *Man in the Attic.* It was a remake of the famous Lowndes story and the script was co-written by Barrie Lyndon, who also wrote the 1944 version for John Brahm. This picture runs along very similar lines to *The Lodger;* the settings are almost identical and the beautiful Constance Smith (who plays Lilly Bonner) injects the glamour as an actress appearing in a naughty French revue. The lodger, who spends many hours in the attic conducting his experiments, shows great affection towards the young actress but the repressed side of his nature surfaces towards the end of the film when he attempts to murder her. Chased by the police he takes a carriage and lashes his way through the darkened streets, eventually turning the carriage over. Mr Slade wades into the dark waters of the river where his torment ends forever. Apparently, his unfaithful mother was at the root of his problems and ultimately the reason for his murderous mission. *Man in the Attic,* directed by Hugo Fregonese, holds up well and Palance gives a solid performance as the mysterious lodger, though not as sinister and broody as that offered by Cregar.

The opening sequence of the 1959 black and white film *Jack the Ripper* shows a streetwalker leaving a pub and walking along a foggy Whitechapel street. She meets the Ripper who is searching for a woman named Mary Clark. He realises that she is not the intended victim, but he murders and then mutilates her all the same and all within a few seconds. He disappears into the mist carrying his black bag. There is no mysterious lodger in this film but a whole host of suspects in their roles as doctors and surgeons who work at the Mercy Hospital for Women. The film runs along the lines of a whodunnit, and its two focal points are the music hall and the hospital - just the right ingredients for Jack as a decadent aristocrat or a surgeon. It's a quality film and has some good punches. Being controversial for its day, the film received and X certificate rating when it was released in Britain. (In fact it was nearly banned and censors warned film enthusiasts not to see it!)

The finger of suspicion points at the calm and collected Dr Tranter, played by John Le Mesurier, who appears back at the hospital with his surgical instruments shortly after another murder is committed. 'Cut deeply,' he says, 'that's the secret of surgery these days.' If Tranter seems too obvious, there's the deformed, mute, hunchback assistant who looks like something from a Frankenstein film. This is hardly surprising considering that Jimmy Sangster wrote the screenplay and then went on to write for Hammer horror films.

Actor Denis Shaw leads the vigilantes and they pursue the hunchback Louis Benz (Endre Muller in real life) as far as the hospital gates. Benz is far too ridiculous to be the Ripper and he can't speak, so who are we left with? Well, there's the sharply spoken Ewen Solon, who is the Governor of the Mercy Hospital. He doesn't seem to be a nice chap at all, but must have some redeeming features as he is Sir David Rogers, no less! The fearless Rogers thinks nothing of verbally thrashing Assistant Commissioner Hodges who mistakenly believes Louis Benz to be the Ripper.

The faintly romantic side to the film is afforded by actress Betty McDowall, who accepts an invitation to the music hall from American detective Sam Lowry, played by Lee Patterson.

Eventually, Mary Clark is tracked down by the Ripper, who turns out to be Sir David. He is determined to avenge his son's suicide, which was triggered by Clark. Whether she was really a prostitute is not made clear; Rogers merely says he must 'kill the virus'. Clark dies on her own bed and Sir David makes off to the hospital, stabbing the porter on the way in. By this time the police are hot on the trail of Jack the Ripper. Back at the hospital, Inspector O'Neill (aptly portrayed by actor Eddie Byrne) asks Rogers to help save the porter's life. The last sequence is memorable. Sir David, in a desperate attempt to escape, ends up trapped in the space beneath a lift. The lift (yes, you guessed) descends and crushes him to death. (A pressing moment for 'Jack'). The case against Rogers is unproven. *Jack the Ripper* was produced and directed by Robert S Baker and Monty Berman.

The film *A Study In Terror*, based on the characters created by Sir Arthur Conan Doyle, was made by Columbia Pictures in 1965. The fictional detective Sherlock Holmes is challenged by a real criminal from his own time period. John Neville is excellent as a young, energetic Holmes, and actor Donald Houston does a fine job as the ever-faithful Watson. *A Study in Terror* was made in colour and realistically captures the sordid Whitechapel setting of the Ripper murders. The quality of the film is improved even further by fine actors, notably Anthony Quayle, Robert Morley and Frank Finlay. (Quayle and Finlay met again in 1979 for the Holmes/Ripper film *Murder by Decree*.) Barbara Windsor plays a cheeky, busty Annie Chapman and Georgia Brown captures the essence of the bawdy pub singer with her raucous songs.

No time is wasted in introducing the viewer to Jack the Ripper. Even before the opening credits a prostitute is murdered on a quiet street. This is followed by the film title which forms out of a swirling mist. The accompanying music adds a sense of sadness to the film and has a haunting quality. East End squalor is excellently depicted with its soup kitchens, dim back alleys, ruffians, whores and pickpockets - a splendid film set for the Ripper and the great detective.

A Study in Terror, produced by Henry E Lester, is more straightforward than the eponymous novel by Ellery Queen as there is no sub-plot, and the lavish colour production helps to enhance those horrific moments. The harshness and depravity of the period comes over strongly and is due to the skill of British director James Hill. You may be wondering who the Ripper was in this film. Lord Carfax is the culprit and his identity is revealed in the final moments as he engages in a fierce struggle with Holmes. It is a truly great film.

The Victorian murderer took time out from the movies and his terrible impulses were passed on to his daughter in the 1971 Hammer production, *Hands of the Ripper*. The film is taken from an original story by Edward Spencer Shew and stars Eric Porter and Angharad Rees. The opening scene shows a typically top-hatted Ripper running away from an outraged mob. He then goes on to murder his wife, who suspects him, but the murder takes place in view of their little daughter, Anna. In later years the teenage Anna (played by Rees) is rescued from the evil clutches of a fake medium who is exploiting the innocent girl in order to make money. The scholarly Dr Pritchard (Eric Porter) takes Anna into his care after she murders the medium by impaling her to a door. He soon realises that her disordered mind has been caused by a terrifying experience from her childhood days. Mistakenly believing she can be cured by psychoanalysis, the doctor entrusts her into the care of the maidservant, who also becomes a victim of the girl's madness. Anything that shines or sparkles sends Anna into a trance – but beware, any kiss or close contact brings back the image of her father, whose spirit then possesses her.

Later on, Anna manages to escape from Pritchard's home and finds herself amidst the squalor of Whitechapel, where a friendly Long Liz takes the lass back to her own lodgings. Liz is stabbed in the eye with a bunch of hatpins and Anna is rescued by Pritchard, who decides to take her to Madam Bullard (a royal medium), in a final attempt to discover the truth. Bullard senses the presence of Jack the Ripper and shortly after embracing the young Anna she is murdered. Pritchard looks on in horror and disbelief as Bullard slumps to the floor. By now the girl is insane and the kind doctor, who never gives up on her, ends up being stabbed with a sword.

Anna eventually finds herself in the company of the younger Pritchard's fiancé, who takes her to the Whispering Gallery at St Paul's Cathedral. In the final dramatic scene, Anna jumps from the parapet as Dr Pritchard agonizingly beckons her to come to him. *Hands of the Ripper* is accompanied by sad, but embracing music. It was directed by Peter Sasdy and is undoubtedly a classic Hammer film production.

Roy Ward Baker's *Dr Jekyll and Sister Hyde* (1971), is a daring mix of both fact and fiction. The setting is a very foggy Whitechapel in 1888, with an array of attractive prostitutes. Ralph Bates, who plays Dr Jekyll, is the leading actor in this enjoyable picture. Jekyll is searching for the elixir of life in order to prolong his research into disease prevention. The secret for his new formula lies in the chemistry of female hormones, and so its off to the mortuary to see the real-life resurrectionists Burke and Hare. There is a problem, though. The doctor's experiments with the hormones turn a male insect into a female: What will the outcome be when the concoction is used on Jekyll himself? The final potion is duly tested and the result is Sister Hyde. Actress Martine Beswick was chosen for the role because of her remarkable likeness to Ralph Bates.

Meanwhile, the gruesome activities of Burke and Hare become known to the locals, who proceed to murder them. Jekyll must find the essential female body parts for himself and so the Ripper is born. Jekyll becomes Jack and he begins to stalk the young unfortunates of the Whitechapel streets. As time passes, Sister Hyde assumes greater dominance and Jekyll's internal conflict becomes apparent when the brother and sister from the upstairs flat become interested in the opposite gender transformations: the brother fancies the sexy Sister Hyde and the sister falls for the dedicated Dr Jekyll. As the murders continue, Jekyll comes under suspicion and Jack becomes Jill (nobody would suspect a woman). Hyde's personality becomes even stronger and the Ripper murders continue.

Eventually, one of Jekyll's colleagues (Professor Robertson) believes him to be involved with the murders. He relates his suspicions to the deadly sister, but she disrobes in front of the stately professor. The anticipation of sex causes Robertson (who is trembling and no doubt weak at the knees) to be drawn into the evil clutches of the seductress. He suffers a fatal blow.

In a frantic attempt to rid himself of the malicious 'sister', Jekyll destroys his apparatus, but the police learn the identity of the Ripper from a blind beggar. The final scene has Bates dangling from a roof-top but he loses his grip as his physically weaker alter ego takes over. He falls to his death.

Dr Jekyll and Sister Hyde was produced by Albert Fennell and Brian Clemens (who also wrote the screenplay). The best line has to be from Martine Beswick when she receives a visit from the brother upstairs. He asks how Jekyll is keeping, to which Sister Hyde replies, 'He hasn't been himself of late.'

Murder by Decree (1979) happens to be my favourite JTR film. It has Holmes and Watson on the trail of a sinister murderer in a very foggy and studio-bound London. The intense atmosphere of the film, along with its oppressive music, never fails to capture my attention. The director was Bob Clark who also produced it along with Rene Dupont. Stephen Knight's conspiracy theory is given full treatment here, but *The Ripper File* (1975), written by Elwyn Jones and John Lloyd, appears in the end credits instead.

Filmed under the working title *Sherlock Holmes and Saucy Jack*, the film benefits from an excellent cast of actors. Christopher Plummer gives a fine performance as Holmes and probably benefited from his appearance in the British television adaptation of Conan Doyle's *Silver Blaze*, shown in 1977. Plummer's Holmes is different to the original; the detective in Doyle's stories comes over as cold and calculating but in *Murder by Decree* we see a sympathetic and passionate Sherlock who occasionally shows his humorous side. I found Christopher Plummer's alternative version was actually quite refreshing.

James Mason is simply delightful as Watson and he commented that the role of the faithful doctor was totally within his range. Mason saw Watson as an honest and dependable man – a man whom he would have liked very much. The actor was thankful that Watson was Holmes's equal in this picture. John Gielgud plays the Prime Minister and Anthony Quayle and Frank Finlay meet again in their roles as Sir Charles Warren and Inspector Lestrade respectively.

The foggy atmosphere and confined studio set actually add to this film, giving it an eerie appeal. Christopher Plummer is blatantly not a pipe smoker and mistreats his calabash in an early sequence which places Holmes and Watson at the theatre. News of the ghastly murders soon reach the ears of the detective, but he is not willing to take up the case unless asked to. Disgruntled with the inefficiency of the police in their investigation, the Citizens' Committee pay Holmes a visit. Watson is surprised at his friend's apparent disinterest in the matter.

Messages from an anonymous adviser manage to persuade Holmes to take action and the duo head off to the latest crime scene. Holmes discovers a grape stem and he senses something suggestive about the victim's mutilations. Back at Baker Street he examines the stem whilst Watson, who has just eaten, is trying to corner the last pea on his plate.

Another tip-off from their secret adviser sends them to the home of Robert James Lees (played by Donald Sutherland), whose 'visions' of the crimes are taken seriously by Holmes. By now, the 'Juwes' message has come to the attention of the great detective, who senses a dark force behind the murders and speculates that the message may have been written by some person who is using the crimes for his own purposes. And so the Baker street sleuth sets off on a deadly trail of murder, intrigue and corruption. The solution to the mystery is close at hand when the pair visit Annie Crook at a sombre and depressive asylum.

The story stays fairly close to Stephen Knight's original work. The essence of *Murder by Decree* is based on the secret marriage of Prince Albert Edward, Duke of Clarence and Avondale, to a common Roman Catholic girl who bears him a child. This indiscretion is seen as a threat to the monarchy and a plan evolves with the aim of eliminating Mary Kelly and her associates. Holmes is saddened after seeing the torment that has befallen Annie. Back in London, Warren has resigned and the indefatigable duo begin their search for the wretched Kelly.

There are some minor revisions in this excellent production. Inspector Foxborough (David Hemmings) is the secret informant who has been manipulating Holmes by steering him in various directions. As head of the radical movement, his aim was to bait the detective in the hope that he would expose the corruption and abuse of power as shown by Sir Charles Warren and the government. Sir William Gull becomes Sir Thomas Spivey in the film, and his ruthless accomplice and coach driver is William Slade.

Holmes's powers of observation and deduction inevitably lead him to the appalling truth; he even discovers a particular variety of grape used by Spivey to induce unconsciousness in his victims. In the end he is summoned by Prime Minister Salisbury who, though offended by Holmes's attitude, actually succumbs to his conclusive proof and offers to resign.

Murder by Decree is a great Sherlock Holmes film which manages to avoid the all too familiar Holmes–Watson clichés. As a Ripper film it is intense and contains a strong emotional force throughout: splendid entertainment.

Jack the Ripper is alive and well and killing in San Francisco – in 1979. This was the basis of Nicholas Meyer's *Time After Time*, made in that year. It is a mixture of fact, fiction, humour and romance. The principal actors are Malcolm McDowell (as H G Wells) and David Warner, who plays a surgeon named John Stephenson. Warner was playing 'Jack' for the second time and in this offering he gave a worthy performance.

Wells is entertaining guests at his home in London. The year is 1893 and he tells of his new invention: a time machine, for which you need to have a key or there's no coming back! Stephenson (H G's colleague) arrives at the house shortly after committing a murder but he is followed by the police. They notice his black bag and the Ripper makes off into the future using the time machine. Fortunately, the machine reappears in Wells' basement, minus Stephenson of course, and the intrepid time traveller goes off in search of the Victorian madman. His destination turns out to be a museum in San Francisco where his invention is displayed as an exhibit. Stephenson feels at home in his new world of sex and violence but is unaware, initially, that his new adversary is hoping to find him.

Whilst trying to track down the surgeon, Wells meets bank clerk Amy (Mary Steenburgen), who eventually falls in love with him. There are amusing scenes where Wells fumbles his way into a taxi and grapples with an electric toothbrush. He finds the technological world bewildering and at the same time he is thrown off balance by the brutality of contemporary life. Meanwhile, the Ripper scours the streets for more victims and is not to be disappointed. The headline for the next murder reads: Prostitute Murdered in North Beach. Victim of brutal slaying.

The story deepens as Amy and her eccentric friend become emotionally involved, but she cannot accept his story about the time machine. The plot thickens when the Ripper visits her and asks for the key to be left at the exhibition centre. Wells manages to convince Amy that he is indeed from a past age. He takes her forward in time but to their horror they discover a newspaper containing an account of Amy's murder. Wells uses the information to try and trap the Ripper at Amy's apartment, but he fails to get there, owing to a tyre puncture. The police now suspect him, and a friend of Amy is murdered instead. The mutilations make it impossible to identify her and the investigating officers mistakenly assume the victim to be Amy.

The last scene takes place at the 'Wells Exhibition' where the Ripper is sent into infinity by his ex-colleague, who activates the machine from the outside. The intellectual dreamer decides to return to his own age where he can write his books. He takes Amy with him after summing up, 'Every age is the same – it's only love that makes any of them bearable.' And so Jack the Ripper survives. He will, I'm sure, come back another day.

In 1988, on the centenary of the murders, there was talk of a film which was to reveal the true identity of the Whitechapel murderer. It was simply called *Jack the Ripper*. It has a strong cast of actors, notably Michael Caine, Lewis Collins, Ray McAnally and Jane Seymour. David Wickes was the producer and director and the tantalising build-up to the TV screening had me wondering, could this be the final answer? What stimulated my interest even further was the introductory note saying the story was based on extensive research and a review of the official files on the case by special permission of the Home Office. There had to be something new in this centenary production, but after only several minutes into the story I realised that the events portrayed were not entirely accurate.

The reign of terror starts with the murder of Polly Nichols who is examined at the mortuary by Dr Llewellyn. He states that Polly had her kidneys and uterus removed. Abberline (Michael Caine) is described as one of the Yard's best detectives – so why is he summoned to investigate the slaying of a common whore? Furthermore, the inquest into Polly's death is held only a day or two after the murder, leaving Abberline and Sergeant Godley (Lewis Collins) very little time to gather evidence. Meanwhile, the psychic, Robert Lees (whose visions are symbolic), is 'seeing' a killer with two faces.

A *Star* newspaper journalist by the name of Benjamin Bates uses his influence not only to stir local feeling against the police but also to capitalise on any rumour regarding the killer's identity in order to increase newspaper sales. George Lusk is portrayed as an anarchist whose activities bring him face to face with the tough Inspector Abberline. The conflict created by Bates and Lusk serve well to keep the tension on the boil. Significantly, an air of secrecy becomes apparent very early on in this picture. One gets the impression that Abberline's superiors already know something about the murders (or murderer). If the murdered women aren't important then the killer must be!

Jane Seymour is Miss Emma Prentice, who becomes an admirer of Richard Mansfield. He is the toast of London in Robert Louis Stevenson's *Jekyll and Hyde* stage production. Armand Assante gives a fine performance as Mansfield, who becomes a suspect after Abberline witnesses his remarkable transformation from Jekyll into Hyde at the Lyceum Theatre.

The ever-faithful Sergeant Godley checks out the more mundane suspects: sailors, butchers, slaughtermen and chefs, whilst Abberline searches for a more mysterious killer. There is certainly no shortage of suspects in this active drama. The Prince of Wales makes a brief appearance and the finger of suspicion also points at Dr Acland (Gull's son-in-law), Lusk, Bates, Lees, Dr Llewellyn and Superintendent Arnold. Inspector Abberline tries to nail Mansfield for the murders but finds himself being irritated by Emma's involvement with the dubious actor.

Ray McAnally is superb as the semi-retired physician, Sir William Gull, and with all the talk about the killer being left-handed I wondered if McAnally's apparent left-handedness was a tempting clue to the Ripper's identity. Although many events and details from the actual investigation are included in the film (e.g. the Goulston Street message and the Ripper letters), they are introduced in such a way as to support the plot of the story, this being that two people are involved with the murders. *Jack the Ripper* is, in fact, very contrived and although it keeps the viewer guessing - with its doctors, surgeons, anarchists, penny whores and police officials - it comes across strongly as a whodunnit in the last half-hour or so. Although I could detect shades of the royal conspiracy scenario (and I was disappointed when the Ripper was revealed to be Sir William), the film was executed with style and imagination. Caine and Collins come across as strong characters and their comradeship and light-hearted banter makes the film even more enjoyable. The hollow breathing sound, which can be heard as the Ripper prepares for his mission of death, adds a sense of menace to a film that is laced with colourful actors and some authentic settings. The true facts surrounding the Ripper case may be distorted, but for all its fiction, *Jack the Ripper* stands as a highly entertaining drama. I have watched it several times since its original showing in 1988.

Jack's Back, released in the same year, is a lukewarm attempt at using the Ripper murders in 1988 Los Angeles where prostitutes are being slaughtered in the same way as the original victims. James Spader is John Wesford, a medical student working at a clinic. He becomes a suspect but dies at the hands of a fellow medical student who makes it look like a suicide. The cops close the case but Spader turns up again, this time as Rick Wesford (John's twin brother.) Rick attempts to discover the truth about the murders and is ably helped along by actress Cynthia Gibb, who plays Christine Moscari. The police latch on to the idea that Rick is somehow involved, but he manages to avoid arrest. With the help of a doctor, Rick is put under hypnosis and discovers who the real Ripper is. He turns out to be the head of the clinic where John Wesford was working. *Jack's Back* was written and directed by Rowdy Herrington.

Deadly Advice (1994), produced by Nigel Stafford-Clark, is an entertaining black comedy set in modern times. The location is Hay-on-Wye, a small and charming town on the Welsh border. It's a story about two sisters in their twenties who live with their domineering mother. One of the sisters, Jodie (Jane Horrocks), is visited by Major Herbert Armstrong at the local bookshop. Armstrong was hanged in 1922 for murdering his wife by poison. He tells the girl how his wife spoke to him in the same nasty way as the sisters' own mother. If the seeds of murder were planted in Jodie's mind by the appearance of this manifestation, they were to bloom and blossom with the arrival of three more real life killers: Dr Crippen, Kate Webster and George Joseph Smith – all experts in their field. Miss Webster has the biggest impact on Jodie. Her axe-wielding ways are taken on board by the frustrated girl, who eventually whacks mother over the head. The film is enhanced by the inclusion of a male stripper who comes to stay with the two girls.

Jodie's murderous tendencies become heightened and, for one reason or another, her sister and the stripper both end up dead. Actors Edward Woodward and Hywel Bennett play the parts of Armstrong and Crippen and lines like 'What sort of poison did you use?' and 'Trust me, I'm a doctor,' add to the black humour which is apparent throughout.

With the mother and sister both dead, Jodie finds herself in a precarious situation. Sooner or later, her dark secret will be discovered. Enter Jack (Sir John Mills), who tells her he was a hairdresser in his day. Inspector Abberline himself was one of his customers! 'I was the only one they never caught,' he tells Jodie. His not-so-deadly advice is simply to be the kind of person nobody suspects. Sounds reasonable. Jodie ends up in court and receives a 'not guilty' verdict, thanks to Jack the Ripper. *Deadly Advice* was directed by Mandie Fletcher.

Ripper Man (1994), sees the reincarnation of the Whitechapel murderer in 1990s San Diego. Screenplay writer and director Phil Sears has the deranged Charles Walken (Timothy Bottoms) carrying out the mutilation murders and at the same time wondering if he is really the original Jack the Ripper. In a seedy downtown bar he is entertained by hypnotist Mike Lazo (Mike Norris), who plods through his unconvincing act. Lazo, an ex-police officer, meets Walken after the show and decides to help him discover if his bloodline is the stuff of legend. The film is straightforward enough with no red herrings or surprises.

Another hypnosis session reveals a 'George' from his previous life and Lazo becomes convinced of his subject's guilt. Walken seeks the attention of Tony, another hypnotist and friend to Lazo, who discovers the truth. Walken is the reincarnation of the Victorian murderer George Chapman. (Well, that makes a change.)

Tony is murdered, but not before passing this startling information onto Lazo, who is now a suspect himself due to his intimate knowledge of the recent murders. Walken (a physician with no licence to practise) retires to his lair at the condemned psychiatric hospital from where he originally escaped, taking Lazo's girlfriend as hostage. The last moments show the Ripper battling with Lazo, who he manages to beat down as the girlfriend looks on in horror. Finally, Walken takes his own life by stabbing himself. In keeping with the film's plot of an immortal Ripper, Chapman/Walken shouts, 'I never die!' *Ripper Man* was, in my opinion, better than *Jack's Back* – only just.

The Ripper (1997), filmed in Australia, delves into the murderous activities of Prince Albert Victor, the Duke of Clarence. The role of the Prince was given to actor Samuel West, who appears at the beginning of the film amongst the inhabitants of a busy Whitechapel street. Michael York is Sir Charles Warren, who is cast as a rather hollow character with practically no enthusiasm for solving the case. Inspector Jim Hansen (Patrick Bergin) mingles with the drabs of the East End and members of the refined Benton Club, which has as its members the likes of Warren, Lord Henry Smith and the Prince himself.

The Ripper's identity is all too obvious from the outset, the most significant clue as to his identity coming from actress Gabrielle Anwar who plays Florry Lewis. She notices the smell of apricots as the Prince, who has just taken the life of another unfortunate, passes by her. The clue of the apricot smell lies in the use of arsenic, which can give rise to this odour when used on patients suffering from syphilis. The treatment is expensive and Hansen believes the murderer may be well-to-do. Enter our old friend Sir William, in fact *Dr* Sir William Gull in this offering, whose list of syphilitic patients is examined by Hansen. Five members of the Benton Club also appear on this list, so that narrows the field down. Florry recognises the Prince from a photograph and plans are then made to capture the Ripper.

For me, *The Ripper* (directed by Janet Meyers) never really got off the ground. With a little more imagination it could have made a fairly interesting story.

In 2001 20th Century Fox gave us their rendering of Stephen Knight's royal conspiracy theory. *From Hell* is heavy on style and features Johnny

Depp (as Inspector Abberline) in the lead role. The appearance and personality of Abberline is completely different to the actual man himself. In the film we see him as an opium and absinthe addict, and he has psychic powers akin to those possessed by Robert Lees who features in the chapter 'Black Bags and Top Hats.' The film is loosely based on a comic book series which uses Knight's theory as its premise. The book series, entitled *From Hell*, was written by Alan Moore, with artist Eddie Campbell who provided the drawings.

The film comes across as a fantasy horror story. There is no real sense of a deranged serial killer on the loose amongst the inhabitants of Whitechapel. What helps to drive this film along, in my opinion, is the appearance of several fine actors. Ian Richardson aptly plays Sir Charles Warren as a somewhat stiff character whose temperament is at odds with Abberline's laid back demeanour. However, the inspector's powers of reasoning, coupled with his psychic visions, are rarely questioned by his trusty companion Sergeant Godley, played by Robbie Coltrane. Jason Flemyng is superb as the simple-minded coachman who lures the Ripper's victims to their deaths, and David Schofield is an admirable choice for his role as McQueen, head of the notorious Nichols gang who extort money from Kelly and her colourful friends. The most chilling moments are provided by Ian Holm as Sir William Gull. He portrays his character with a certain edginess: a product of his temporal madness that simmers beneath a veneer of respectability and regal composure.

With its infusion of Masonic lore, foul-mouthed harlots, strong-arm tactics and a potential love match between Abberline and Mary Kelly (played by Heather Graham), *From Hell*, directed by Albert and Allen Hughes, provides an enjoyable two hours of viewing. I actually went to the cinema to see this film and was particularly struck by the intro music which intensifies, then gently cascades into a rich, hypnotic sea of sound. *From Hell* gets a thumbs-up from me!

Some people might ask, why should the crimes of Jack the Ripper be used in such a way so as to provide fun? Why has the Ripper been used so many times by the film industry? Is it just and proper that we should dress him up in fine clothes and give him a top hat and a knife? It's almost as if we justify what he did and we make light of it. Films about the Ripper have helped to immortalise him and it is the chilling trade name, the brutality of the crimes and their inexplicable cessation, which help to explain the imaginative folklore that has distilled itself into our harmless TV viewing which, it has been said, is so playful and innocent.

I for one enjoy films about the Ripper, along with millions of other people. It is difficult to appreciate how shocking those crimes really were, how deranged the Ripper's mind really was. The films do not make his crimes easier to comprehend and they certainly do not bring us closer to knowing his identity. It is the 'other' Jack the Ripper who we see on our TV screens and in the fictional writings. The real truth is not entertaining; it is frightening and repulsive. The difference is, none of us like serial killers - we just like watching films about them.

That, I'm afraid, is human nature.

Jack the Ripper – based on the author's preferred suspect and eyewitness reports

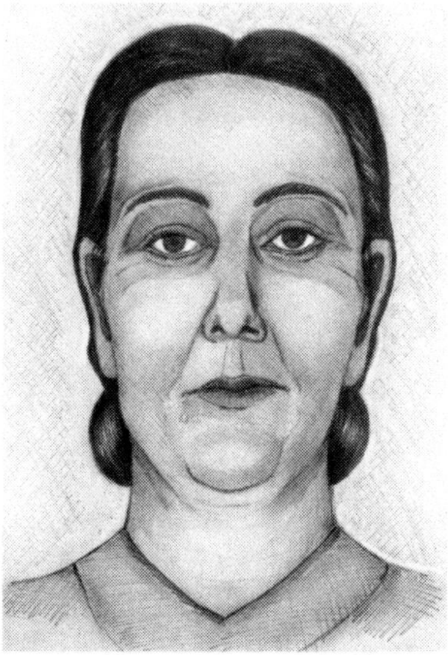

Mary Ann ('Polly') Nichols – the first canonical victim, discovered in Buck's Row

Annie Chapman – the second victim, discovered in the backyard of 29 Hanbury Street

Catharine Eddowes – the fourth victim, discovered in Mitre Square

Mary Jane Kelly – the last canonical victim, murdered in 13 Miller's Court (Reconstruction of the victim's mutilated features)

Mary Kelly's final resting place, St Patrick's RC Cemetery, Leytonstone, London (Author's photo)

The archetypal Ripper as he appeared in the 1959 film Jack the Ripper (Mid-Century Productions)

Barbara Windsor as Annie Chapman in the 1965 film A Study in Terror (Courtesy of Euro London Films Ltd)

A typical East London street (circa 1900)

The Whitechapel Bell Foundry
Practically unchanged since the Ripper's day (Author's photo)

Durward Street (formerly Buck's Row). Mary Ann Nichols' body was discovered on the pavement to the left of the corner of the wall (Author's photo)

Mitre Square – the scene of Catharine Eddowes' murder. Her body was discovered just to the left of the flower bed, on the pavement close to the kerb (Author's photo)

Sandy's Row, Spitalfields. This street is similar to the way it would have looked in 1888 (Author's photo)

6
Holmes and the Ripper

'Another Jack the Ripper if you ask me – a homicidal maniac.'
'No Watson. In the case of Jack the Ripper there was one thing in common; his victims were all from one walk of life living in the same section of the city.'

Basil Rathbone and Nigel Bruce, *The Woman in Green*, 1945

Sir Arthur Conan Doyle was born in Edinburgh in 1859. His greatest achievement was, of course, his creation of Sherlock Holmes who shared lodgings in Baker Street with his faithful companion, Dr John H Watson. Doyle died in 1930 but his creation lives on. Holmes is the most famous character in the literature of crime and in his adventures we find a world full of sinister characters who emerge from the fog-bound streets of London with its clattering hansom cabs and gas lamps – a delightful setting in which to let your imagination take wing. It was inevitable that sooner or later the greatest detective of all time would have to pit his wits against the evil and cunning Ripper.

In 1978, *The Last Sherlock Holmes Story* appeared. Written by Michael Dibdin, this ingenious tale sees Holmes and Watson pushed to the brink of madness as the Ripper's identity comes into focus.

The story opens in the year 1976 when a metal dispatch box is rescued from the vaults of a bank. Amongst the people present are the bank manager and Dr Watson's great-nephew. The box contained a series of typed notes (the 'Watson papers') and those who became acquainted with the content of the papers were deeply shocked.

Here is the gist of Dibdin's plot. Holmes receives a telegram on 28 September 1888 from Inspector Lestrade of Scotland Yard. (Lestrade was involved in more than a dozen of Holmes's cases.) The Whitechapel killings are mentioned in the telegram and also a request from Scotland Yard asking for some assistance. The good doctor is surprised the great detective should take an interest in the case, but the audacity of the crimes and the horrible mutilations that have by now become the hallmark of the Ripper convince Holmes that whoever the villain is, he is no ordinary criminal. Enter Lestrade himself. He is disappointed with the investigation because one of the Yard's suspects, John Pizer, has an unbreakable alibi on the night of a particular murder. There is a new clue, though - the 'Dear Boss' letter. Its content convinces Holmes that the writer is likely to be a well-spoken gentleman rather than a low-class tough. Dr Watson has his own thoughts regarding the murderer and thinks that he is probably like 'Tonga'. (At this stage readers who are familiar with the Holmes' stories will recognise Michael Dibdin's intimacy with Doyle's famous detective. 'Tonga' was a native of the Andaman Islands who helped the convict Jonathan Small to escape from a penal settlement in the story called *The Sign of Four*.) Watson supports his own theory by saying that the murders took place close to the docks. His hypothesis finds favour with Holmes, who draws attention to the arrangement of objects around Annie Chapman's corpse: a heathen rite, perhaps? Then there was the discovery of part of an envelope bearing the letter 'M'. Another clue? We shall see. Watson records his companion's every move in this chilling novel - as much as he is allowed to - for Holmes spends a good deal of his time investigating the case on his own. Dibdin cleverly creates a thread of intrigue as the story progresses: one wonders why Holmes is so eager to keep Watson at bay.

As the novel progresses, Holmes tells Watson that they are being followed by one of the three most dangerous criminals in London. He is Professor Moriarty, described in Doyle's stories as the 'Napoleon of crime'. Moriarty is amusing himself by committing the murders but at the same time he has tempted his ultimate adversary into a challenge to the death. Again Holmes races off into the fogs of mystery leaving Dr Watson to his own devices. Meanwhile, Lestrade receives another letter and the handwriting is identical to the writing of a previous postcard sent in by the Ripper. A short while later he shows this to Holmes, who explains that a clear pattern becomes evident if one studies the dates of the murders. Using Tabram as the first murder (on 7 August), it is obvious that there is a gap of one week and then three weeks between the murders. The inspector is quick to point out that no murder occurred in the week following the double murder, but to the great detective it is merely the exception that proves the rule. The 7 October victim had already been murdered on 30 September - two for the price of one! He goes on to explain that because the killer of Elizabeth Stride was disturbed by the arrival of Louis Diemschutz, his timetable of murder was altered and so he was compelled to move his next murder forward by one week.

Shortly after the double murder, Inspector Lestrade receives another letter and part of a human kidney. The writing in this recent communication is different to that of the previous letters and Lestrade concludes that there must be two murderers. The plot thickens. At this point Sherlock Holmes does not make any worthwhile comment or contribution to the Yard's investigation. He decides to keep Moriarty entertained until the next murder and so he leaves town for Wiltshire. It is probably a good move, for Watson writes that Holmes is better off out of London and away from Moriarty's henchmen. And so the detective duo are separated yet again.

The foundations of the Ripper's anonymity begin to crumble as the reader prepares for the answer in this chilling tale. Before the finale, events take an unusual turn. Watson is shown a simple diagram of the locations for the last four murders (omitting Tabram for some unknown reason), and there is a letter 'X' marking the spot for the next unknown victim. The diagram clearly shows the letter 'M' by linking the murder sites ('M' for 'Moriarty'), and by a series of clever deductions Holmes has pinpointed the time and place of the next murder. The location is close to the new market, and at this very spot Sherlock Holmes will meet Jack the Ripper – or so we are led to believe. Oddly enough, Inspector Lestrade is not informed of this astounding prediction. On the night in question, Holmes and Watson call in at the police station after trudging the foggy streets and alleys of Whitechapel: an arduous task for Watson, as his old army wound begins to trouble him. In an instant Holmes dashes out into the streets followed by the faithful doctor. At last the Ripper passes by and carries on down the street opposite. Watson is told to return to the station and warn Lestrade, but as the pair make off in opposite directions Watson hurts his ankle. After recovering he decides to follow his companion and Moriarty. Sherlock's stratagems had given him cause to be suspicious and now was the time to find out what the devil was going on. Moriarty disappears down a street but a figure emerges from a house in Dorset Street and approaches the doctor. Watson observes the shadowy figure from the recess of a doorway. As the figure passes, Watson recognizes that it is Holmes himself.

These are deep waters indeed, and as Holmes had adopted a disguise to protect himself against Moriarty and his henchmen, Watson attempts to alter his appearance by applying mud to his face and turning his coat inside out so as not to attract attention to himself. An hour or so later, Watson sees his friend stop and talk to a woman; there is another man close by. Could this be a trap? Would the woman lure the great Sherlock Holmes to her room so he could be murdered by an accomplice? The truth seemed to be dawning on the good doctor. The whole situation has been engineered by the evil genius Moriarty, who will meet his arch-enemy in that tiny room in Miller's Court where Holmes had been lured. Watson waits silently outside the room when he suddenly remembers that Jack the Ripper must kill twice on the same spot – Holmes and the woman are about to die. The doctor falls asleep but awakens with the realisation that Holmes might be in desperate need of help. He reaches his arm through the broken glass pane of the apartment and moves the cloth to one side. At first glance it appeared that somebody had exploded. Sherlock Holmes was wearing only his undergarments and was smoking his pipe. The woman was quite dead and lay on a blood-drenched bed.

In the following weeks Dr Watson finds himself alone at Baker Street, waiting for Holmes to return. A communication reveals that he is still on the trail of Moriarty, but is the trusty biographer losing his mind? Could Sherlock be Jack?

In keeping with the Sherlock Holmes stories, as written by Sir Arthur Conan Doyle, Michael Dibdin cleverly brings Holmes, Watson and Moriarty together for the final confrontation at the Reichenbach Falls. Watson cries, 'It's all over – I know everything!' The astonishing, stunning truth is finally revealed – Holmes *was* the Ripper and he releases himself into the torrents of the Falls. It's a marvellous story. Dibdin's conclusion uses a quote from Sir Arthur's story 'The Final Problem', which reads:

> Any attempt at recovering the bodies was absolutely hopeless, and there, deep down in that dreadful cauldron of swirling water and seething foam, will lie for all time the most dangerous criminal and the foremost champion of the law of their generation.

In 1965 Columbia pictures presented *A Study in Terror* (mentioned in the previous chapter) and, as was fairly customary in the 1960s, the movie distributors became interested in the novelisation of their film. In 1966 the film appeared in book form, written by the famous fictional detective Ellery Queen, who was created by the detective writers – and cousins – Frederick Dannay (1905-1982) and Manfred B Lee (1905-1971). The book carries the same name as the film and has been described as a small masterpiece.

The story opens with Ellery Queen receiving a manuscript written by Dr Watson. It relates the case of how Sherlock Holmes stalked Jack the Ripper. The novel has two themes running throughout: the actual story of Holmes and the Ripper (as taken from Watson's manuscript), and the modern-day investigation by Ellery Queen, who attempts to exonerate Watson's suspect and name the real murderer.

The great Holmes receives a parcel at his lodgings in Baker Street and his curiosity is aroused by its contents: a surgeon's instrument case minus the post-mortem knife. Using his marvellous powers of deduction he determines that the case was taken to a pawnshop which faces south on a narrow street. The discovery of a coat of arms under the velvet lining sends the duo off to Devonshire and the Shires Castle, where they meet Kenneth Osbourne, the Duke of Shires. The Duke, a forbidding man, reveals that his younger son, Michael, was the owner of the case but has been 'dead' for six months. On their way out, Holmes and Watson encounter the other son, Lord Carfax, who promptly replaces all the instruments into the surgical case after Holmes purposely drops it.

It transpires that Michael had disgraced the family name by marrying a prostitute; his father then disowned him. The surgical kit is returned to Lord Carfax, and Holmes returns to London. It occurs to him that the missing post-mortem knife may be a symbolic and subtle allusion to the Whitechapel murders.

A little later in the story, the Baker Street Irregulars are sent to locate the 'pawnshop on a narrow street'. The shop in question is situated in Whitechapel. (The 'Baker Street Irregulars' were a band of street urchins who helped Sherlock on various occasions.) It's off to the pawnshop in Whitechapel where the owner, a middle-aged man named Joseph Beck, says that a woman with a disfigured face bought the surgical case. 'The set was complete when the woman redeemed it,' he answers them.

Beck furnishes them with another clue. The lady who originally pledged the case was called Sally Young, who gave her address as the Montague Street Hostel in Whitechapel. The trail leads them to Montague Street where they meet Inspector Lestrade at the mortuary there. They discover that the Ripper has struck again.

Lestrade introduces Holmes and Watson to the morgue superintendent, Dr Murray, and they proceed to view the body of Annie Chapman. Before leaving the mortuary they are allowed to see Dr Murray's hostel. They also meet his niece, Miss Sally Young. She is questioned by Holmes, who learns that the surgical case belonged to Pierre, a poor wretch of a man who turned up mysteriously at the hostel. Pierre had suffered a severe head injury but he was allowed to stay there, where he seemed to be happy enough. Sally pawned the case as the hostel was running on a tight budget. Surprisingly, Lord Carfax enters the hostel and it transpires that he had placed some of his own funds into the upkeep of the establishment.

Back on the lonely, dark streets of Whitechapel and the Baker Street sleuths are attacked by three street toughs. Fortunately, they manage to beat them off. This takes place almost half way into Ellery Queen's novel, and at this stage Dr Watson writes down a résumé of suspects. Only one is unidentified and this is the disfigured woman who bought the instruments from Joseph Beck. Could she hold the key to the identity of Jack the Ripper? What is also curious is the fact that Lord Carfax confidently replaced the surgical knives when Holmes dropped the carrying case.

Mycroft Holmes receives a visit from his brother, Sherlock, and Dr Watson at the Diogenes Club. Mycroft surmises that their investigation is not proceeding without notice; hence the murderous attack by the East End ruffians. The two brothers are in agreement regarding Pierre - he is the Duke of Shire's second son, Michael. Watson feels that Pierre is the Ripper.

The notorious Angel and Crown public house is situated in the heart of Whitechapel and it was at this bawdy establishment that three of the Ripper's victims went drinking before their deaths. Watson is told to go there to see what, if anything, he can find out. Adopting his own disguise he winds up in the pub in question where he sees Max Klein, the proprietor. He notices that one of the punters is Joseph Beck. During the carousing, the unfortunate doctor is befriended by Polly Nichols. Eventually, she leaves and is followed by Holmes in disguise. Watson follows the pair but soon finds himself being attacked by Holmes, who thinks that Watson is the Ripper. Meanwhile, Polly escapes - only to meet the true killer. Realising what has happened, Holmes and Watson dash off to Beck's pawnshop, where Holmes quickly concludes that Beck is not the murderer. He would not have had sufficient time to clean himself up and change into his nightclothes.

Later on, Holmes visits Murray's mortuary whilst a curious Watson finds himself in a nearby abattoir where the slaughtering of pigs is occupying the attention of a pathetic Michael Osbourne.

As the story gains impetus we learn that Michael had studied medicine at the Sorbonne in Paris. During his stay he met and fell in love with a prostitute named Angela Osbourne. She had a friend who was also her protector - the unsavoury Max Klein. No doubt Klein saw the chance of making some easy money for himself and so he forced Angela into marrying Michael. The Duke of Shires and Lord Carfax already knew about the marriage and kept it a closely guarded secret, but Klein's plan was to extort money from the Duke by advertising the marriage and exposing Angela for what she was.

Michael retaliated but he received a severe beating. Angela tried desperately to protect Osbourne but her interference riled the merciless Klein, who mutilated her face with a knife. The three of them returned to Whitechapel and Max Klein bought the Angel and Crown public house with the money he took from Michael. Angela was kept prisoner at Klein's pub, and Michael was taken to the hostel instead of being done away with. However, one of Angela's friends overheard someone discussing Sally Young and the surgical case. It was to be taken to a pawn shop. Angela bought the case and, after removing the scalpel, sent it to Sherlock Holmes in the hope that he would be sufficiently intrigued to investigate the Jack the Ripper murders.

The final scene sees Holmes and Watson in the clutches of Klein. Watson is tied up in the same room as Angela. He is very concerned for his friend who, along with Michael Osbourne, has been taken into another room presumably to be killed. Enter Lord Carfax, who stabs Angela, proceeds to mutilate her and then sets fire to the room. Carfax and his brother both die in the flames and Sherlock manages to escape as the growing flames cause the collapse of the staircase. Klein and his henchman are killed by the falling timbers. The truth at last? It very much looks like Carfax had been insanely trying to eliminate all prostitutes until he finally caught up with Angela, the woman who had initiated the blackmailing scheme.

The story does not end there. Watson's unpublished account of the Whitechapel murders eventually came into the possession of Lord Carfax's daughter, Deborah Osbourne Spain, who took it to Ellery Queen for his final analysis. The final answer to the Ripper's identity is given – the Duke of Shires, who had his own room in Whitechapel. Lord Carfax had discovered his father's guilt, and when he set eyes on Angela he murdered her, mistakenly believing her to be the sole mastermind behind the plot to extort money from the family. After he killed Angela, he told Watson to spread the news that *he* was Jack the Ripper. He was merely trying to protect his father's name and reputation.

In 1962, William S Baring-Gould's *Sherlock Holmes of Baker Street* was printed in America. Baring-Gould had been, for a long time, the doyen of Holmes enthusiasts and his sumptuous *Annotated Sherlock Holmes* (1967) serves as a valuable reference manual for fans and scholars alike.

His 1962 book was described as a unique reconstruction of the great detective's life. In its pages the reader was treated to Watson's accounts of fascinating problems for the first time. His chapter on the notorious Ripper murders was named: 'Jack the Harlot Killer: Friday, November 9 - Sunday, November 11, 1888'. The story opens with the great detective receiving a visit from Inspector Athelney Jones. He was the Scotland Yard detective to be credited with solving the case of *The Sign of Four,* and now he has received instructions from Sir Melville Macnaghten. His orders are to seek Holmes's assistance in solving the Ripper mystery. The seventh murder had just occurred in Dorset street, not far from where Mary Ann Nichols was slaughtered.

The latest victim is Mary Kelly who, twelve months previously, rented Number 13 Miller's Court from a man named McCarthy. She shared the room with her husband, Joseph Kelly. Holmes listens intently as the inspector describes her injuries. Jones then said, 'And to think, Mr Holmes, that only ten hours before she had been so young, so rosy, so happy that she was singing.'

Sherlock is reminded of other notorious murderers and one in particular - Joseph Phillipe, the French ripper who robbed and killed his victims in Paris in the 1860s. Jones then goes on to explain that all clues, no matter how far-fetched, must be followed up, and to this end three of the Ripper's victims had their eyes photographed in the belief that the last scene they witnessed might be imprinted on the pupils of the eyes. The Baker Street sleuth accepts the case and his plan of action is to take place late at night. He insists that Watson does not accompany him.

In a pub, somewhere in Whitechapel, a tall woman with blond hair finishes her drink and ventures onto the foggy streets. She is followed by a broad, burly man who wears a black cloak and hat. He carries a small black bag and his woollen muffler covers the lower part of his face. The hag leads the mysterious stranger into a dark and secluded court where, after a few words, he lunges at her with a knife. In an instant the woman retaliates by pulling a long sword from inside her walking stick. It is Holmes, no less, who has successfully snared the Whitechapel murderer. A final, desperate attempt to kill Holmes is foiled by Watson, who arrives just in time.

Every credit to Doctor Watson in Baring-Gould's neat little story. The doctor had deduced, as one would have expected his companion to have done, that Athelney Jones was the murderer. How on earth could he deduce such a thing? Well, the inspector mentioned that Mary Kelly was plump, rosy and had been singing - ten hours *before* she was murdered. The fact that she was singing *Sweet Violets* was reported in *The Times* the day after her death. The person who gave this information to the newspaper spoke to nobody else after the interview and it was not published in any other newspaper. Jones had never seen Kelly, so how could he have known that she was plump, rosy and singing when it had not appeared in print? The answer to this question could only be that Jones was Jack the Ripper. The affair was kept quiet by Scotland Yard who did not want to admit that one of its own men was the culprit. Well done Watson... Elementary my dear Holmes!

The year 1994 was a bad one for Sherlock Holmes fans due to the publication of *The Baker Street Irregular: The Unauthorized Biography of Sherlock Holmes.* Written by Austin Mitchelson and published both in England and America, the introduction to this book tells us that although Watson was accustomed to making commendable statements about his friend he did not attempt to conceal the true nature of the detective. The doctor wrote openly about Holmes's cocaine and morphine addiction. There were also instances when murderers were allowed to walk free and occasions when Holmes took to committing burglaries.

The author goes on to say that a careful study of the cases, as written by Dr Watson, reveals that Sherlock Holmes was not the cool and fair-minded Victorian gentleman-adventurer that many people believe him to have been. A particular chapter illustrates this point most aptly: 'The Curious Incident of Sherlock Holmes and the Whitechapel Murders'. The one man who surely could have been instrumental in catching the Ripper was 'haunted by fears of madness' and had been suffering as a result of months of failure and self-doubt. Mitchelson gives a very brief and reasonable account of the murders and there is mention of some of the suspects, for example the Duke of Clarence. It seems curious that our greatest detective did not become involved in the hunt for the Ripper and, as the author points out, we know that Holmes was in London at the time of the atrocities. In the adventure of *The Hound of the Baskervilles*, Holmes was reluctant to leave London during September 1888, which was the month when Stride and Eddowes were murdered. At that time it was imperative that somebody should go to Devonshire with Sir Henry Baskerville, and Dr Watson was chosen to accompany him in the absence of Holmes. Perhaps he was in some way connected with the murders. Yet to suppose that this may have been the case is simply ludicrous speculation.

Mitchelson embarks on a careful analysis of the emotional side of Holmes. By the April of 1888 he was badly in need of a case and his cocaine habit was in full swing. So, would the constant use of this drug have affected the detective's way of thinking? Apparently yes. The side effects can cause delusions of persecution and paranoia; other aspects of its use may include anxiety and depression. Holmes's behaviour had changed and the symptoms just mentioned were noticeable in 1887 and 1888. The Ripper murders occurred at a time when Sherlock needed to prove himself. Attention is drawn to eyewitness testimony of people who actually saw the murderer and there is no escaping the fact that the Ripper looked like Sherlock Holmes. He even wore the familiar deerstalker cap. So, we have an interesting comparison between the detective's physical appearance and that of the dreaded Ripper. Furthermore, Detective Sergeant White gave a description of a man he believed to be the killer and it fitted the description of Holmes. (White was involved in the investigation of the Whitechapel murders and was supposedly the only officer to come face to face with Jack the Ripper.) The only difficulty in comparing White's description with that of Holmes lies in the estimated height of the suspect. White's suspect was about five feet ten inches tall whereas Holmes was allegedly over six feet in height. Mitchelson explains the discrepancy by referring to the case of 'The Three Students'. In the latter case there is evidence to suggest that Watson overstated Sherlock's height, though what is perhaps more significant, to my way of thinking, is that White reported his suspect as being slightly bent at the shoulders. This would make him look shorter than he actually was. Holmes would undoubtedly have made a desperate attempt to alter his physical appearance in such circumstances.

These comparisons in no way make Holmes and the Ripper one and the same, but there are other points of interest to be considered. It is clear from post-mortem reports that the killer possessed some basic skills in anatomy, and it is fairly certain that he knew the area intimately. Mitchelson also states that he would have needed the physical ability to overcome his victims. Holmes had an accurate knowledge of anatomy and had spent some considerable time in the East End. He was always in training and was well versed in Baritsu (a form of Japanese wrestling), so the task of overcoming his victims would have been simple. All of this is circumstantial but Mitchelson discovered a tantalising clue contained in the case of 'The Five Orange Pips'. In his recollections of this adventure, Watson wrote that a man named John Openshaw received the orange pips before he was murdered. Matthew Packer, who owned the shop on Berner Street, sold a bunch of grapes to a man who was with Liz Stride shortly before she died. An examination of Stride's stomach contents revealed that she had not eaten any fruit that night: it was Holmes who placed the grape seeds by the victim as a warning of impending death. Only Holmes could have left such an evocative clue.

Another discovery that was carefully considered at the time was the message referring to the 'Juwes'. Mitchelson makes an interesting comment regarding this in saying that if the Ripper wanted to leave a message he would probably have written it close to the victim's body. This would have left no doubt as to its authorship. It is highly unlikely that he would leave a chalked message on a wall in a darkened passage a few blocks away.

Austin Mitchelson's hypothesis goes like this. Holmes was becoming paranoid and needed to prove to himself that he had not lost his powers. He assumed the identity of Aaron Kosminski, a pathetic imbecile, in order to facilitate his campaign of murder. There is the circumstantial evidence, already outlined, and the clue of the grape seeds. When the Metropolitan Police finally arrested him, under the alias Kosminski, they did not know who he really was because at that time he was not famous. He was taken to the seaside convalescent home for police at Bexhill on Sea where Detective Sergeant White had been sent to recuperate from his exhaustive investigations into the Ripper murders. White immediately recognised the suspect and was told that his name was Kosminski, but he would not testify against Kosminski because he was a fellow Jew. (This is assuming that White was also a Jew.) Holmes was taken back to Whitechapel and set free but the true suspect was kept under surveillance by the City of London Police. They had been issued with Kosminski's name and address and told that he was suspected of being the Whitechapel murderer.

Fortunately for Sherlock Holmes, the City Police and the Met were not aware that the man identified by White as the Ripper and the man the City Police were watching were two separate individuals. Kosminski was eventually sent to an asylum whilst the real Jack the Ripper remained at liberty.

Austin Mitchelson compares Holmes's character with the psychological profiling of serial killers and concludes that he showed all the classic symptoms. Personally, I'm surprised that witness statements about the killer's appearance did not describe him as smoking a calabash pipe. Perhaps Holmes decided to keep it in his pocket along with his magnifying lens and surgical knife.

It would be interesting to know how Sir Arthur Conan Doyle himself would have tackled the Jack the Ripper case. Strange as it may sound, the author admitted that he would not have made a good detective. In 1894 an American journalist asked him how Holmes would have tracked down the notorious fiend. Doyle replied that, not being particularly observant himself, he would endeavour to 'get inside the skin of a sharp man and see how things would strike him.'

Having been to the Scotland Yard Museum and studied the Ripper letter preserved there, he thought Holmes might have deduced that the letter-writer had been in America and was accustomed to the use of a pen. The paper was good quality and the writing was of a round, 'clerkly' hand. (Doyle couldn't have been closer to the truth, for it is now known that a journalist from the *Star* wrote the letter. Doyle said that the letter could have been a hoax.) He suggested that Holmes would have reproduced the letters in facsimile form and have them printed in the leading newspapers of Great Britain and America, with the offer of a reward to anyone who could produce a letter or specimen of the same handwriting.

In 1904 Conan Doyle was made a member of the Crimes Club. It had been formed the previous year and its members debated famous criminal cases including the East End murders. As a result of his membership, Doyle was invited to visit Whitechapel. The actual visit was arranged by Dr Frederick Gordon Brown and one of his colleagues; it took place on 19 April 1905. A small group of men, including Doyle, were taken to the murder sites by three City detectives who were well acquainted with the facts of the case.

The idea for Sherlock Holmes's deductive powers came about when Doyle joined the Medical Faculty of Edinburgh University in 1876. He was fascinated by one of the tutors, Dr Joseph Bell, who not only gave lectures in surgery but impressed his students by explaining how the diagnosis of a patient could commence the instant he walked through the door. Bell, an outstanding doctor and scientist, became equated with Conan Doyle's detective creation and was frequently asked to help out in solving real crime mysteries. With the help of a colleague he investigated the Ripper murders. They both came to the same conclusion but their findings were never made public.

If Sherlock Holmes had been a real person there is little doubt that somebody from Scotland Yard would have asked for his assistance. I feel that by using his methods of observation and deduction, he might have been able to channel the massive police investigation in a new and fruitful direction. His methods would have been different in this enquiry and he would have adopted a more conventional approach. To end this chapter we shall imagine that the great Holmes of Baker Street really did solve the riddle of the Ripper's identity.

(Extract from the Journal of John H Watson, MD)

It is with a certain amount of sadness that I take up my pen to write this entry, on a dull morning in January 1894. There was a gentle patter of raindrops against the window to my right side and I could see those great clouds rolling and rising like some grotesque serpent above the roof tops. My wife had died two years ago to this very day. Not only were my thoughts concentrated on her, but on those earlier days of adventure with my dear friend Sherlock Holmes, the best and wisest man I have ever known. I felt that the time had come to reveal the facts of the dreadful case of the Whitechapel murderer – a case that drove Holmes almost to the brink of mental destruction and, I hate to say, almost cost him his life.

During the period of the so-called 'Jack the Ripper' murders, my friend and I were engaged in three other cases: *The Sign of Four, The Greek Interpreter* and *The Hound of the Baskervilles* – one of very few adventures in which I participated without the constant presence of Holmes. During the latter case he remarked, 'In a modest way I have combated evil, but to take on the Father of Evil himself would, perhaps, be too ambitious a task.'

One morning, at the beginning of September, I found myself standing in the bow window studying a recent murder. The unfortunate woman was Mary Ann Nichols who was savagely attacked in Buck's Row. I distinctly remember Holmes gathering together his leftover pipe dottles from the night before and loading the black mess into his calabash. I could tell by his quick glances that he had noticed my agitation as I altered my gaze between the morning bustle in Baker Street and the columns of the newspaper.

The woman in question was of the 'unfortunate' class and the police constable who discovered her found her throat cut from ear to ear. The unusual feature about this murder were the terrible wounds inflicted upon her abdomen. The attack had been carried out with great force. The motive for the crime was a complete mystery and the police surmised that a gang of street ruffians may have been extorting money from the streetwalkers. In this instance Nichols was unable to offer anything and she suffered the ultimate penalty of death at the hands of the ruthless bullies.

Tabram and Nichols were both murdered in the same month. What did Holmes think? Before I had the chance to ask that very question he fell back into his armchair and said, if I remember correctly, 'I cannot offer an explanation, Watson, and really it is impossible to tell whether or not the three murders were committed by the same hand.'

I did not seek an explanation for my friend's deduction and nothing more was mentioned about the Whitechapel murders until the morning of 8 September when Police Constable Dooley, of J Division, entered 221b Baker Street and summoned both Holmes and myself to take a cab to Hanbury Street in Spitalfields.

We duly arrived there to find a crowd of people on the pavement and in the road outside Number 29. There was a feeling of intense excitement in the air. It was obvious that another murder had occurred and it was with great difficulty that we were escorted down a narrow passage to the scene of the crime. I cannot recall having ever looked upon a person who had been so brutally murdered as this pitiable woman. The police surgeon had already made a preliminary examination and he invited me to study the injuries. It was a cloudy morning and whilst I endeavoured to take notes, Sherlock Holmes took his magnifying lens and made a detailed examination of the backyard and adjoining yards. He then spoke quietly with Inspector Chandler, the duty officer from Commercial Street Police Station. Before leaving the scene my friend knelt beside the corpse - it turned out she was Annie Chapman - and stared intently at her terrible injuries. He was particularly interested in the mutilations and in the small arrangement of the woman's possessions lying beside her feet.

It was obvious to me that Holmes had discovered something in that little backyard off Hanbury Street, but he declined to tell me what it was. Following the Chapman murder, Holmes consulted Inspector Helson and Frederick Abberline in order to gain as much information as possible about the investigation. At a later date I learned that Holmes had left instructions with Helson. Police Constable Dooley, who was a keen admirer of my friend's methods, agreed to follow certain lines of enquiry in our absence. A number of people were carefully questioned and their answers were placed at Holmes's disposal. Glancing over my notes from the time of the Jack the Ripper murders, I see that four names were mentioned several times by Holmes: Timothy Donovan, Albert Cadosh, Elizabeth Long and a street beggar by the name of Joe Wilson. Holmes had known Wilson for some years.

Looking back to those dreadful months when my companion's nerves were stretched to their limit, I realise now that I should have attempted to retrieve him from the evil clutches of his drug addiction. He spent very little time at our lodgings during the interval when I was at Baskerville Hall, and on my return our landlady told me that he had hardly slept. The correspondence, that was usually fixed with a jack-knife to the mantelpiece, had grown in thickness, and there were numerous anatomical drawings and maps strewn about the room. All of this was evident upon my return from Devonshire and I waited patiently for the opportunity to sit peacefully by a blazing fire and smoke a pipe with Holmes. That moment did not occur until the case had come to a close.

I will commit to paper the few facts that I can remember in relation to Sherlock Holmes's investigation of the Ripper murders. Firstly, Holmes was of the opinion that the murderer had gained some medical knowledge, and though the extent of the mutilations indicated a very violent and deranged person, he would be capable of acting naturally in his day-to-day activities. Secondly, in the back yard of Hanbury Street, or rather just over the fence at the far end of the yard, my friend discovered a pocket-size leather case with two letters, possibly initials, burned into it. Holmes revealed that the Ripper had searched Annie Chapman's pocket – he was looking for something that belonged to him. Thirdly, the beggar known as Joe Wilson said that he had seen a man leaving 29 Hanbury Street on the morning of the murder. Holmes could not match the description of the man with any of the known occupants of Number 29. There was a strong possibility that this man was the murderer.

Towards the end of October, Holmes was fortunate enough not only to have been given access to the Yard's papers on the case, but to have been afforded the help of three constables from J Division. They were given specific instructions that had to be followed to the letter. The Baker Street Irregulars also played their part in the hunt for the formidable Terror of Whitechapel.

To say that it was a difficult case would be an understatement, for the unfailing efforts of Holmes to name Jack the Ripper almost brought him to a state of collapse. He had spent several nights trudging the streets and alleys of Spitalfields and Whitechapel disguised as a Lascar. During the day he sought the help of doctors and police surgeons and had spent some considerable time at the London Hospital and in mortuaries in the district.

At the beginning of November we received a visit from Helson who was eager to speak with Holmes concerning recent developments in the Ripper investigation. It very much looked as if an arrest was imminent. However, the arrest of a man whose address was given as Tenter Street, soon proved to have been a mistake. On 9 November the awful news of another murder filtered through. The latest victim, Jane Kelly, was the seventh one in the series, and by all accounts this slaying had been executed in a most fiendish manner. Holmes was taken to the small room in Miller's Court where the unfortunate woman had met her end. He took great care when examining the contents of the room and afterwards he spoke to John McCarthy, who was the owner of the houses. A few days later Holmes returned to the court and visited the residents there. He interviewed them individually and on his return he told me that the whole ghastly affair would soon be over.

Sherlock Holmes left Baker Street at midday on 17 November. He indicated that he knew the identity and whereabouts of the Whitechapel murderer and he would gather enough evidence to send the monster to the gallows. By this time my friend was absolutely exhausted and my efforts to change his mind and send someone in his place were futile. I offered to go myself but Holmes insisted that only he could successfully capture the man who was now known to the whole country as Jack the Ripper.

Most of what occurred that night was related to me by Inspector Helson. In the early hours of the following morning I looked from our window and saw a cab racing down Baker Street. A few moments later it was followed by another cab and they both came to a sharp halt outside 221b. Three men stepped out onto the pavement and I immediately recognised the lean figure of Holmes, who seemed to be in a rather befuddled state. I ran downstairs and into the hall where I met Helson, Constable Dooley and Holmes, who had several scratches upon his blackened face. I helped him to the bedroom where I tended to his cuts and gave him a mild sedative to help him sleep.

Holmes had been making his way to a house in Palmer Street, Spitalfields, and was seen to be in a very excitable if not agitated state. Fortunately, the appearance of the detective was relayed back to Helson. It was feared that Holmes was not in full control of his faculties. A short time later Helson himself was approaching a tiny court just off Palmer Street when he was shocked to see smoke rising from one of the houses. A fire had started in a room which was below ground level and could only be reached by climbing down a narrow set of stone steps. Halfway down the steps there was a grimy window through which Helson could see that two men were fighting amongst the flames. The inspector instinctively knew that Sherlock Holmes was in desperate need of help. The door at the bottom of the steps was jammed and soon cracked open from the force of Helson's shoulder. The heat and smoke were becoming unbearable. Holmes turned and looked at the inspector, who cried out, 'Get out, for God's sake man get out!'

Sherlock Holmes turned quickly and fired a bullet into the contorted face of his quarry before he was forcefully pulled from the inferno by the frantic inspector.

It was by no means certain that the man who lived and died in that squalid room was Jack the Ripper. Helson had only just been informed that a man had been arrested on suspicion of being the Whitechapel murderer, but because of the suspect's unsound mind and violent nature he was sent to an asylum. No other information about this suspect was forthcoming. Analysis of all the evidence and information eventually led Holmes to a man named Nigel Kilpatrick. Kilpatrick was thirty-five years old; he was a stout, unsavoury looking character with a pockmarked face. He had worked as a mortuary assistant and had previously spent some time helping out at the London Hospital. He possessed the anatomical knowledge needed to carry out the mutilations, lived alone and was a frequenter of the seedy East End public houses where he caroused amongst the prostitutes. Holmes discovered that on numerous occasions he had beaten up streetwalkers, but more importantly, Kilpatrick was acquainted with Annie Chapman and was seen drinking with her the night before she died. He was the man seen drinking with Jane Kelly and was subsequently described as having a carroty moustache. Though Kilpatrick had red hair, Holmes told me that he had no moustache when he confronted him in his lair. There was a deathly silence in that stinking room and Holmes could barely make any sense of what Kilpatrick was saying. When questioned about the contents of the two jars that stood on a shelf, Kilpatrick exploded with anger and threw an oil lamp across the room; he then lashed out with his knife. Holmes, in a moment of tremendous rage, shot the odious creature.

The proof that Holmes needed was lost forever and many senior police officers are now convinced that their suspect, caged safely in an asylum, is the man known as Jack the Ripper. Did the greatest detective of all time shoot an innocent man? Helson and Dooley sided with Holmes, as I did, and kept quiet about the events they had witnessed.

Only recently Inspector Helson paid me a visit and we spoke about the Whitechapel mystery. It transpired that the small, leather case found close to Chapman's body had the letters 'NK' burned into it. What was disconcerting for me was that the suspect arrested by the City Police had the initials 'NK' and so it is possible that Sherlock Holmes may have made a terrible mistake. At this point in time there is no further information regarding the police suspect, and the prospect of making a comparison between their man and Kilpatrick seems remote. Holmes was finally convinced of Kilpatrick's guilt when he noticed two jars on a shelf in his room. He could not be sure, but he thought they contained human organs.

7

Jack's Diary?

Initially, one journalist wrote, 'Diary has experts quaking.' The diary, or journal, as it is sometimes referred to, was supposedly written by a Liverpool cotton merchant, James Maybrick, and is signed 'Jack the Ripper'. Another newspaper wrote that a diary had been discovered in a house which had undergone electrical repairs. It further stated that the man who had written it had been married and had children. Could this be the answer to the mystery? My initial reaction was one of scepticism, but being a collector of Ripper material I simply waited to see if a book emerged out of these startling revelations. It did. The book was called *The Diary of Jack the Ripper* and it was published in 1993. It was written by Shirley Harrison, a researcher and journalist. The story of the diary goes back to 1992 when Robert Smith, of Smith Gryphon Publishers, was invited by a literary agency to study a journal which was signed by Jack the Ripper.

The owner of the diary was Michael Barrett, an ordinary working man from Liverpool, and it was apparently given to him by a friend in 1991. His friend, Tony Devereux, did not reveal how it had come to be in his possession and he died shortly after parting with it. Robert Smith tells us, in the introduction to Shirley Harrison's book, that he soon became aware of the high level of skills that would be required to forge such a complex document. If a hoaxer was involved, then he would have to possess detailed knowledge of the physical and psychological effects of arsenic addiction and its long-term effects.

Perhaps the biggest downfall of the diary is the fact that a comparison of James Maybrick's handwriting (from his two-page will) with the handwriting of the diary shows that the two types do not match. However, Shirley Harrison investigated the possibility that the 'will' may have been forged by James's brothers. Robert Smith also points out that up until 1987 nobody knew that the Ripper had removed Mary Kelly's heart, yet the diary mentions Kelly by name and shortly afterwards are the words 'no heart, no heart'. There is also mention of an 'empty tin box' in conjunction with Catharine Eddowes' murder. There had not been any published reference to this particular item prior to 1987. Another development in favour of the journal's authenticity came about in 1993 when two gentlemen turned up at Smith's London office. They were brothers and had brought with them a gold pocket watch which had a signature and some initials scratched on it. The signature was 'J Maybrick' and the initials were of the five victims of the Ripper. The words 'I am Jack' were also scratched into it.

There has been much debate concerning the authenticity of the journal and more books were to follow. For this reason, I have decided to dedicate a full chapter to the enigma of the diary. Jack's diary? Well, perhaps you would like to decide for yourself.

Mike Barrett had spent time as a merchant seaman and had worked on oil rigs. In the early 1990s his friend, Tony Devereux, gave him a parcel and told him to 'do something with it.' The parcel contained what appeared to be an old scrapbook from Victorian times. The pages appeared to show evidence of glue stains which pointed to the possibility of the book having once been used for photos or postcards. The first forty-eight pages had been removed; the remaining sixty-three pages contained words which stirred Mike's emotions. He told his wife, Anne, that he could not believe what he had just read: not in a million years. The first clue to understanding the contents of the 'diary', as it came to be known, was furnished in a book entitled *Murder, Mayhem and Mystery* by Richard Whittington-Egan. Mike Barrett happened to come across this book during his research into the Whitechapel murders. The book mentions the Maybrick family and their home, Battlecrease House. The house is situated in a suburb called Aigburth, south-east of Liverpool's city centre. It was at this house where James Maybrick and his wife Florie spent their final years together. Mike wondered if it was possible that this respectable middle-aged cotton merchant was in some way connected to the Whitechapel murders. He ended up taking the diary to a literary agent, Doreen Montgomery, of Rupert Crew Limited, London. She wanted a second opinion regarding Mike's story and so she asked Shirley Harrison to look at the evidence of the diary. I ought to mention here that although the name 'Maybrick' does not appear in the journal, there are various clues throughout its pages which make it quite certain that James Maybrick is the apparent author. At first, Doreen and Shirley were suspicious about the diary - only too aware of the well-known scandal of the 'Hitler diaries'. They turned out to be forgeries. It was decided that expert advice was needed so Mike went along with Shirley Harrison to the British Museum. The diary was shown to the museum's curator, Robert Smith (not to be confused with Robert Smith the publisher). He suggested that they take it to a document examiner as a proper examination was needed to verify that a) the diary had originated from the Victorian period, and b) the writing within it was over 100 years old. Dr

Nicholas Eastaugh examined the diary. He is a scientist who is well versed in the techniques used to date the materials used in manuscripts and old documents. With great care, he obtained tiny samples of ink from the pages in order to assess the chemical composition. He also conducted tests on the paper to ascertain its age. His preliminary findings showed that there was nothing in the ink and paper which would suggest a widely different date than 1888 or 1889. The contents of the diary were also studied in detail by Dr David Forshaw, who is a consultant in forensic and addiction psychiatry. He summed up by saying that for somebody to have faked the diary, he would have needed an exact understanding of criminal psychology and the effects of drug addiction. Several experts in the field of 'Ripperology' offered their expertise to Shirley Harrison during the research and writing of *The Diary of Jack the Ripper.* Three of the experts, Paul Begg, Martin Fido and Keith Skinner, wrote *The Jack the Ripper A to Z,* which is a standard reference book for serious students of the Ripper murders.

Not wanting to skim over what could become a fascinating story, Shirley Harrison researched the lives of the Maybricks. James Maybrick was born in 1838 and died in the May of 1889. His American wife, Florence, was accused of poisoning him with arsenic. The judge at her trial was Sir James Fitzjames Stephen, who was the father of James Kenneth Stephen. James Kenneth has been named as being involved in the Ripper murders. In 1972 Michael Harrison's book, *Clarence,* proposed J K Stephen as being a likely candidate for committing the Whitechapel murders. Florence Maybrick was found guilty of murder and condemned to death, but Home Secretary Henry Matthews granted her a reprieve and she served fifteen years in prison.

Battlecrease House still exists today. It is a twenty-room building standing opposite the Liverpool Cricket Club in Aigburth. The Maybrick family had originally come from the West Country and one section of the family had settled in the Whitechapel area in London. James had four brothers. William was the eldest; the three younger brothers were named Michael, Thomas and Edwin. Michael became a fine singer and songwriter. He adopted the stage name 'Stephen Adams' and by 1888 he was one of Britain's most admired composers of popular songs. The story goes that William ran away and went to sea, whilst the other two brothers, Thomas and Edwin, went into commerce.

In her book, Shirley Harrison reveals details of a treatise which was published in 1891, two years after Florence Maybrick's trial. It was written by a Scottish lawyer, Alexander William MacDougall, and entitled *Treatise on the Maybrick Case.* This document tells of a woman who called herself Mrs Maybrick; she claimed to have been James Maybrick's real wife. Her usual address was given as 265 Queens Road, New Cross, London SE. Harrison consulted the census records for 1891 and was able to establish, for the first time, the occupants of 265 Queens Road. There was a 69- year-old widow named Christiana Conconi and her 18 year old daughter; a 14-year- old visitor and the old widow's niece, 44-year-old Sarah Robertson. Christiana had married a watchmaker and moved to Mark Lane near the Tower of London. Harrison thinks it likely that Sarah joined Christiana and her husband in Mark Lane.

Did James Maybrick meet Sarah Robertson on one of his trips to London's East End where his ancestors had lived? Whitechapel is very close to Mark Lane and if Maybrick committed those murders he would already have been familiar with the streets and alleys. Christiana's husband died in 1863 and three years later she was to remarry. Her new husband was Thomas David Conconi, and a witness at the wedding signed her name as 'Sarah Ann Maybrick'. A codicil to Thomas Conconi's will stated that if his wife was to die in his lifetime then the house goods (and other items) should go to his friend Sarah Ann Maybrick, wife of James Maybrick of Old Hill Street, Liverpool and now residing at 55 Bromley Street, Commercial Road, London. In her book, Shirley Harrison points out that no marriage certificate for James or Sarah could be traced for that time period. For 1871 the census lists Sarah as living in Bromley Street; there is no mention of Maybrick being there. Records show that he was in Liverpool and working for Gustavus Witt, a commissioning agent.

When he was thirty-six Maybrick went to Norfolk in Virginia to open up a new branch in cotton trading. In 1877, while still in Norfolk, Maybrick caught malaria. He was given quinine for his condition but it didn't seem to make him any better and so the chemist shop dispensed small amounts of arsenic and strychnine. At that time Thomas Stansell was Maybrick's servant. He later recalled, at Florence Maybrick's trial, that Maybrick would order him to make some beef tea into which Maybrick would stir small amounts of arsenic. In Victorian times some women used arsenic preparations for their complexions. It was also used for medicinal purposes to treat people suffering from headaches or fever.

In 1880 Maybrick sailed from New York to Liverpool on board the *Baltic.* It was on this voyage that he met 18-year-old Florence Chandler. Florie, as she was known, was travelling to Paris with her mother, the Baroness Caroline von Roques. Florie's father died in 1863 and she may have perceived James as a fatherly figure. By the time they had arrived at Liverpool he had already proposed to her, and in July the following year they were married at St James's Church in Piccadilly. Eight months later their first child was born. He was named James, later to be referred to as 'Bobo'.

From 1882 to 1884 the Maybricks went backwards and forwards across the Atlantic, living in Norfolk, Virginia, and in Liverpool. Before this time period the cotton merchant was well and truly hooked on arsenic and it was an addiction that was to stay with him for the rest of his life.

In 1884 the cotton industry changed and coal was to be exported in place of cotton. The Maybricks decided to move back to Liverpool for good, and they rented a detached house in the suburb of Grassendale. Maybrick became a Freeman of the City; his drug habit, however, played a very significant part in his life. 1884 saw a decline in Britain's economy. Maybrick became concerned about the family's finances - a situation which was only worsened by Florie's expensive taste for clothes.

In July 1885 there was a new addition to the family. A daughter was born and she was named Gladys Evelyn. The timing couldn't have been worse. The foundation of the marriage was beginning to crumble, as Florie had found out that her husband was having an affair and this fact is echoed in the diary. Shirley Harrison wrote that the other woman may not have been Sarah Ann Robertson. It is likely that she was abandoned in London. Florie was also aware of his drug abuse. James referred to it as his 'medicine'.

In 1887 Maybrick employed a servant by the name of Alice Yapp. She was also a nurse. It was an extremely stressful time for Florie, especially with the new servant. Florie herself was running out of money; she was concerned about her husband's adulterous ways and his drug addiction. It was at this time that she met Alfred Brierly. Brierly was a cotton broker and his company was in Old Hall Street, just around the corner from where Maybrick worked. The Brierly family was well respected in the community. Evidently, Florie had made a beeline for Brierly at a social function. It had been noted on several occasions that Florie was flirtatious and enjoyed being in the company of men. In early 1888 the Maybricks moved from Grassendale to Aigburth where they took out a 5-year lease on Battlecrease House. The servant line-up was: Nurse Yapp; a gardener named James Grant; Alice Jones (a housemaid who became the wife of Grant); and a maid named Mary Cadwallader. Battlecrease House was situated in Riversdale Road, a road which housed businessmen and professional men alike. It was at this house where Maybrick had his den. It was reached by going through the main bedroom and it was always kept locked. James's brothers sometimes called round to see him, except William the eldest. Michael had always been regarded as the brains of the family and James seems to have been very jealous of him - a fact that is revealed in the writings of the diary. Edwin, the youngest brother, worked with James and there were rumours at the Cotton Exchange that Florie and Edwin were having an affair.

The Poste House is a public house situated in Cumberland Street, Liverpool. It is situated close to a street called 'Whitechapel'. James Maybrick used to go drinking in that pub and it was there, as Shirley Harrison tells us, that the bloody trail of Jack the Ripper began. It is thought that Maybrick saw his wife with Brierly in that particular street. Maybrick assumed that they were seeing each other.

In the diary, Brierly is referred to as 'the whoremaster' and his wife as 'the bitch' or 'the whore'. It was the writer's insane jealousy that eventually drove him to murder. He had motive enough; it only remained for him to choose the location where he could commit his heinous crimes. He decided on Whitechapel in London, although his first murder occurred in Manchester. James had reason to visit his brother, Thomas, who lived in Moss Side, so it was in this city that his murderous desires were to take effect for the first time. The diary reveals that he did not gain any pleasure from this particular murder. He strangled his victim, but there was no ripping or abdominal mutilation as with the later victims. Harrison points out that the method of strangulation, as used by the Ripper, was first suggested in Donald Rumbelow's *The Complete Jack the Ripper*. Rumbelow is a retired sergeant who worked for the City of London police. He is now a crime historian and author. His work on the Whitechapel murders and Jack the Ripper has served as an anchor for subsequent authors.

It seems that Maybrick wrote his diary in his own office, probably when everybody else had gone home, for he speaks about 'returning' (presumably back to Battlecrease). During some of his visits to London he stayed at Michael's home in Regent's Park. It is interesting to note that Gustavus Witt, a former partner of James Maybrick, had an office in London's Cullum Street, which was only 400 yards from Mitre Square.

In the summer of 1888 Maybrick visited his doctor several times as his health had gradually worsened due to his excessive drug abuse. He was taking both arsenic and strychnine and in those days there was little knowledge available on the long-term effects of their use. Strychnine pills were used for various medical purposes but Maybrick took them in the same way as a child would eat sweets. The severely handicapped marriage did not continue without comment. The diary though is not concerned with any mishaps or arguments between Florie and her husband, but with his campaign for revenge. The only way that Maybrick could punish Florie was by punishing other women, and by the August of 1888 his sadistic sexual fantasies could no longer be contained in his mind; he needed to fulfil those desires and this could only be achieved by turning the fantasy into reality. In April and August of that year Emma Smith and Martha Tabram were murdered. Smith was attacked by a street gang and died from her injuries.

Harrison believes that Tabram was probably killed by an unidentified soldier. In that Autumn the murders of Smith and Tabram were linked to the Ripper crime series. A contemporary forger would have mentioned these two killings, but there is no mention of them in the diary. Importantly, Maybrick could have been in London when a Ripper murder was committed. This has been confirmed by doctor's appointments and by various social events. In August 1888 Maybrick went to London again and he rented a room in Middlesex Street, Whitechapel. The diary reveals that he spent some time getting to know the streets. It was obvious that he was preparing for his 'campaign'. Middlesex Street runs almost parallel to Goulston Street and it was an ideal location to have as his base. On 18 August his brother, Edwin, left Britain for America. This event would have given Maybrick a feeling of emotional freedom, a feeling that nobody was looking over his shoulder. The time was nearly right for James Maybrick. His second victim was Mary Nichols, and the writings of the diary indicate his frustrations in not being able to cut her head off. Reference is also made to his medicine and the 'whore' and 'whoring master'. It seems that he was quite content in leaving Florie behind in the arms of Alfred Brierly. The murder of Nichols is described as a 'triumph' and he simply could not wait to continue his murderous activities.

Following Nichols' murder the cotton merchant travelled back to Liverpool but after only one week he was back in London again. Shirley Harrison writes that James Maybrick harboured a deep feeling of inferiority and the reason for his entries in the journal were his way of proving himself to the world. The next victim was Annie Chapman, and if you remember from the chapter entitled 'Murder in Whitechapel', part of an envelope was found in the backyard of 29 Hanbury Street . The envelope had a letter *M* written on it which was supposedly in a man's handwriting. Two pills were also found in a piece of paper. These two aspects of the Chapman murder scene, the pills and the *M* are mentioned in the diary. Harrison suggests that it was this piece of torn envelope which gave Maybrick the idea of leaving the initial of his surname. It seems that more of the name and address were originally on the envelope, but we are told that by the time Maybrick left it [the envelope] only the *M* had survived. The absence of Annie's brass rings suggests that the murderer may have taken them. Again, reference is made to 'rings' in the diary and Maybrick wrote that he removed them because they reminded him of his wife.

After Chapman's murder, he was enjoying the glory that was his, and although he was ageing rapidly, and suffering from the effects of his drug abuse, he waited with eager anticipation for a chance to commit yet another horrible murder. This was to occur in Dutfield's Yard where Liz Stride met her end. The noise of Diemschutz's pony and cart had disturbed Maybrick before he could begin the mutilations on the poor woman. He was literally only seconds away from being discovered and he could not believe that he hadn't been caught. His escape route probably took him towards his rooms in Middlesex Street, but he carried on into Aldgate and crossed the boundary between the Metropolitan and City Police jurisdictions.

By this time he was a desperate man because he had failed to complete his task in Dutfield's Yard; his blood lust, if we can call it that, would be even stronger at this stage. His next victim was only a matter of minutes away. He met Catharine Eddowes at Church Passage, but this time he was seen by Joseph Lawende, who estimated his age as being 30. (Maybrick was 49 at the time of this murder.)

Dr Brown's post-mortem report on Cathy's injuries mention a cut on each side of the cheek which, when peeled up, formed a triangular flap. This was a clue to the Ripper's identity and it was in the form of an initial. If you join the two inverted V's together they form a letter 'M' – a detail which is comparable to the envelope clue at the scene of Annie Chapman's murder. The police made a list of Cathy's possessions and it reveals that she carried an empty tin matchbox. This list of effects was not published, not even in any of the local newspapers at the time. The list itself became available for public viewing in 1984, but not before. The emtpy tin matchbox becomes highly significant because it is mentioned in the diary; only the murderer himself could have had such specific knowledge.

Middlesex Street is only a short distance from Mitre Square but Maybrick did not proceed directly back to his lodgings because early morning workers would be preparing their stalls. Instead, he walked down Stoney Lane which brought him out onto Middlesex Street. Then he crossed over to a street almost directly opposite, which brought him out into Goulston Street. It was here that Maybrick was forced to hide in a passageway which led into Wentworth Model Dwellings. He wiped his hands and bloodstained knife on the piece of apron that he had cut away from Cathy's clothing. He threw this onto the pavement and then took a piece of chalk from his pocket with which he wrote a message on the wall just inside the passage – the now famous 'Juwes' message. We have already seen how Jews came under suspicion when John Pizer was taken in for questioning and this was reported by the press. Maybrick took delight in leaving clues; the 'Juwes' message was his way of 'toying' with the police. The strange spelling of the word 'Juwes' appears to be important. The addition of the letter 'e' coupled with and inverted 'm' are both in themselves suggestive. Could it be that he had written his Christian name 'James' in such a way that it appeared to read 'Juwes'?

Other clues which appear to link the diary to the Ripper murders are to be found in Maybrick's style of writing. The handwriting of the 'Dear Boss' letter would be disguised for obvious reasons. Shirley Harrison relates the use of 'down on whores' and 'funny little games' (used in the 'Dear Boss' letter), to the mocking tones of the diary. Also the Americanisms used in the letter, such as 'dear boss' and 'fix me', would be terms which were known to Maybrick from his days in America and from conversation with his American wife.

During October there were no more murders. His drug supply had not been as plentiful as in the past and consequently he lacked the strength needed in order to continue with his campaign. He returned to Whitechapel in November and stayed at his brother's house. During his stay he took a large dose of arsenic, more than ever before. Within a very short time he had butchered Mary Kelly with unbelievable ferocity and returned to Liverpool. Mary was the youngest and prettiest victim of the Whitechapel murderer and she resembled Florence Maybrick. This resemblance drove Maybrick to commit his ultimate crime. It was the final revenge and beyond that savage and horrendous act of murder there was nothing left to be done.

It is interesting here to look again at George Hutchinson's description of the man he saw with Kelly on the night of the murder. He described him as wearing a necktie with a horseshoe pin and a gold chain. Shirley Harrison's *Diary of Jack the Ripper* shows a photograph of Maybrick with his horseshoe pin and gold chain. Furthermore, her book (and the updated version), show the police photograph of Mary Kelly's body as she was found in her room in Miller's court. On the wall just above the corpse, one can make out the letter 'M'. Just in front of it there appears to be an 'F'. Are these Florence Maybrick's initials written in blood by her husband? The letter 'M' had appeared at three separate crime scenes and indeed the diary mentions initials having been placed here and there.

James Maybrick hid the diary in the hope that one day it would be discovered. It ended up with Mike Barrett who said he received it from a friend - but where did *he* get it from? The mystery of the origin of the diary was to continue.

Dr Nicholas Eastaugh was one of the experts who used various analytical techniques in an attempt to date both the ink and the paper components of the diary. He pointed out that even if both the age of the ink and the paper could be determined with reasonable accuracy, this still would not be enough to tell us when the diary was actually written. He concluded, after all the tests were carried out, that the age of the ink and diary did not conflict with the dates 1888–89. He admitted that, in view of the evidence at his disposal, a sophisticated modern forgery could not be ruled out. The proof of the authenticity of the diary is not conclusive. Shirley Harrison delved further into the mystery of the Maybrick journal by seeking the advice of medical experts in order to ascertain whether or not it could have been written by somebody suffering from arsenic addiction. She learned that the diary revealed an understanding of the mental and physical effects of arsenic abuse. A modern hoaxer would find it extremely difficult to invent such precise medical details.

Two forensic document examiners studied the handwriting of the diary. One of them was Anna Koren, who is a member of the American Association of Graphologists. Koren looked at the handwriting and came up with a character analysis of the author of the diary. The report is very detailed but, interestingly, it lists such traits as inferiority, tendency to despotism, low self-esteem and extreme mood changes. The handwriting of the diary is free flowing and in the person's natural hand. Furthermore, as Dr David Forshaw pointed out, the writing would be considerably different from the same person's formal handwriting style if he was keen to disguise it. Apart from the possibility that the handwriting in the diary is not that of James Maybrick, there does not seem to be anything about it that immediately gives the impression of a forgery.

If the diary is genuine then it solves the mystery of the identity of the Ripper once and for all. Believers in the diary were further convinced of its authenticity when a watch turned up - a watch that belonged to Jack the Ripper! In April, 1993 the *Liverpool Daily Post* featured the story of Maybrick, the diary and the Ripper. Shortly after the appearance of the article, Albert Johnson contacted the *Post* and said that he owned a watch that once belonged to Jack the Ripper. The news of the watch filtered through to Paul Feldman, whose dedicated research into the Ripper crimes and the Maybrick diary culminated in the publication of his book *Jack the Ripper: The Final Chapter* (1997). He was the Director of Research and Executive Producer (along with Laurence Ronson) for the video called *The Diary of Jack the Ripper* (1993). The watch was examined by Feldman and various other people, notably Keith Skinner and Martin Howells (co-authors of *The Ripper Legacy*).

Albert Johnson had purchased a gold Verity watch at a jeweller's in Wallasey in 1992. It was an investment for his granddaughter. He showed the watch to his work colleagues who spotted some scratch marks on the inside back of the watch. They subjected it to a further examination under a microscope and noticed the name 'J Maybrick'. One of his friends, who had read the Maybrick article in the *Post*, remarked to Albert that the watch may have belonged to the Ripper. The owner of the shop from where Mr Johnson bought the watch was Ronald Murphy, who had been the previous owner of the watch for a couple of years. It had been given to him by his father-in-law, who ran a jeweller's shop in Lancaster. Mr Murphy was contacted and asked about the scratches on the watch. He felt sure they were there when he sold it. Albert's younger brother, Robert, became involved with the watch. It was his opinion that the watch was genuine but the diary was a fake.

By this time certain questions were beginning to form in Paul Feldman's mind. Was it possible that the Barretts and Johnsons knew each other and was it just by chance that Albert Johnson bought James Maybrick's watch seemingly at just the right time? Publisher Robert Smith had been contacted, and the relevant details concerning the watch were passed on to him and Shirley Harrison, who were preparing for the publication of *The Diary of Jack the Ripper.* They told Mr Johnson that for the watch to be included in the book he must have it examined in order to verify the age of the scratches. He took their advice and the watch ended up in the very capable hands of Dr Turgoose, a metallurgist and lecturer at the University of Manchester Institute of Science and Technology.

The results of the examination were faxed to Paul Feldman and they contained considerable details. In essence Dr Turgoose concluded that whilst his results did not indicate a recent origin of engravings (i.e. scratches), there were no observable features which would prove without doubt the age of the engravings. He went on to say that the scratches could be recent but in order to make them appear to be a lot older, considerable skill and scientific awareness would have been needed. Would Albert Johnson risk taking the watch to an expert if he knew that it had been recently tampered with?

In June 1994, Mike Barrett agreed to be interviewed by Harold Brough of the *Liverpool Daily Post.* The surprising outcome of the interview was published a few days later in the newspaper. Mike Barrett related details of how he had faked the 'Ripper Diary'. The report quoted him as saying that he was the greatest forger in history. These revelations came about at a time when Mike Barrett was apparently drinking heavily. His wife had left him, and that in itself is enough to turn some men to drink. She said that Mike had admitted to the forgery in order to get back at her, but as Shirley Harrison pointed out in her updated version of *The Diary of Jack the Ripper,* why would the fake diary be used against her? Not unless *she* was involved with the diary's fabrication. Shortly after the appearance of the newspaper article, Mike Barrett's solicitor issued a rebuttal saying that when Barrett's confession was made he was not in full control of his faculties.

Paul Feldman was not at all convinced that Mike's confession was true and so he telephoned Harold Brough and told him to ask Mike five questions. If he could answer them correctly then Paul Feldman himself would go public and admit that Barrett had forged the diary. The questions were related to James Maybrick and the Ripper's victims. Mike could not answer the questions, and on a previous occasion he was unable to explain a) how he could write a diary which would fool experts, b) how he had obtained a diary with old paper, and c) how he managed to obtain old ink with which to write the diary.

The story of the diary has become more and more complex as time moves on particularly as Paul Feldman's book, *Jack the Ripper: The Final Chapter*, introduces more characters from the Maybrick lineage including living descendants. For a complete picture of the diary, the watch and all those involved with this intriguing story, I would advise you to read the books by Harrison and Feldman. For a useful summary of the facts relating to Maybrick, his wife and the diary, the DVD entitled *The Diary of Jack the Ripper* (presented by Michael Winner), is extremely useful. Just as a matter of interest, the actor Martyn Whitby (who played James Maybrick in this production) looks somewhat like the Canadian actor, Laird Cregar, who played 'Jack' in the 1944 film version of *The Lodger*.

In this chapter I have tried to cover some of the essential points regarding the authenticity of the diary and the watch. The debate continues and there are those who would strongly disregard the validity of the diary's origin. It remains for you to decide. There is much to be said in favour of 'Jack's Diary', but I must admit there have been other theories regarding the identity of the Whitechapel murderer which are more persuasive. If the diary is a forgery then it has to be said that a tremendous amount of work has gone into producing it. Scientific examination has not been able to show conclusively that the diary is a forgery or otherwise, and various experts on ink analysis have offered contrary findings.

8

They Say I'm a Doctor Now

Over the years there have been many theories concerning the identity of the man who was responsible for the deaths of those five women in London's East End in 1888, and there may be many more to come. Over the last thirty years or so various documents have come to light, and these papers, coupled with the diligent research of crime historians and enthusiasts, have given us not only a better insight into the investigations of the time, but access to a number of 'key' suspects.

It is not my intention to cover every 'solution' that has emerged (that in itself would take up many more pages), but to look at some of the theories proposed by ardent enthusiasts who have taken up the pen in their quest for an answer.

What has tended to happen with books about the Ripper's identity is that a theory is proposed and the suspect is announced for consideration, only to be exonerated by the author of the next Ripper book, who then proceeds to give his reasons why his suspect is the right one. It is not very difficult to tear down somebody else's theory. It is not my intention to do so in this chapter, but rather to present a brief outline of the lesser known and more widely known suspects - with a view to impartiality.

Leonard Matters' book *The Mystery of Jack the Ripper,* along with Edwin T Woodhall's *Jack the Ripper or When London Walked in Terror,* have been mentioned in 'Black Bags and Top Hats', and they are among the first three full-length books to appear in this country. The third book (now extremely rare) is *Jack the Ripper: A New -Theory*. It was written by William Stewart and published in 1939.

In order to construct his theory, Stewart poses several questions. What sort of person could be out at night without exciting the suspicion of family or neighbours and who could walk through the streets heavily blood-stained and not be arrested? And what sort of person could possess the anatomical knowledge evinced by the mutilations, who could risk being found by the dead body and have a perfect alibi? The only answer could be that Jack the Ripper was a woman who was or had been a midwife. Stewart wrote that 'no violence' (in the sense that masculine energy had been used) was apparent in the murders of the Ripper. The killer could only have been a midwife because of the knowledge which was displayed in the performance of the mutilations and because 'the mutilations were performed by a hand unpractised in surgery but at the same time possessing a knowledge and manipulative dexterity which the calling of a midwife calls for'. A similar theory was aired in 1972 and was published in the *Sun* newspaper. Written by ex-Detective Chief Superintendent Arthur Butler of New Scotland Yard, the solution to the mystery was simply that the women died because of bungled abortion attempts. The mutilations were merely added afterwards to cover up the mistakes.

There was a break of twenty years following William Stewart's book; then came *The Identity of Jack the Ripper* (1959), by Donald McCormick. His book refers to a set of handwritten documents written by Dr Thomas Dutton and entitled *Chronicles of Crime*. Dutton was a man of considerable ability and intelligence and was, amongst other things, a member of the Chichester and West Sussex Microscopic Society. He supposedly used microphotography to study the handwriting contained in the numerous Ripper letters received by the police. Although his chronicles were not published they contained other case studies as well as the Whitechapel murders. The doctor's writings have long since vanished (Dr Dutton died in 1935), but McCormick had made notes of them in 1932, and in his book he wrote, 'Dutton and Abberline were friends and the latter sought the doctor's advice.' Inspector Abberline believed that Polish-born Severin Klosowski (who changed his name to George Chapman) was the man responsible for the Whitechapel murders. Chapman was a wife poisoner and was hanged in April 1903. He had previously worked as a feldscher (a surgeon's assistant, commonly known as a barber-surgeon) and he was living in the East End at the time of the murders.

According to Dr Dutton, Abberline changed his mind in respect of Klosowski being the Ripper. McCormick wrote that the inspector changed his mind because he came across a man who was Chapman's double (a dead ringer). This man was a Russian and also a barber-surgeon. McCormick makes reference to William Le Queux, who was a writer and journalist. He was also the author of a book on Rasputin, *The Rascal Monk* (1917), which was apparently based on documents found amongst Rasputin's personal belongings. One of these documents stated that Dr Alexander Pedachenko was Jack the Ripper. Donald McCormick speculated that Abberline's Russian barber-surgeon could have been Pedachenko. The reason for the murders was that Pedachenko was a secret agent working for the Russian police; he was sent to Britain to discredit the British police force. I ought to mention that in those days, particularly in Poland and Russia, a barber might engage an assistant who would perform simple surgery like removing warts. Hence the term 'barber-surgeon'.

The year 1965 saw the publication of *Jack the Ripper in Fact and Fiction,* written by True Crime author Robin Odell. His book gives an accurate account of the murders and though it was written with no particular suspect in mind, the author concentrated on what type of person the killer may have been. I found this book immensely interesting and have always had a high regard for its content. Odell wrote,

> Many doubtful, if not fantastic stories were concocted, and the public created an image of Jack the Ripper that corresponded well with the villains of Victorian melodrama who nightly trod the boards of the East End's cheap music halls and theatres.

This statement, along with similar statements from other writers, has to be seen as one of the reasons for 'Jack's' metamorphosis into the imaginary creature that he ultimately became. In 1995 Odell wrote that amidst all the fiction and fantasy there must be 'some nuggets of truth'.

Odell suggests the murderer may have been a shochet. A shochet (Jewish slaughterman) would use a long steel knife called a khalef for the ritual slaughter. They possessed anatomical knowledge and knew how to use a knife. Also, they knew how to avoid being spattered with blood; it was a technique they employed daily when cutting the throats of animals and so it is not unreasonable to assume that their perfected method of killing could have been used by the Ripper. His theory is based on three important observations: the Ripper possessed at least some anatomical skill, the throat cutting was carried out with perfected ease, and he knew how to avoid being covered with blood. These three factors would be compatible with the methods employed by a slaughterman.

In 1965 American journalist Tom Cullen wrote his *Autumn of Terror: Jack the Ripper – His Crimes and Times.* Cullen's book is the first to feature the 'Macnaghten Memoranda', but apart from this he had studied numerous newspaper articles as part of his research and he used his information wisely and accurately. Cullen's suspect has already been mentioned in this book and the same suspect features widely in Dan Farson's *Jack the Ripper* (1972). The suspect named by both authors was Montague John Druitt - the name mentioned in Macnaghten's notes. His notes (the 'Memoranda') were written in 1894 with the aim of refuting a series of newspaper articles which appeared in the *Sun* newspaper, implicating a man named Thomas Cutbush with the murders in Whitechapel. His report was headed 'Confidential' and forms part of Scotland Yard's file on the murders. His notes, contained in the official version at Scotland Yard, are reproduced here:

> I may mention the cases of three men, any of whom would have been more likely than Cutbush to have committed this series of murders.
>
> 1) A Mr M. J. Druitt, said to be a doctor and of good family, who disappeared at the time of the Miller's Court murder, whose body (which was said to have been upwards of a month in the water) was found in the Thames on 31st December – or about 7 weeks after that murder. He was sexually insane and from private information I have little doubt but that his own family believed him to have been the murderer.
> 2) Kosminski, a Polish Jew, & resident in Whitechapel. This man became insane owing to many years indulgence in solitary vices. He had a great hatred of women, specially of the prostitute class, & had strong homicidal tendencies; he was removed to a lunatic asylum about March 1889. There are many circumstances connected with this man which made him a strong 'suspect'.
> 3) Michael Ostrog, a Russian doctor, and a convict, who was subsequently detained in a lunatic asylum as a homicidal maniac. This man's antecedents were of the worst possible type, and his whereabouts at the time of the murders could never be ascertained.

In 1959 Daniel Farson visited Lady Christabel Aberconway (Macnaghten's daughter), and she allowed him to view her personal typewritten (and partly handwritten) copies of her father's original documents. In that same year Farson presented a TV series called *Farson's Guide to the British.* Two episodes featured material on the Whitechapel murders, and in one of them Sir Melville's main suspect was covered in some detail, but only his initials (MJD) were shown to the viewing public. During the showing of the series Mr Farson made an appeal for information on the Ripper crimes and as a result he received many letters. One in particular was from a Mr Knowles, who lived in Australia. Apparently,

Knowles had seen a document titled 'The East End Murderer – I Knew Him', written by Dr Lionel Druitt or Drewett. Dr Lionel Druitt, who was Montague's cousin, was practising medicine at a surgery in the East End of London in 1879, and in 1886 he emigrated to Australia.

Dan Farson was excited about the possible existence of this Australian 'document'. It had been privately published by Mr Fell of Dandenong in 1890. Was it still in existence? Farson travelled to Dandenong where he discovered that Lionel had indeed practised there in 1903; he had also set up practice in New South Wales and Victoria at various times. The crucial document, however, could not be traced.

Druitt was a popular suspect for many years. He was a barrister, a good cricketer and a teacher at a boys school in Blackheath in 1880 from which he was dismissed in 1888 for getting into serious trouble. It has been conjectured that he was involved in homosexual activities. There was insanity in his family and, as we can see from the 'Memoranda', Macnaghten wrote that Druitt was 'sexually insane' (i.e. homosexual). Montague's body was recovered from the river Thames by waterman Henry Winslade on 31 December 1888. The verdict at the inquest was suicide while the balance of the mind was disturbed.

Although this chapter is concerned with the many suspects who have emerged over the years, it would be unforgivable not to mention True Crime author and crime historian Donald Rumbelow, who I was fortunate enough to meet at the Jack the Ripper Conference in Norwich in 1998. His book, *The Complete Jack the Ripper* was published in 1975 and has since been revised and updated. It is a valuable and important contribution to the mystery. Rumbelow, one of the world's foremost authorities on the case, did not set out to prove who the murderer was. His aim was to present the hard facts of the case and to cut away the legends and inaccurate theories that have fogged the issue. His book goes back to basics and looks at the crimes in their true historical settings. He was the man who discovered one of the two remaining photographs of Mary Kelly's mutilated body and he has undertaken much work in preserving material from police archives which would otherwise have been destroyed. Richard Whittington-Egan's *A Casebook on Jack the Ripper* was also published in 1975. Again, this book is not concerned with a particular suspect; it is a scholarly account of the murders that took place in 1888.

Martin Fido is a crime historian and author of *The Crimes, Detection and Death of Jack the Ripper* (1987). Fido, who is very keen on using reliable sources, started out with the idea of writing a general survey of the case. His painstaking research may have brought us a lot closer to establishing the identity of the Ripper because Martin Fido identified the man named in Macnaghten's memoranda - Kosminski.

In considering Fido's theory one must be aware of the 'Swanson Marginalia' referred to in the first chapter. Swanson wrote that 'Kosminski' was the suspect and that when the suspect was sent to Colney Hatch he died *shortly afterwards.* As Fido has pointed out in his writings, Anderson's conclusions explain why the suspect could not be charged: the suspect had already been certified insane and the witness would not give evidence against a 'fellow-Jew'. The second suspect listed in the Memoranda was Kosminski, a Polish Jew who was resident in Whitechapel and ended up in a lunatic asylum. Many circumstances made him a *strong* suspect. Fido concluded that Anderson's 'Polish Jew' and Macnaghten's 'Kosminski' must be one and the same person, and so he made a meticulous search of asylum records plus searches from admissions and discharge books. His findings were extremely interesting. Three names surfaced:

1) Nathan Kaminski. He was a Polish Jew and lived at 15 Black Lion Yard in March 1888. He was a bachelor and had been treated for syphilis. The similarity to the name 'Kosminski' is plain to see. Kaminski could have been Anderson's suspect but no record of his death could be found.
2) David Cohen. In December 1888 this derelict Jew was wandering aimlessly in the streets of Whitechapel. Clearly, he was unable to look after himself and the Metropolitan Police had him taken to the Whitechapel Infirmary. The records showed him to be twenty-three years old and a tailor. He was a dangerous fellow, both to himself and to others. He was sent to Colney Hatch Asylum where he died in October, 1889.
3) Aaron Kosminski. When considering Kosminski, Fido was acutely aware of the fact that Macnaghten wrote how this suspect (i.e. Kosminski) 'was removed to a lunatic asylum about March 1889'.

So, using this date he searched the asylum records for a Polish Jew who lived in Whitechapel. He wrote in his book, *The Crimes, Detection and Death of Jack the Ripper*, that 'no East End or City pauper lunatic called K-anything-ski was held in a public asylum from 1888 to 1890'. Significantly, he did find an entry for Aaron Kosminski in the Colney Hatch asylum records for 1891. Kosminski was admitted on 7 February 1891. He was twenty-six then and his occupation was given as a hairdresser. He had been suffering from mania for six years and had not attempted work of any kind during that period. Aaron's next of kin was his brother-in-law Woolfe, who resided at Sion Square just off the Whitechapel Road.

In July the previous year, Aaron was sent from the latter address to Mile End Old Town Workhouse Infirmary. He was suffering from delusions that he knew the movements of all mankind and that he must not accept food from people. (This was probably the reason why Kosminski ate bread from out of the gutters.) The records also indicate that he was not dangerous and that he practised 'self-abuse' (masturbation). However, at one time he had threatened his own sister with a knife. His mental condition deteriorated and in 1894 he was sent from Colney Hatch to Leavesden Asylum (for imbeciles), where he died in 1919.

Fido considered Nathan Kaminsky to be a very plausible suspect and almost certainly the man to whom Anderson referred. Kaminski's address was central to the murder sites; he was taken to a lunatic asylum shortly after the murders stopped and he died in the asylum not long afterwards. Now the problem was, no record of Kaminski's death could be found at St. Catharine's House - not unless a different name had been assigned to him when he entered the asylum. This is of course, if he was the suspect. The relentless Fido noticed three things about a Jewish lunatic named Aaron Davis Cohen (aka David Cohen). Like Kaminski he had no relatives and he was the same age. He had been taken to an infirmary by the police because he was wandering about and unable to care for himself.

Fido concluded that Kaminski and Cohen were the same person, and because the authorities could not make out Kaminski's name they labelled him 'David Cohen', a name commonly applied to Jews who's names caused difficulty. But remember, 'Kosminski' was the name mentioned in the 'Swanson Marginalia', not 'Cohen'. A possible solution to this discrepancy was afforded by Martin Fido. The Metropolitan Police took Nathan to the Whitechapel Workhouse and he was registered as 'David Cohen' (who subsequently was identified as being the murderer). At a later date Aaron Kosminski (the City Police suspect) came to the attention of the Metropolitan Police, who assumed that the City suspect, Kosminski, was the same as the Met's suspect Cohen - because of their similar ages and the apparent similarity between the names 'Kaminski' and 'Kosminski'. When the Met wrote their report on Cohen they (wrongly) entered details which were applicable to Aaron Kosminski. As Fido's theory indicates, the murders stopped after Cohen had been picked up and he was violent enough to have been the Ripper. Importantly, he died *shortly* after his incarceration.

Another suspect surfaced in the same year as Fido's important contribution to the case in a book called *Jack the Ripper: The Bloody Truth* (1987). The suspect was re-examined by Melvin Harris who, to his credit, had written two other books on the subject of the Ripper murders. After carefully scrutinising many proposed theories, Harris became convinced that the murderer was probably someone unsuspected. In the end he conceded that there was one person who needed to be examined again and this particular person was the only one who could be regarded as a serious candidate for the Ripper.

Robert Donston Stephenson was born in Yorkshire in 1841. His parents were fairly wealthy people. He referred to himself as Dr Roslyn D'Onston, and during his life he had studied chemistry, medicine and black magic. In fact, as a schoolboy he showed a keen interest in astrology and witchcraft. Occultist Aleister Crowley (1875-1947) wrote that he knew the identity of the Ripper. The Ripper, he said, 'disappeared' after each crime and, significantly, Crowley was under the impression that Stephenson was a master magician.

At the time of the murders Stephenson visited Scotland Yard and told police officials about a Dr Morgan Davies of the London Hospital, who had demonstrated how the Ripper sodomised and then murdered his victims

Stephenson also worked as a freelance journalist when in London and wrote articles for the *Pall Mall Gazette*, some of which were concerned with black magic and the Whitechapel murders.

As Harris points out in his writings, the idea of a black magic connection with the Ripper's crimes is not a new one. The 1930s crime reporter Bernard O'Donnell was a friend of Aleister Crowley and pressed him to name his 'suspect with the magical powers' - but to no avail. However, O'Donnell was aware that Crowley once possessed a box that belonged to Jack the Ripper. The story of the box was related to Crowley in 1912 by Vittoria Cremers, who was involved with the running of his 'magical' society. In the 1880s novelist Mabel Collins, who was a noted follower of Madame Blavatsky, embarked on an intimate friendship with Cremers. Whilst Cremers was away in America, Collins contacted D'Onston and arranged to meet him. She was greatly impressed by this 'marvellous man', this 'great magician'. Eventually the three of them set up a cosmetic company - paid for by the ladies - for which D'Onston concocted his secret recipes for their beauty cream and rejuvenating products. They lived together on premises in Baker Street, but as time went on Mabel's fondness for the black magician subsided and turned into fear. She had seen something belonging to D'Onston and from what he had told her she became convinced that he was Jack the Ripper. She told Vittoria about her suspicions but would not reveal what it was she had seen.

Cremers became extremely curious about D'Onston and she wanted to know more. She waited until he had gone out and then entered his room to have a sneaky look round. In the room she came across a deed-box that she was able to open with one of her own keys. Inside the box were some books and some black ties which were stiff and hard. They had stains upon them, and at a later date she became convinced that the stains were blood. D'Onston, who was not aware of her discovery, told her that the Ripper hid his victim's organs under his necktie as he escaped from the scene of the crime.

The story about Dr Davies was probably told many times by D'Onston, who was recounting his own wicked deeds. When asked why he used the name 'Tautriadelta' to sign some of his articles on magic, he said that the reason would cause a sensation and nobody would ever find out.

Harris's interest in the FBI's study of serial killers led him to create what he calls a 'Master Profile'. Dr Roslyn D'Onston fits perfectly into it. His murders were almost certainly connected with the rituals of black magic; maybe his hidden desires were finally released in that autumn of terror. Harris suggests that the murders may have stopped because the outcome of them was simply nothing! No magical powers had been bestowed. It must have been a disappointment for the great magician. After the murder of Mary Kelly he became seriously ill and had to spend a few weeks in the London Hospital. He wrote a book, *The Patristic Gospels* (1904), and after its appearance the man simply vanished (not into thin air). Melvin Harris asks in his book *Jack the Ripper: The Bloody Truth*, 'Did he quietly settle in some foreign part?'

In 1995 a new book appeared about Jack the Ripper, and in its pages was the name of a suspect who had not been mentioned in previous Ripper books. In February 1993 a Suffolk policeman, Stewart Evans, received a phone call from Eric Barton, a book dealer in Richmond, who had some letters for sale. The letters, which pertained to the Whitechapel murders, were of great interest to Evans, who had been interested in the Ripper mystery since his days as a teenager. The letters soon came into his possession; there were four of them and they originated from the beginning of the 20th century. They were written to the author George R Sims, and one letter in particular was signed by Chief Inspector John Littlechild, who was head of the Secret Department at the time of the Ripper's reign of terror. There is no question that the letters are authentic and the 'Littlechild letter' (as it is often referred to) has passed stringent tests that confirm it as being genuine and of the correct period. The letter is three pages long and is typewritten. What is of tremendous importance to Ripper historians is the mention of a completely new suspect – the possibility of solving the riddle of the Ripper's identity seemed very strong. The result of the investigation was a book, *The Lodger: The Arrest and Escape of Jack the Ripper* (1995), co-written by Stewart P Evans and researcher Paul Gainey. It is an important book that has evolved as a result of the recognition of an historical, genuine document.

The suspect was known to have been a sadist, and it was common knowledge amongst his acquaintances that his feelings towards women were bitter in the extreme. He was arrested at the time of the murders on account of 'unnatural offences' but he jumped bail and escaped to Boulogne. The man was a contemporary suspect and the 'Littlechild Letter' reveals his name – Tumblety. As far as can be ascertained, Francis J Tumblety was born in 1833 in Canada and he moved to Rochester, New York, with his parents. As a teenager he sold books containing porno literature. He left Rochester only to return there in 1860.

Francis Tumblety came to England in June 1888 and stayed at a number of hotels in London's East End. By this time his dress had been toned down and he was no longer conspicuous. Evans and Gainey believe that he took up lodgings in Batty Street in 1888. Batty Street was ideally situated because it gave access to all the murder locations. As they wrote in their book, Tumblety had 'engineered a safe bolt hole for himself right in the heart of the East End'. He murdered Polly Nichols and then ceased killing for a short while. Meantime, he merely trudged around the East End streets formulating his plan as he watched the drabs and destitute women wandering about. He murdered Annie Chapman on 8 September and Cathy Eddowes on the 30th. As he made his way back to Batty Street he would have been extremely nervous as the police were combing the area due to another murder – that of Elizabeth Stride. (Evans and Gainey devote a full chapter to Stride. They concluded that her murder was most probably the result of a domestic dispute.) When Tumblety reached his lodgings he immediately began to change his clothes but was confronted by his landlady while doing this. Needless to say, he began to search for new accommodation. The police though were already on his trail and on 7 November 1888, he was taken into custody and charged with gross indecency offences. As Evans and Gainey point out, this was two days before the Kelly murder, and it looks like he was released on police bail on the same or the next day. He was arrested on suspicion of being the Whitechapel murderer on 12 November.

A report in the *New York World* for 2 December 1888 stated that Tumblety was arrested on suspicion of being connected with the murders in Whitechapel, but the police, unable to gather the necessary evidence against him, decided to detain him for other offences. He was remanded on bail on 16 November on counts of gross indecency against men, but before his trial came up he headed for the Channel ports and travelled to Boulogne. He was to adopt the name of Frank Townsend and ended up being pursued on his way to New York by Inspector Walter Andrews of Scotland Yard.

Tumblety proved to be the ultimate fugitive. There was no hard evidence against him; he left no clues and there was no apparent motive for his crimes, yet the police held strong suspicion against him. He completely evaded capture. I spoke to Stewart Evans on a couple of occasions and he told me there was a possibility that Mary Kelly may not have been a Ripper victim. (This is mentioned in the 1996 updated version of their book, *Jack the Ripper: First American Serial Killer.*) Evans and Gainey agree that Joseph Barnett may well have killed Kelly and then mutilated her in such a way as to make it look like a Ripper killing. Stewart told me, at the Jack the Ripper Conference for 1998, that he was convinced Francis Tumblety was responsible for the deaths of Nichols, Chapman and Eddowes. The elusive Tumblety was featured in a TV documentary in 1996.

The author William Beadle proposed a different suspect in his books, *Jack the Ripper: Anatomy of a Myth* (1995) and *Jack the Ripper Unmasked* (2009). Beadle, who is chairman of The Whitechapel Society in London, wrote that William Henry Bury was Jack the Ripper. Bury and his wife Ellen had moved to Dundee from London in January 1889, and after only a few weeks William woke up to find his wife dead. She had a length of rope around her neck. Five days later he went to the police station and told two detectives that his wife had committed suicide. The police visited his flat on Princes Street and found his wife's naked body in a wooden trunk. She had been strangled with rope and her body had been mutilated with a knife. A doctor's report revealed that there were ten knife wounds in the abdomen, pubic region and the perineum. Ellen's body had been mutilated after death and the police surgeons who conducted the post-mortem both concluded that she had been dead for several days and definitely had not strangled herself. William Bury was charged and convicted of her murder.

When the police visited his flat they discovered two chalked messages. One was behind a tenement door and read, 'Jack Ripper is at the back of this door,' and the other message, situated on the stair wall leading down to the flat, read, 'Jack Ripper is in this sellar'. Beadle mentions the fact that, according to the papers kept at the Scottish Public Record Office, Bury did not make a statement in his own words, or at any rate if he did then it is not contained in the file. What Bury told the two detectives (on 10 February) was written down by them and dated the following day, but there is no mention of why Bury mutilated his wife after death or of the chalked 'Jack Ripper' messages.

As Beadle wrote, it looked like the Dundee police were keeping the possibility of a Ripper connection at arm's length until Scotland Yard was called in. Abberline himself was brought in to investigate this one, the reason being that Bury had been in East London, and of course his wife Ellen had suffered abdominal mutilations. It looks like Abberline did not connect William Bury with the atrocities in the East End.

Bury lived in Bow, East London, from October 1887 to January 1889. In April 1888 he married Ellen; shortly after the wedding he persuaded her to sell some of her shares, (worth £20,000 in today's money), keeping a considerable amount of her money for his own purposes. He used some of the money to buy a pony and cart, and no doubt much of it was spent on beer. The pony and cart were used by him to peddle sawdust in the East End.

Abberline's enquiries brought some interesting facts to light. It transpired that William met Ellen (supposedly a servant) at premises on Quickett Street, and she was a prostitute. Bury was aware of her sordid occupation and, ironically, he passed venereal disease onto her. She was very frightened of him and feared that he might kill her. In March 1888, he stole money from his employer and demanded money from Ellen. He made an attempt to cut her throat but was stopped in time.

Beadle gathers many more facts in support of his theory that Bury was the Ripper and he makes a strong case against him. There are marked similarities between Bury and the FBI's profile of Jack the Ripper. To sum up: 1) Bury was twenty-nine at the time of the murders; 2) He lived close to Whitechapel/Spitalfields; 3) His job of hawking sawdust provided him with a good knowledge of the area; 4) He associated with prostitutes and kept late hours; 5) He hated women and married Ellen *only* for money; 6) He slept with his wife and his knife.

Ellen probably suspected her husband of being the Whitechapel killer and so she wrote the chalked messages. Unfortunately, she signed her own death warrant in doing so. Bury had made plans to go abroad and so he placed his wife's body in the trunk in order to dispose of it from aboard ship. However, after reading an article about a couple who had committed suicide, he changed his mind. Maybe he could convince the police of his wife's suicide and inherit the rest of his wife's shares. When he was arrested he was carrying an agreement to transfer all shares to him!

By 1997 the next suspect had arrived and once again I found myself digging deep into my pockets and purchasing this fairly hefty tome: *The Secret of Prisoner 1167: Was This Man Jack the Ripper?* It was written by James Tully, and it contains some interesting maps in one of the appendices. Tully investigated a man named James Kelly who was born on 20 April 1860 in my home town of Preston in Lancashire. As a lad he worked in Liverpool but it seems that he acquired no friends, male or female. Soon enough, mental instability began to set in. He had no sexual experiences at all when in Liverpool because he disliked and distrusted most women; however, during a visit to London he was introduced to a girl named Sarah Brider, who he later married. In 1882 Kelly lived with her at her home in Cottage Lane, off City Road, London, but the house was also inhabited by her parents, brothers, a sister and a lodger.

Kelly had little chance to be with Sarah, and to make matters worse she supposedly suffered from a vaginal disorder making intercourse very difficult. The sexual frustration became unbearable and this drove him to the East End for some cheap sex. It wasn't long before he caught a sexually transmitted disease. This led to severe headaches and discharge from the ears.

In 1883 he married Sarah and they lived at Cottage Lane as before. His mental condition rapidly deteriorated, so we are told, and his hatred of women intensified. At times he blamed his wife for everything that had gone wrong. He started brooding and 'his mind filled with all manner of suspicion'.

In June 1883 James and Sarah had a violent row which terminated in Sarah being stabbed in the throat. Kelly was charged with attempted murder but this was soon to change. On the evening of 24 June Sarah died, and now he faced a murder charge. He was due to face the hangman. However, because of his deteriorating mental health, his solicitors conceded that he may not have been fully responsible for his actions. The Criminal Lunatics

Act of 1884 had just come into force and Kelly's case was re-examined shortly before he was due to hang. James Kelly was reprieved and certified as being insane. He was sent to Broadmoor Asylum, which opened in May 1863. Kelly was admitted to Block 4 and his number was 1167. Block 4 was for prisoners who were 'quite mad and suicidal'. Kelly was depressed and showed signs of religious mania; in fact he said it was God's helping hand that made his escape from Broadmoor possible. This event occurred on 23 January 1888.

According to author James Tully, Kelly came to believe that his wife was a prostitute and that, with the help of her mother, she was merely trying to get her hands on his money. (He had inherited money from his grandmother's estate.) Tully poses the question why, if Kelly was the Ripper, did the first murder occur over six months after his escape? It seems that, being short of money and on the run, the thought of committing murder would not have entered his mind.

At the time of the Nichols' murder Kelly was living with friends on Collingwood Street, not far from Buck's Row, and an item in the *Echo* stated that certain police officers had a suspect in mind - a man who lived not far from the scene of the crime. Tully describes his suspect as a 'lust killer' and says that he must have felt sexually satisfied after he had removed Annie Chapman's entrails and womb.

Assistant Commissioner James Monro wrote to Broadmoor in February 1888 concerning Kelly's whereabouts, and he had informed officials at the asylum that Kelly's mother-in-law's house was being watched but no information regarding him could be obtained. Monro's resignation from the post of Assistant Commissioner had taken effect from August 31st, the day when Polly Nichols died. He continued his role as Head of the Secret Department and was responsible to the Home Secretary. As Tully says, Monro's interest would still have been stimulated by the unfolding events in the Ripper case. The Home Secretary wrote a memorandum to his Private Secretary, Evelyn Ruggles-Brise, saying that he should 'stimulate the police about the Whitechapel murders. Monro might be willing to give a hint to the CID people if necessary'. It very much sounds as if Home Secretary Matthews and Monro were in possession of information which the police on the ground were not aware of. James Tully wrote that 'the James Kelly penny finally dropped with the authorities on the day after Mary Kelly was murdered'. On that day the police raided Number 21 Cottage Lane and Kelly's mother-in-law was vigorously questioned. James Kelly was not there. Kelly remained on the run for thirty-nine years and returned to Broadmoor to give himself up. He died there in 1929. James Tully does not categorically state that Kelly was the Ripper, but he believes that he is the most likely candidate.

Another solution to the mystery came along in 1998 when ex-magistrate Bob Hinton gave his account of the murders in his book, *From Hell . . . The Jack the Ripper Mystery*. In Chapter Ten of his book, called 'When you have eliminated the impossible, whatever remains, *however improbable*, must be the truth', he sets out his theory and explains why George Hutchinson had to be Jack the Ripper. The title of this chapter is a Holmes' quotation from *The Sign of Four* by Sir Arthur Conan Doyle. Hinton discounts many previous suspects but to his credit he does give some of them a fair mention. He takes a very close look at the man who he thinks was the Ripper.

Hutchinson was born in Shadwell, only a few miles from Whitechapel itself. The reader's attention is drawn to, what we might refer to as, the 'leading victim' – Mary Kelly. Apart from being the last victim of the Ripper, she was the youngest, the prettiest and she was literally 'wiped out' in her own room. As Bob Hinton says, her face was so badly hacked and cut that Joseph Barnett could only identify her by her hair and eyes. (Barnett's inquest testimony revealed that he identified her by the *ears* and eyes. He probably said 'hair' but was misheard. Mary's hair was a feature that made her so recognisable.) Mary had caused an intense violence to erupt in the Ripper and Hinton asks an important question: 'What was so special about her, what did she do?' He tells us that Mary was a 'user' of other people. Her ex-boyfriends called in to give her money and this was probably the reason why her landlord, John McCarthy, allowed her to get into debt with her rent payments. Mary Kelly could manipulate people to a certain extent and would use flattery to get her own way. Most men would recognize such a situation and react accordingly, but in rare instances a certain type of person will draw an entirely different meaning from what has been said. Such people live in a world of their own; they have obsessive personalities and are termed 'stalkers'.

Hinton states that Hutchinson was the 'archetypical stalker' and he would have caused Mary to feel uneasy. Of course she was not to know that Hutchinson was the Ripper. To him she was pure and wonderful, but as time went on, and after numerous knock-backs, the love obsession would turn to hate.

His theory hinges on the acceptance of Mary Kelly being a user of people and Hutchinson as being a stalker. In essence George Hutchinson was infatuated with this woman ('infatuated' in this sense meaning an intense and morbid fondness), and because she should have felt the same way about him - but didn't - then somebody was preventing them from having a successful relationship. This is the illogical way in which stalkers think. The story of Kelly, a respectable Irish girl being sucked into the degradation of the East End slums, would be entirely believable to her stalker. And who was to blame? Prostitutes.

In the early hours of Friday, 9 November, Hutchinson came across Mary Kelly after a long trawl from Romford where he had probably been working. Instead of greeting him by putting her arms around him, she asked him for money. He didn't give her any. She was obviously drunk, and almost immediately after leaving him she stopped and spoke to a man. This caused utter turmoil in Hutchinson's mind and so he followed them back to Miller's Court and waited until Mary's client had left. And the rest you know. Kelly was, after all, just like the rest of them… and now she had to pay the price. Her killer lost control completely and literally wiped away the person who was Mary Kelly. All that remained of her was a butchered mess. It was the stalkers last revenge.

Hutchinson was seen loitering opposite Miller's Court by Sarah Lewis, who didn't recognise him. Hinton suggests that rather than keeping quiet and risk being a key suspect in a murder enquiry, Hutchinson decided to bluff it out at the police station. He concocted a story 'that would legitimately put him outside Miller's Court at that time'. His fantastic description of the man he saw with Mary was made up. If this man really existed, then the description of him is almost identical to the archetypal villain of the stage and represents the image created by the press. If Hutchinson was Jack the Ripper, his bluff certainly paid off.

During the last decade the mystery of the Ripper's identity was apparently solved by best-selling crime writer, Patricia Cornwell, who is famous for her Kay Scarpetta novels. Her book, *Portrait of a Killer: Jack the Ripper – Case Closed* (2002), received much publicity. Her theory was also aired in an Omnibus TV documentary.

Patricia Cornwell's interest in the Ripper murders began in 2001 when she visited Scotland Yard. John Grieve, the Deputy Assistant Commissioner at that time, offered to take her on a tour of the crime scenes. (Perhaps she could introduce forensic investigator Scarpetta to the Ripper case in her next novel.) Mr Grieve took her on a tour of the crime locations, adding factual details as he went along. He also mentioned some of the suspects. One of them was the artist Walter Sickert. He is discussed in the chapter entitled

'From a Jack to a Queen,' which contains an overview of Stephen Knight's theory. According to Knight, Sickert was involved in the murders but did not actually kill any of the victims. The ex-chief mentioned one of Sickert's paintings, 'The Camden Town Murder,' which shows a man sitting on the edge of a bed with the body of a nude prostitute lying on it. When studying some of his paintings Ms Cornwell felt that they portrayed a sense of morbidity, violence and a hatred of women. She wrote that there were unsettling parallels in the life of the painter and the crimes of this fabled Victorian killer.

Walter Sickert was in his twenties when he ended an acting career in the pursuit of art. His work was first exhibited in London in 1881. In the following year he became a student under the guidance of American artist James McNeill Whistler, and they both enjoyed a deep and lasting friendship. In her book, Cornwell tells us that Sickert was very much dependent on women, and saw them as 'objects to manipulate, especially for art or money.' He hated women, too, for they reminded him of his horrible deformity. Sickert was born with a penile fistula, and various operations to correct it left him with a deformed penis. Cornwell writes, 'He may not have had enough of a penis left for penetration, and it is quite possible he had to squat like a woman to urinate.'

Eventually, James Whistler got married. This would have been a massive blow to Sickert's stability and happiness. These ingredients may have been all that were needed to make him the most infamous serial killer of all time.

What seems to be the starting point for Cornwell's investigation – indeed, her suspicions – is to be found in some of the artist's paintings. One of them, entitled 'Le Journal' (1904), shows a lady lying down, apparently holding a newspaper or magazine. She is wearing a necklace. Cornwell connects this piece with a mortuary photograph of Catharine Eddowes, and says that the necklace reminds her of a negative of beads of blood which could symbolise Eddowes' cut throat. I have to admit, the two images do show a certain similarity. Sickert's 'Camden Town Murder' is actually part of a series of drawings and paintings that he created in 1908-9. The title refers to the murder of Emily Dimmock in Camden Town, London, in 1907. The man who was put on trial for her murder was acquitted by the brilliant barrister Edward Marshall Hall. Ms Cornwell links this crime with those committed by Jack the Ripper. Other paintings by Sickert show women in vulnerable, naked poses and she believes that he was reliving some of his violent crimes through his paintings.

The next stage in her research was to try and link Sickert's letters with the so-called Ripper letters stored at the Public Record Office. The idea was to see if any DNA had survived from 'Ripper' letters which could be compared with DNA from the Sickert correspondence. (Of course, one has to assume that the chosen Ripper letters were penned by the killer himself.) The DNA tests were carried out at the Institute of Forensic Science and Medicine in Richmond, Virginia. The tests were negative: no nuclear DNA had survived. The next step was to examine one of Sickert's paintings for forensic clues. This also proved negative. Undeterred, Ms Cornwell decided to test for mitochondrial DNA. In nuclear DNA an exact match between two different sources can be one in billions, but with mitochondrial DNA that statistic is greatly reduced. A mitochondrial gene sequence on one of the Ripper letters was found to match sequences extracted from two letters penned by Sickert. This evidence was by no means conclusive. Further investigation unearthed a particular Ripper letter that had the same watermark as one of the artist's own handwritten letters, but this was a tenuous link.

Towards the end of her research Ms Cornwell received a letter from the Manchester City Art Gallery inviting her to view a little-known Sickert painting called, 'Jack the Ripper's Bedroom.' By this time it was apparent to the famous writer that all the circumstantial evidence was coming together in a positive way. The painting in question is dark, eerie and provocative. Was Walter Sickert saying, 'This is *my* bedroom, and I am Jack the Ripper.'? Well, Patricia Cornwell is certain that he was.

In 2007 a retired CID detective came up with an entirely new suspect. In his book, *Jack the Ripper: The 21st Century Investigation* (2007), Trevor Marriott poses the question of why the killings occurred at weekends. This is an interesting point because back in those times many people worked a six or even a seven-day week. Of course, the reason could be mere coincidence. After eliminating his prime suspects – Druitt, Cutbush, Kosminski, Maybrick, Tumblety and Sickert – Marriott speculates that the killer could have been a merchant seaman. He writes, 'The dates of the Whitechapel murders could fit in with the voyages of a seaman in respect of both the gaps between the murders over the initial four-month period of killings and the gaps between the later murders of Alice McKenzie and Frances Coles.' Marriott believes the Ripper murdered eight women between August 1888 and February 1891. His assessment of Stride's murder (30 September 1888) led him to believe she was not a Ripper victim. He mentions the crime location as being different to the rest, and points out that a different type of knife was used in this murder.

Marriott found no evidence to support the idea that the police pursued the 'merchant seaman' line of enquiry. (In fact Edward Knight Larkins proposed a strikingly similar theory at the time of the murders. Larkins, who was a clerk in HM Customs Statistical Department, believed the murderer to be a Portuguese cattleman who sailed regularly to London. His theories were thoroughly investigated by the police. They even scrutinized the River Thames boatmen too.)

Marriott says, quite rightly, that ships use docks and prostitutes are attracted to them. The murder locations were close to St Katharine's Dock and the London Dock. His research uncovered newspaper reports of the unsolved murders of prostitutes in Nicaragua's capital, Managua. They occurred in January 1889 and the victims were mutilated in a similar way to those of the Ripper.

A pattern was beginning to emerge. After searching through the appropriate records, Marriott came across a German merchant ship named the *Reiher*. It was berthed in St Katharine's Dock on the dates of the Whitechapel murders, excluding 30 September. Importantly, the *Reiher* was present on 17 July 1889 when Alice McKenzie was murdered, and two vessels from the same line were present in London when Frances Coles was murdered on 13 February 1891. Was he a step closer to unmasking Jack the Ripper? Well, he managed to trace all the relevant maritime documents, and in particular the crew listing for the *Reiher* – but it was incomplete. However, the ex-cop's quest was not over. He uncovered Ripper-like murders with a similar MO that occurred between 1891 and 1894 in America and Germany. The perpetrator of one of the murders (that of Juliana Hoffman) had used a long knife with a razor-sharp blade. The woman suffered a cut throat which left a six-inch wound. She was almost decapitated. Her killer was Carl Feigenbaum. He was executed in 1896. This method used by Feigenbaum was suggestive. Marriott believes he had killed before, and he was well aware that the same method had been employed by the Ripper.

Carl Feigenbaum was born in Germany in 1840, give or take a year or two. He had worked as a fireman on German merchant ships. During his trial he mentioned two steamers operated by the Norddeutscher Line of Bremen. These two vessels were from the merchant line that operated merchant vessels sailing between Bremen and London at the time of the Ripper murders. Furthermore, Marriott discovered that Feigenbaum had worked as a fireman on ships sailing between America and Germany when murders were occurring there. After his arrest in 1894, the Ripper-like murders stopped. William Sanford Lawton was Feigenbaum's attorney.

After his execution he told the press that he believed Feigenbaum was Jack the Ripper. He had told him of his all-absorbing passion to kill and mutilate every woman who came his way.

Joseph Lawende's description of the man he saw talking to Catharine Eddowes shortly before she was murdered mentions that he had the appearance of a sailor!

M J Trow, novelist and author of several respected historical biographies, eventually focused his attention on the Ripper murders. I suspect that this scholarly gentleman's interest in the case goes back many years. His theory certainly deserves a mention in this updated volume. His book, *Jack the Ripper: Quest for a Killer* (2009), created enough interest for his theory to be aired on a Discovery Channel documentary.

In his book Trow tells us about 38-year-old Annie Millwood who lived in Spitalfields. In February 1888 she was attacked by an unknown assailant and sustained stab wounds to her legs and lower body. Her injuries somewhat echoed those of Martha Tabram in the August of the same year. Annie died in the following month. Her body was taken to the Whitechapel Infirmary's mortuary in Eagle Place, along Old Montague Street. The keeper of this mortuary was to become M J Trow's suspect – Robert Mann, a pauper inmate of the Whitechapel Workhouse. Mann's job was to strip and wash corpses in readiness for the post-mortems. Mann would have had lots of time to look at Annie's wounds. He may even have witnessed her bloody injuries before she died. Trow writes, '. . . and something clicked in his brain.' The fact that Mann was keeper of the mortuary would have given him a sense of power over the other inmates, and, importantly, his presence on the streets of Whitechapel day or night could be explained by saying he had been called to unlock the mortuary.

Trow says the first victim of the Ripper was Martha Tabram, who was stabbed thirty-nine times. One wound only was inflicted by a different instrument which may have been a dagger or bayonet. Martha had already been stabbed once by a soldier from the Coldstream Guards when Mann came across her body. He then stabbed her repeatedly using his clasp knife. Mei Trow uses geographical profiling to explain Mann's presence at the Tabram crime location (a south-east direction from his workhouse), and then in a south-west direction where he came across Polly Nichols on 31 August. By this time he was feeling more confident and in control. He used one of his mortuary instruments: a catling or cartilage knife. Such knives have stronger blades than the one used in the Tabram murder. After Nichols' body was taken to the mortuary, just around the corner in Eagle Place, Mann would be called to discharge his duty, and he would have taken delight in viewing the abdominal mutilation.

After describing the murder of Annie Chapman, Trow goes on to the night of the double event when Stride and Eddowes were killed. He includes Stride as a Ripper victim and says that this murder was south of his preferred killing zone, but by now he has gained even more confidence. The Stride murder is unfinished business (the arrival of Louis Diemschutz prevents the mutilations) and so Mann heads off towards Mitre Square where he meets Catharine Eddowes. Interestingly, Trow tells us that Eddowes was admitted to the Whitechapel Workhouse in June 1887 and may have come into contact with Robert Mann.

I should mention that Trow describes Mann as wearing a billycock hat and overcoat. This description is taken from the inquest report on Chapman's murder. Elizabeth Long saw a man talking to Annie shortly before her death. She did not see his face, but went on to say, 'He was wearing a brown low-crowned felt hat. I think he had on a dark coat, though I am not certain. By the look of him he seemed to me a man over forty years of age.' She further added that he looked foreign and his appearance was shabby-genteel. This is Trow's Ripper. This is Robert Mann. The description is different to the one given by Joseph Lawende, who saw a man talking to Catharine Eddowes shortly before her murder. He was described as thirty years old, fair complexion, wearing a pepper-and-salt loose jacket and a grey cloth cap. Mann was fifty-two at the time of the murders. The two descriptions cannot have been of the same person, and Trow casts doubt on Lawende's description.

Mary Kelly's murder is covered in some detail and following on from this we learn about Alice McKenzie – Robert Mann's final victim, murdered on 17 July 1889 in Castle Alley, Whitechapel.

In his book, Mei Trow delves into the criminal mind and offers a profile of the Ripper. Mann's workhouse home and mortuary were close to the scene of the first canonical victim, Poly Nichols; he possessed anatomical knowledge and knew how to administer knife cuts without being spattered with blood; he wasn't conspicuous in a crowd, and he spent much time working alone. Trow compares Mann's habits and lifestyle with the FBI's profile of the sort of person who committed the crimes. The FBI's profile regarding the Ripper's occupation states that he might have worked in a job whereby he could indulge his violent destructive fantasies, perhaps as a butcher . . . or mortuary attendant.

The theories on the Ripper's identity, or what kind of person he may have been, go back literally to the time of the murders. Hundreds of working-class and professional people were detained and questioned in 1888, and since then many authors and crime historians have sifted through the evidence and decided on a particular person. It has been said that some writers have chosen a suspect and then selected - sometimes distorted - the evidence to fit their case. This is probably true in some instances. When I wrote this chapter it occurred to me that there was an unusual assortment of characters roaming around the East End in the autumn of 1888: 'Dr' Tumblety, M J Druitt, Roslyn Donston Stevenson, James Maybrick, Nathan Kaminski, George Hutchinson, Aaron Kosminski and William Bury - to mention a few. These are only the ones we know about; there must have been dozens of others. A person's chosen suspect depends very much on his or her interpretation of the evidence, and throughout the years I personally have changed my mind on several occasions. After speaking to enthusiasts and theorists at the Ripper Conference I noted that some of them would fervently protect their candidate for the Ripper - and who can blame them?

At one time my mind was firmly set on Aaron Kosminski as being responsible for the murders but these days I'm not so sure. Maybe I have read too many books on the subject and I have to ask myself, Why do I need to know? I often wonder just how many Whitechapel murder books would be on my shelf if the name 'Jack the Ripper' had not been thought of.

The 'Dear Boss' letter quoted in the chapter entitled 'Murder in Whitechapel' had a postscript to it:

Don't mind me giving the trade name.

Wasn't good enough to post this before I got all the red ink off my hands curse it. No luck yet. They say I'm a doctor now ha ha.

The laugh may still be resonating today.

9
Sidelines

The mystery of the identity of the Whitechapel fiend has been a source of interest for over one hundred and twenty years, and some of the world's most brilliant criminologists have been drawn into the complexities of the crimes. Even today the mystery exercises a fascination over many people and I very much doubt that Jack the Ripper, whoever he was, will be completely forgotten. A prolonged and detailed study of the Whitechapel murders inevitably leads one to question other aspects of the case. In this chapter I shall be looking at some of the minor conundrums that are associated with the Ripper mystery. Was the Ripper really responsible for both murders on the night of 30 September? And how can we explain the sighting of Mary Kelly when she was supposed to have been dead?

Many authors have accepted that Liz Stride was murdered by the Ripper but there are some, including myself, who do not subscribe to this view. I must add that I am in no way trying to discredit the beliefs and views of anyone else; these are only my opinions and of course the reader will reach his or her own conclusions. One might be tempted to say how can all this be of any importance so many years after the events? The fact remains: the Ripper puzzle and all its intricacies is still as thought-provoking today as it was back then.

The International Working Men's Educational Club was once an ordinary dwelling house and could hold up to two hundred people. It was a meeting place for all nationalities, including Russian, Jewish, Czech and Polish. The club was not popular amongst the local inhabitants due to the arguments amongst its patrons which, on occasion, could be heard in the early hours. Following the Stride murder some of the newspapers reported that the dead woman was clutching some grapes. This aspect of the case formed part of Stephen Knight's theory, and the business with the grapes was featured in the film *Murder By Decree.* In reality there were no grapes or grape stems found on the body or within one foot of it. Dr Phillips and Dr Blackwell conducted a post-mortem examination on Elizabeth Stride and it was concluded that the woman had not eaten any grapes within many hours of her death. The whole point about the grape seeds is this: as we have already seen, in the first chapter, Liz and her companion entered a greengrocer's shop at around midnight on the night of the murder and the man purchased some grapes. The owner of the shop was Matthew Packer, and he gave a statement to a senior detective on 4 October regarding the appearance of Stride's companion.

Louis Diemschutz, who discovered the body, gave an interview to *The Times* on the day after the murder and reported that Stride was holding some cachous (breath sweeteners) in one hand and grape stalks in the other. So, there is the possibility that Stride's man was her attacker, especially if she had received grapes from him. There are bound to have been grape skins and stalks in Dutfield's Yard, as people passing by and entering the Yard would have used it for disposal purposes (taking into account the fact that Packer's shop was only a few feet away). Though Stride had not eaten any of the grapes, this does not preclude the possibility that the man who bought the grapes was her murderer; and yet Matthew Packer was not called to testify at the inquest. Whichever way you look at it, the episode with the grapes is not an important factor in itself; it becomes very important when viewed in the context of who bought them from Packer and what he looked like.

What is of great importance is the incident involving the attack on Stride that took place at 12.45 am. The attack was witnessed by an Hungarian Jew named Israel Schwartz. Remember, Schwartz crossed to the other side of the street during the altercation, and Stride's attacker called out 'Lipski' – apparently to another man who was watching the incident. Schwartz soon made off but started to run as he was under the impression that the other observer was following him. About ten minutes later Stride was dead.

There are many problems associated with this murder, but one theory that has been suggested by several authors is that the woman was murdered by her lover, Michael Kidney. A significant feature about her murder is highlighted in Bob Hinton's, *From Hell . . . The Jack the Ripper Mystery.* Schwartz was walking behind a man who stopped to talk to Stride and then, within seconds, was dragging her all over the place. Hinton wrote, 'It is almost impossible to imagine an argument *between strangers* deteriorating so quickly into physical violence'.

This was certainly not the way that Jack the Ripper operated. He would not have pulled a victim about in such a fashion, risking the chance of her screams ringing out, nor would he have attempted an assault in public view and drawn attention to himself by calling out 'Lipski'. It has been suggested that because Liz did not scream out very loudly, she must have known her attacker.

Up until her murder Kidney had lived with Stride in Dorset Street for three years. On a few occasions she had left him, and by September of 1888 she had taken up lodgings at Flower and Dean Street. Liz had appeared in court on charges of being drunk and disorderly and was not averse to using foul language. Likewise, Kidney had used obscene language and was accustomed to heavy drinking bouts. In July 1888 he spent a few days in prison for being drunk and disorderly, and in the previous year Liz had charged him with assault but failed to appear against him at Thames Magistrates' Court. There is no doubt that Kidney showed his nasty side to his girlfriend and knocked her about.

On 1 October, the day after the murder, he went into Leman Street Police Station and asked to see a detective. He was drunk at the time and said that he would have killed himself had he been the policeman patrolling the area at the time of the murder. In his book, *Jack the Myth* (1993), A P Wolf draws the reader's attention to an interesting fact. The inquest on Elizabeth Stride opened on 1 October and at that time the body had *not* been identified. Kidney must have known that Liz had been murdered otherwise he would not have called in at the police station ranting about the latest murder. As Wolf says, he was playing the part of the outraged upright citizen before anyone even knew that the body was that of Stride. If the dates are correct then this makes Kidney the number one suspect for his girlfriend's murder.

There are other pointers with this particular homicide that deserve consideration. Before looking at these I must add that although the man who was seen throwing Liz Stride onto the ground *probably* killed her shortly afterwards, there remains the possibility that somebody else committed the murder, though this seems highly unlikely. It is very unusual for a person to be attacked by two different people within the space of ten minutes.

The knife used to mutilate Catharine Eddowes was sharp and pointed, which was in contrast to the weapon used on Stride. The knife used in this instance was short and broad and had a rounded end. This is interesting because if the same man murdered both Stride and Eddowes then it clearly shows that he carried two knives quite different in shape and length. The fact that Stride was not mutilated does not preclude the possibility of a Ripper attack, because the evidence shows that she had only just received the fatal cut as Diemschutz entered the Yard with his pony and cart. If the Ripper had been at work then it would have been impossible for him to continue the onslaught; but whoever killed the woman the chances are that he was hiding in the shadows as Diemschutz looked upon the body.

Unlike the previous victims Nichols and Chapman, there was nothing to suggest that Stride had been asphyxiated. Part of the Ripper's modus operandi was strangulation. Reports of the murder tell us that the poor woman was wearing a silk scarf that had been pulled very tightly and the bow was turned to the left. Her open right hand was lying upon her chest and had blood upon it whilst the partly closed left hand was lying on the ground and contained a small packet of cachous. The scarf and cachous give us a possible insight into how Liz Stride was attacked - but what was she doing there in the first place? She seems to have taken the trouble to look fairly smart that particular evening, and if we accept the times of her presence in Berner Street it looks like she was hanging round the International WMC for about forty-five minutes. It is my belief that she was waiting for somebody who was inside the club, and meantime she was seen with a friend or potential customer who eventually left her.

After the minor attack, witnessed by Schwartz, she entered the Yard with the intention of gaining safety but turned back after being confronted by her attacker. Her scarf was pulled from behind and she was dragged to the ground. She raised both hands to her scarf in an attempt to free it and fell to the ground during the struggle. The cachous were still in her hand as the knife cut was administered. At this point Louis Diemschutz's cart would have been approaching, causing the attacker to hide.

That the Whitechapel murderer took unbelievable risks during the execution of his murders is obvious to see, but a serial killer like the Ripper would not grapple with his victim prior to murdering her - in the presence of observers. I would also look at the location factor in this series of crimes. The other four victims led the Ripper to places of their choice, but this was not the case with Elizabeth Stride and she does not appear to have been soliciting on this tragic occasion. According to other authors, Berner Street itself was not frequented by prostitutes.

In less than two hours Catharine Eddowes was murdered in Mitre Square and this event further enhanced the belief that the dissatisfied killer, having been unsuccessful with Stride, went on to find another victim and satisfy his grotesque urges. It is my humble opinion that the murder in Dutfield's Yard was not committed by Jack the Ripper; but this creates another problem. Before going any further it ought to be mentioned that many authors have stated that Schwartz was not called to testify at the inquest into Stride's death; and there is nothing to suggest that he did, apart from the fact that, in a written memo, Dr Robert Anderson wrote that Schwartz gave evidence at the inquest. It would seem highly unlikely for Schwartz not to have been called to give his evidence. Michael Kidney did give evidence and if he was seen in court by Schwartz then he certainly was not recognised as being Stride's attacker. The inference being of course that they never saw each other in court or, if they did, Kidney was not the murderer. The only other option is that Israel Schwartz attended the inquest at a different time to that of Kidney.

If we accept that Elizabeth Stride was not murdered by the Ripper then the identification of Aaron Kosminski at the Convalescent Police Seaside Home in West Brighton needs to be re-examined. Let us briefly look again at what Anderson, Macnaghten and Swanson wrote about Kosminski.

Sir Robert Anderson (from page 138 of his autobiography of 1910):

> I will merely add that the only person who had ever had a good view of the murderer unhesitatingly identified the suspect the instant he was confronted with him, but he refused to give evidence against him. In saying that he was a Polish Jew I am merely stating a definitely ascertained fact.

Sir Melville Macnaghten (writing in 1894):

> He had a great hatred of women, with strong homicidal tendencies. He was (and I believe still is) detained in a lunatic asylum about March 1889. This man in appearance strongly resembled the individual seen by the City PC near Mitre Square. There were many circs. connected with this man which made him a strong suspect.

Chief Inspector Donald Swanson:

> (Swanson made notes in his personal copy of Sir Robert Anderson's autobiography, *The Lighter Side of My Official Life*, regarding Anderson's Polish Jew.) Adding to the sentence in Anderson's book about the witness refusing to testify, Swanson pencilled in:
>
> *...because the suspect was also a Jew and also because his evidence would convict the suspect, and witness would be the means of murderer being hanged which he did not wish to be left on his mind.*

And on the endpaper Swanson wrote:

> *Continuing from page 138, after suspect had been identified at the Seaside Home where he had been sent by us with difficulty in order to subject him to identification, and he knew he was identified. On suspect's return to his brother's house in Whitechapel he was watched by police [City CID] by day*

and night. In a very short time the suspect with his hands tied behind his back, he was sent to Stepney Workhouse and then to Colney Hatch and died shortly afterwards – Kosminski was the suspect – DSS

As mentioned in a previous chapter, author and researcher Martin Fido discovered the *only* Kosminski to be entered in the Colney Hatch Asylum records – Aaron Kosminski. Aaron Mordke Kosminski (to give his full name) was born in Klodiva, in the Province of Kalish in central Poland, on 11 September 1865. He arrived in England in 1882. Here is a brief picture of his life from 1890 onwards:

July 1890

Sent to Mile End Old Town Workhouse Infirmary for treatment. Admissions register states that Kosminski had been insane for two years. After a few days he was discharged into the care of his brother-in-law Woolfe Abrahams who resided at 3 Sion Square, Whitechapel.

4 February 1891

Taken back to the Infirmary by his family. He was certified as being insane.

7 February 1891

Entered the Colney Hatch Lunatic Asylum. The Register of Patients lists his occupation as a hairdresser. (A lay witness for the certification of Kosminski stated that he picks up bits of food from the gutter and eats it. He is dirty and will not be washed. He has not attempted work for years. Kosminski threatened his own sister with a knife.)

April 1894

Transferred to Leavesden Asylum for imbeciles. He was demented and incoherent by this time and suffered with aural/visual hallucinations.

March 1919

Died at Leavesden from gangrene of the leg.

We can be certain that Macnaghten and Anderson were referring to Aaron Kosminski. There are many inconsistencies and problems arising from what Macnaghten and Swanson wrote in connection with Kosminski. Macnaghten wrote from memory and obviously got mixed up with his dates; also he was mistaken in saying that Kosminski resembled the individual seen by the City PC near Mitre Square. He probably meant PC Smith of the Met, who saw a man with Stride in Berner Street on the night of her murder. Swanson was wrong when he wrote that Kosminski was sent to *Stepney Workhouse* and that he died *shortly after* being taken to Colney Hatch. His pencil notes were written some years after the events and I am sure the mistakes were due to faulty memory after the passage of time. The problem now is: Who was the witness who *unhesitatingly* identified Kosminski at the Seaside Home?

The first annual report for the Seaside Home (as it became known) still exists for the year 1890 to 1891. It opened in March 1890 and the report says that from its opening until 1 March 1891 the Home received 102 visitors, including two who were admitted by special request. After being identified, Kosminski returned to his brother's house (when he was watched by City CID), and shortly afterwards he ended up in Colney Hatch. Now, we know of two men who could have been the witness at the Seaside Home. One is Israel Schwartz and the other is Joseph Lawende who saw a man with (probably) Cathy Eddowes before she was murdered. Remember, Lawende identified Eddowes by the clothes she was wearing. She had her back to him.

The next point is very important. After the identification Swanson wrote that *in a very short time* the suspect was sent to Stepney Workhouse and then to Colney Hatch. So, the identification must have taken place shortly before Aaron's readmittance to the Infirmary which was on 4 February 1891. If Schwartz or Lawende took part in the identification in Brighton then the time lapse between their sightings and the identification is at least two years. At Catharine Eddowes' inquest Lawende doubted that he would recognise the man again. Would he recognize Kosminski two years later? The answer is a definite *no*!

The other possibility is that Schwartz was the witness. He watched a man ill-treating Elizabeth Stride for only a minute or two. Again – given the two-year time period – it is unlikely that he was the witness, not unless there was some outstanding facial feature which made him difficult to forget. There again, if this was the case then surely Lawende would have remembered it too.

We should also note that while it was understandable for somebody to use the term 'Lipski', it seems odd that one Jew would use the term to insult another Jew. It is unlikely that Kosminski was involved in the murder of Liz Stride, but we must consider this: if Kosminski did commit the Berner Street murder and if he was identified by Schwartz at the Seaside Home then we can understand Anderson's belief that the Ripper had been identified.

My own personal feelings are that Kosminski was identified at the Seaside Home by an unknown witness. It was not Schwartz or Lawende. According to Chief Inspector Swanson, Kosminski was allowed to return to his brother's house in Whitechapel; therefore the police did not have enough evidence to detain him or charge him with one of the murders. The City CID kept a close watch on Kosminski day and night and the only Ripper victim to be murdered on City territory was Cathy Eddowes. This may be interpreted as indicating that there was another Jewish witness whom we don't know about. Unfortunately, existing records do not mention any other witness. Bob Hinton wrote that the police could have gone to a magistrate with the witness and obtained an arrest warrant giving them the power to force the witness to attend a trial merely by serving him with a subpoena. As to the in-depth detail of legal matters I must say that I have no knowledge at all. It would be unwise for me to comment on the implications of a witness refusing to testify and the matter must rest here.

Many researchers and authors, including myself, would be very interested to know the identity of the witness, and exactly what it was Kosminski was seen to be doing that was so incriminating it could have sent him to the gallows. We simply do not have the full story, which is a pity, because now we are left with a big question mark over Aaron Kosminski. Was he Jack the Ripper? Perhaps we will never know. Many authors are convinced that, by virtue of his insanity, he could not have been the Ripper. I shall be looking at Aaron Kosminski again, briefly, in the final chapter.

Another problem, and one that all Ripper authors and enthusiasts are aware of, concerns the time of Mary Kelly's murder. At 10.45 a.m. Thomas Bowyer discovered the body at 13 Miller's Court, Dorset Street. Dr Thomas Bond visited the crime scene at 2 p.m. the same day and reported that rigor mortis had set in *but increased* during the course of the examination. He was well aware that the time of death was difficult to determine, and in a report to Robert Anderson he wrote that the period of rigidity varies from six to twelve hours. In those days they did not have the techniques that modern science has afforded us with at the present time. Though the time of death can be calculated more precisely today, it is important to realise that many different factors can affect the onset and duration of rigor mortis. Generally speaking, rigor mortis is caused by the coagulation of the muscle plasma causing the muscles to become stiff and tense. This occurs in muscles after death. It's onset is rapid after death from exhaustion (e.g. fighting in a battle) or from a weakening disease. The most accurate determination for death time is the cooling of the body, but again this is only approximate. Thin people will cool more quickly than fat ones, weak more quickly than healthy, and naked bodies quicker than clothed. In Victorian times the rate of cooling of a body may have been taken into consideration but this would have been down to the doctor's own personal judgement. Nowadays rectal and liver temperatures would be taken as soon as possible.

The main factors affecting the onset and duration of rigor mortis are the environmental temperature and the extent of muscular activity before death. A low environmental temperature retards onset of rigor. When Mary died the weather was cold and miserable; it is possible that there was retardation in the onset of rigor. Consideration should also be given to the fact that Mary was almost completely naked; this, coupled with the opening of the abdomen, followed by extraction of the intestines and liver, would give rise to rapid body cooling. During Dr Bond's examination at the crime scene, rigor mortis was *increasing* and he concluded that death occurred at 2 a.m.

If his observations were correct in saying that rigor was increasing, bearing in mind he was a distinguished police surgeon, then his estimation of the time of death has to be reconsidered. This is not meant to detract from the doctor's expertise and experience, but today's general guide to commencement and completion of rigor mortis may be more accurate than in those days. I think, with respect, that Dr Bond's estimation of time of death was probably incorrect - based on his observations regarding the progression of rigor.

In average conditions rigor mortis commences within three to four hours after death and is complete in nine to twelve hours. If Mary had been killed at around 2 a.m. then rigor would certainly be fully developed at 2 p.m. and her body would have been rigid. Prolonged muscular activity leads to an earlier onset of rigor but this can be discounted as it is highly improbable that Mary physically exerted herself for any length of time prior to her death. It is impossible to say what the temperature was in her room during and after the period of her murder and mutilation; although a fire had been burning in the grate we can be fairly certain that any appreciable heat would have escaped from that room. There would be little, if any, insulation; and besides, the windowpane was broken, thus facilitating heat loss. We can safely assume that it was 'cold' in her room but it would be unwise to put too much emphasis on this fact when trying to determine the time of death.

Dr Bond's post-mortem report reveals that partly digested food was found in the remains of the stomach. Complete gastric digestion by the stomach depends on what you eat. Potatoes and fish (found in Mary's stomach) would take about an hour. If the time of her last meal was known, then Dr Bond may have been able to conclude the time of death by the state of digestion of the potatoes and fish; but the time her last meal was eaten is not known.

What is certain is that Caroline Maxwell gave a statement to the police on 9 November – the same day the murder had occurred. Apparently, she had spoken to Mary at approximately 8.30 a.m. near Miller's Court. A short while later, at 8.45 a.m., she again saw Mary, this time talking to a man outside The Britannia. In her statement she also mentioned Mary's partner, Joe Barnett, saying that they had split up and she had since obtained her living as an unfortunate. Obviously, Maxwell knew personal details about the couple. This supports my belief that Maxwell had not mistaken someone else for Mary Kelly, and I do not subscribe to the idea that she got the date wrong. Also, Maxwell said that Mary was wearing a maroon crossover shawl which, in fact, was later found in her flat at 13 Miller's Court. The medical evidence was in contradiction to what she said because Mary was supposed to have been dead for several hours. I believe the murder occurred between 9.30 and 10 a.m. The body was discovered at 10.45 a.m. by Bowyer. The dreadful injuries inflicted on the body would surely have taken at least half an hour.

If the Miller's Court murder *had* taken place between 9 and 10 a.m. on 9 November, we are faced with a fairly drastic change in the Ripper's format of murder and this has to be accounted for. The Whitechapel murderer would have gone out onto the streets and alleys in the early hours, from 1 a.m. until daybreak, looking for potential victims. There is obviously a great difference in his preferred schedule for stalking victims to the time of Mary Kelly's murder. There must be a reason for this, and I believe that Jack the Ripper wanted to go all the way in acting out his incomprehensible fantasies. To do this he needed more time so that he could carry out his plan of extensive butchery, which he did – with unbelievable ferocity. The 9 November was a special day. It was the day of the Lord Mayor's Show, and in this we have a possible reason for the change in the Ripper's usual methods. During this event many people would have been out of their homes and out on the streets. Importantly, many policemen would have been on the streets too, involved with the smooth running of activities. This could have been his way of thinking; it was perhaps the only chance he would get to go indoors with his intended victim, whilst everyone else had their minds set on other things. This being the case, it shows us how cunning the Ripper was. Previously, he could only carry out his diabolical crimes on the streets whilst the majority of the Whitechapel inhabitants were in their homes, but now he could have his victim indoors whilst the majority of people would be outside. All of this makes me wonder if Mary Jane Kelly knew her murderer, perhaps as a casual acquaintance.

In the first chapter I quoted part of George Hutchinson's statement to the police. On 12 November, after the inquest was concluded, he went along to Commercial Street Police Station and gave a description of a very well-dressed man of Jewish appearance who went off with Mary Kelly at 2 a.m. on 9 November. Apparently this man, who in those days would have been described as a 'toff', went back to Mary's room in Miller's Court. Hutchinson followed them and waited opposite the Court for forty-five minutes. He saw nobody exiting the Court during this time. Sarah Lewis, who was a witness at the inquest, stayed with a friend in Miller's Court that very night. She arrived there at 2.30 a.m. and remembered seeing a man standing opposite the court as if waiting for somebody. She said he wasn't tall, but stout and was wearing a black hat. There is no description available of what George Hutchinson looked like, but it is likely that the man seen by Lewis was Hutchinson himself as the time of the sighting ties in with his statement. The question is, why should he wait for forty-five minutes to see if the well-dressed stranger came out of Miller's Court? That is a long time to wait, particularly as the weather was miserable.

His description of the stranger is very detailed, even down to the shade of his eyes and eye lashes. The police were very interested in his description and Inspector Abberline took it seriously.

At the time, doctors coming home from the London Hospital were questioned by detectives merely because they were carrying small black bags. Under the circumstances one can well imagine the idea of an upper-class killer being just as plausible as one from the lower-classes.

That Hutchinson was standing opposite Miller's Court is not an odd thing in itself. Occasionally, he gave money to Mary, and it has even been suggested that he may have been a client of hers. By his own admission Hutchinson had just returned from Romford and by the time he reached Whitechapel he would have been very tired. The idea of him waiting for forty-five minutes to see if he could catch another glimpse of the stranger does not seem right. Another explanation for his questionable behaviour that night is that Hutchinson was chancing his luck and was waiting opposite the court hoping to see one of the women who lived there, not necessarily Kelly. After all, that particular area was thriving with prostitutes. Could it be that George Hutchinson was merely hoping to spend the night with a woman? I believe Hutchinson waited for half an hour and, seeing that all was quiet, went back to his lodgings on Commercial Street. I think Mary Kelly was asleep at this time; other authors have mentioned the improbability that Mary would willingly roam the streets at such a late hour when the Ripper could have been searching for women.

The only sensible reason I can think of for his visit to the police station, three days after the murder, was his concern over being roped into the investigation as a suspect, especially as Sarah Lewis had seen him. His description of the well-dressed man had, in my opinion, been carefully considered beforehand. Mary's imaginary companion had to stand out in order to direct suspicion away from Hutchinson and be of any use to the police. Hutchinson is a mysterious character in some ways and there is very little information about him. Bob Hinton wrote that he was the Ripper and gave his reasons for thinking this; personally I believe that George Hutchinson was in the wrong place at the wrong time.

In the first chapter I wrote that George Lusk had received a letter and half a kidney on 16 October 1888. Dr Openshaw, of the Pathological Museum, said that *in his opinion* the specimen was half of a left human kidney. The question is, of course, did the specimen come from the body of Cathy Eddowes? There are many people who believe this to be the case.

The postal kidney was said to have been afflicted with Bright's Disease (glomerulonephritis). The latter term refers to a class of diseases of the kidney. Dr Brown's report confirms that Eddowes' right kidney showed signs of Bright's Disease, describing it as, 'pale, bloodless, with a slight congestion at the base of the pyramid'.

This observation supports the theory that the killer himself sent the kidney to George Lusk and there are other reasons for believing this to be the case. Major Henry Smith wrote that about two inches of left renal artery remained intact in the body of Cathy Eddowes and about one inch was attached to the postal kidney. (In adults the left renal artery is approximately two and a half inches long. The right artery is slightly longer.) Apparently, Smith had shown the kidney to Henry Gawen Sutton who was a distinguished physician and an expert on the kidney and its diseases. Sutton confirmed the kidney showed signs of Bright's disease and was not charged with fluid as would be the case if the body had been sent to a hospital for dissection purposes.

This business with renal artery length becomes irrelevant after reading a report from the *Star of the East* for 22 October. Apart from its original newspaper appearance in 1888, the report was printed for the first time in *The Lodger: The Arrest and Escape of Jack the Ripper* by Stewart Evans and Paul Gainey. The article came about as the result of an interview between a reporter and Dr Frederick Gordon Brown. It reads (in part):

> As has been stated, there is no portion of the renal artery adhering to it, it having been trimmed up, so consequently, there could be no correspondence established between the portion of the body from which it was cut.

In Dr Brown's opinion there was no main reason why the portion of the kidney should not be the one removed from the murdered woman.

The postal kidney may have been the one taken from Cathy Eddowes' body but in the light of modern-day knowledge of the criminal mind it would seem extremely odd for the Ripper, or indeed any other similar murderer, to simply give away an organ that has been intentionally removed.

It is important to remember that serial murderers are acting out a fantasy in the commission of their crimes and the 'high' that is experienced at the time of the murder soon begins to fade away. Some serial killers try to rekindle this feeling of power and triumph by keeping a body part for themselves; the actual organ may be preserved or buried in a chosen spot. In some cases the murderer has even eaten parts of his victim.

Jack the Ripper took certain body parts away with him in order to extend his feeling of accomplishment. There is no way he would give away his 'souvenirs', or even part of one, having gone to the trouble of removing them. The kidney taken from Cathy Eddowes was for him and nobody else.

Going back to chapter one I wrote that PC Alfred Long discovered a piece of Eddowes' torn and bloodstained apron beneath the chalked 'Juwes' graffito whilst on his beat along Goulston Street. The discovery was made at 2.55 a.m. Long had previously passed down the street at 2.20 a.m. and believed the apron was not there at that time. Many writers have suggested he used it to wipe his hands and knife after the murder. It has even been suggested the Ripper purposely left a clue at that particular spot in order to give the impression that he was heading in a certain direction. More to the point is this: Why should the murderer bother to tear off a piece of clothing with which to wipe his hands and knife? He does not appear to have done this during any previous murder, and wouldn't it be quicker and simpler to just wipe his hands and knife on the victim's clothing? The tearing and removal of the piece of apron is suggestive. The Ripper had to cut away the clothing before he could begin the mutilations and organ extraction, and there was much clothing to cut through. Now, if the Ripper cut his own face during the assault, for example whilst cutting upwards, it seems likely he would want to use something to stop the bleeding. (He would appear highly suspicious if somebody saw him with blood running down his face.)

If this is what happened, then one can well imagine the killer hiding in some doorway on Goulston Street, or somewhere nearby, holding the torn apron to his face until the bleeding had stopped. This scenario neatly explains why he spent about thirty-five minutes in the area surrounding Mitre Square, and why PC Long found the discarded material in the doorway on Goulston Street at 2.55 a.m., and said it wasn't there earlier. At the inquest Dr Frederick Gordon Brown said that the blood spots (he used the word 'spots') were of recent origin. Jack the Ripper's blood? I wonder. . .

The study of these minor mysteries, as I like to call them, has helped me to gain a better understanding of the mind of Jack the Ripper. This topic will be discussed in the final chapter. If we are ever to solve the mystery of 'who', we need to know 'why'. My opinions concerning the level of the Ripper's intelligence and format of murder have, I admit, changed over the years. I have finally arrived at my own personal vision of what he must have been like.

I feel that the details of the Liz Stride murder, and the identification of Kosminski at the Seaside Home, are important in that they show us how problematical the Whitechapel murders have become. There is, no doubt, a simple explanation to all the questions that have arisen; the only problem is that there are so many solutions to the mystery. We have, in a sense, been leapfrogging from one suspect to another. The list of possible candidates for the role of the Ripper may be exhausted.

'Sidelines' has been a particularly interesting chapter for me to write and I know that many respected students of the case will challenge me on some of the issues raised. Our interest in the murders and the associated problems has kept the mystery alive for a staggering 122 years. There is no end in sight.

10

Bits and Pieces

People often ask me: Would the Ripper have been caught if the murders occurred today? Another question might be: If the Victorian police had our current knowledge of forensic science and fingerprinting, would the murderer have been caught? This sort of speculation begs many questions. In answering the latter I would say that, in my opinion, the police would probably have nailed their man. Needless to say, times have changed immensely since Jack the Ripper was roaming the streets. If he emerged now, then yes of course it would be possible to catch him, but I very much doubt that he would be searching for destitute women in the early hours of the morning. Such a murderer today would probably operate over a much larger area and over a greater period of time.

Walter Dew has already been mentioned in this book; he was a Detective Constable for H Division (Whitechapel) at the time of the murders and eventually became Chief Inspector. His memoirs, written some fifty years later, are illuminating and show us just how rudimentary the investigation was in Victorian days.

Apart from the Ripper crimes there was a large amount of criminal activity in Whitechapel itself and the surrounding areas. Although the police were working amongst tough and merciless criminals there were no East End areas that they would not enter. This we know from Dew himself, who walked the very streets, alleys and courts that were so familiar to the one man whom the police would loved to have caught. The former Chief Inspector wrote that it was difficult to know who the Ripper's first victim was; however, he seems to have decided on Emma Smith as being the first victim. He added that Emma would never have found a place in the chronicle of great crimes were it not for the events which were about to unfold. In mentioning the murder of Martha Tabram (Dew referred to her as 'Turner'), he was struck by the fact that the deaths of Smith and Tabram both occurred on Bank Holidays. This he found suggestive and he wondered if these nights could have been specially chosen. This is interesting speculation. Emma Smith was actually attacked by a gang of thugs but

Martha's murderer was never brought to justice. Could the holiday period have facilitated the crimes in some way? There was no doubt in Dew's mind that Tabram was a victim of the Whitechapel fiend. During the reign of terror the question of motive was considered by most officers and policemen. The only plausible reason for the killings seemed to be that the murderer was seeking revenge on that particular class of women.

I have always held that if the killer was going to be caught in the act of murder, the backyard of Hanbury Street would have been the place. The ex-Chief wrote that this was the Ripper's most daring murder: if anybody had seen or heard the Ripper and Chapman entering that small yard, he could easily have been caught - literally red-handed. Extra police, both uniformed and in plain clothes, had been on duty that evening; the killer must have passed before their watchful eyes. This gave rise to the belief that the fiend must have been supernatural. How else could he have slipped by without giving reason for concern?

Walter Dew was involved in the investigation on the day of this gruesome murder. He took statements from many people who lived in and around Hanbury Street, making use of an interpreter on some occasions. The police were certain that the murders had not been committed for the purpose of robbery, and although the motive was incomprehensible at that time, certain officers believed that somebody, somewhere, shared the Ripper's terrible secret.

Following the deaths of Stride and Eddowes, policemen were sent onto the streets and alleys in even greater numbers - some of them disguised as women. Any person who was seen to be acting suspiciously was stopped and questioned. How the murderer could kill two women in one night was a complete mystery; furthermore, it was difficult to know what methods were employed that enabled him to outwit so many officers. Going forward to the murder of Mary Kelly, we learn that although her eyes were photographed in the hope of capturing an image of the killer, the police did not really expect any result. They were right of course, but it does show how determined were their efforts to discover any possible clue.

Walter Dew held certain opinions about the witnesses who had seen Mary Kelly before she was murdered. Mary Ann Cox, of Miller's Court, saw a man with Kelly whom she described as having a blotchy face and carroty moustache. Provided that Cox's statement was correct, Dew believed this man to have been the Ripper. Her description of the man was circulated at once. Mrs Caroline Maxwell was considered to be a sane and sensible woman of excellent reputation. Her story about speaking to Kelly sometime between 8.30 a.m. and 9.00 a.m. on the morning of 9 November was thought to have been incorrect. Dew wrote that many people are often mistaken as to date and time. He concluded that George Hutchinson was mistaken also. From this we can infer that Walter Dew believed Mary to have been murdered at 1 or 2 a.m. on 9 November.

Dew's reminiscences show us how basic the investigation actually was: it was a matter of going out and catching the murderer in the act of murder, or at least having the chance to question him immediately after a murder had been committed. That Jack the Ripper was questioned during the investigation has to remain a distinct possibility in view of the strong police presence. If the Ripper had been searched and examined after one of his crimes, there is no doubt whatsoever that an intensive interrogation would have taken place at the station.

Many innocent and law-abiding citizens were frequently stopped and questioned during those dreadful months. Andy Aliffe, who has written articles for *Ripperana* and *Ripperologist* (magazines produced for enthusiasts of true crime and the Ripper mystery), discovered a contemporary piece on the murders entitled, 'The Whitechapel Atrocities: Arrest of a Newspaper Reporter'. It was written by an anonymous Victorian reporter who was arrested twice in the same day. He wrote that many men were arrested on suspicion of being the culprit on the strength of foolish and shallow evidence.

This particular journalist had spent four nights in Spitalfields and Whitechapel in November 1888, with the aim of gleaning information on the lives of the inhabitants. Part of the narrative relates to the occasion when he entered the Ten Bells public house only to be glared at by a desperate-looking fellow with a savage look in his dark eyes. The reporter was mistaken for being a detective and received a powerful punch to the chest. He was told that the police were thought to be fools.

On another occasion the reporter was standing on a corner not far from Dorset Street. It was 2 a.m. and although he waited for five minutes not a single person passed by. This was unusual, even at that late hour.

This poor chap seems to have had a rough time in Whitechapel. He entered a public house early one morning (at 6 or 7 a.m.) and asked if there was any truth in the statement that local women would rush into the beer houses as soon as they opened. As it happened the statement was true, but his question aroused the suspicion of a young man who then proceeded to question him about the murders. Shortly afterwards, amidst a barrage of abuse, the reporter found himself being escorted by an officer to the Leman

Street police station. The journalist had obviously not done anything wrong but a large crowd gathered outside the station and he was allowed to go home – through the back door!

Andy Aliffe has published another facsimile of a previously 'lost' item called 'The Whitechapel Horrors', by Tom Robinson. The latter article was rediscovered by author and researcher Stewart Evans.

Robinson resided in Whitechapel at the time of the atrocities and wrote about the local women being too afraid to venture onto the streets, even to buy food. The male inhabitants would stay indoors in case they were suspected of being Jack the Ripper. Regarding the murder in Buck's Row he wrote:

> At this time, as I have said, public opinion favoured by the press, and even accepted by some expert criminologists, pointed to a mad butcher being the perpetrator of the Whitechapel murders, and a slaughterhouse in the vicinity of Buck's Row had become an object of acute suspicion; so when one of the workmen employed in this place volunteered to give evidence, a thrill of expectant horror crept through the crowded court-room. His name was Henry Tompkins, and he described himself as a slaughterman. He declared that neither himself nor his workmates heard anything about the murder till the policeman came to the slaughterhouse and told them of what had occurred.

Robinson wrote about the 'Jack the Ripper Letter' in his section on the Hanbury Street murder:

> It was about this period that Jack the Ripper was first heard of in connection with these series of crimes. The police received an illiterate scrawl, written in red ink, from some person who boasted of being the Whitechapel murderer, and who declared his intention of continuing his career of bloodshed. He signed himself 'Jack the Ripper' and informed the police that they might expect the next murder to take place early in September. I saw a copy of this precious epistle posted outside Leman Street Police Station, and came to the immediate conclusion that the thing was a very unsavoury hoax. I have, however, long since very much moderated my original opinion. Future events

> proved that the author of the infamous 'Jack the Ripper Letter' knew what he was writing about, even if his identity must forever remain a secret.

Towards the end of his narrative, Tom Robinson wrote that the horrible murders gradually became a thing of the past. Some of the murder sites were still intact at the time of his writing and (to continue from Robinson's recollections)...

> old women, who still ply their infamous trades in the dim-lit slums that lie east of Aldgate, tell queer tales of the grim visions that they have seen (or imagined) when lights burn dimly through the yellow fog.

A policeman told Robinson that he seriously believed the murderer to have been a foreign sailor. Recollections like these show us how easy it was for the Ripper to be transformed into a gaslight ghoul.

Articles about the Jack the Ripper murders have appeared in countless books and magazines over the years. One appeared in *The Fifty Most Amazing Crimes of the Last 100 Years* (1936). The chapter called 'The Fiend of East London', was written by F A Beaumont. He wrote that the Ripper killed six women, each murder being followed by mutilation that took several minutes, and in one case, over an hour to complete. Two suspects are mentioned. They are William Henry Piggott and Charles Ludwig.

Several men had been detained following the murder of Annie Chapman. Piggott was arrested in Gravesend the night after the murder because of some unsavoury remarks he had made about women in general. When he was arrested it was noticed that he had injured one of his hands. Also, a bag belonging to him was found to contain items of clothing including a torn and bloodstained shirt. Piggott explained that he had received the injury in Whitechapel whilst helping a woman who had fallen to the ground and she bit his hand. He was subsequently cleared of having anything to do with the murders.

The German hairdresser, Charles Ludwig, came to the attention of the police in the early hours of 18 September after an incident in the Minories (an area close to Whitechapel). A policeman heard a cry of 'Murder!' coming from a court and went to investigate. On his arrival he found a man standing with a prostitute. She seemed distressed and the man was sent on his way. A short while later she told the policeman that the man had produced a large knife. Unfortunately, he could not be seen anywhere. The person in question was Ludwig, who was arrested later that same night due to another incident in which he had used his knife in a threatening manner.

Ludwig was a certain type of individual who could easily have been implicated in the murders at any time. He fitted Elizabeth Long's description of a man she saw conversing with Annie Chapman shortly before she died; Charles Ludwig was a foreigner and forty years old. He lived in the East End and was known to have gone off with prostitutes, but what makes this man an even more plausible suspect is the information given to a journalist by a hotel landlord. The landlord described the German as bad-tempered and said that he possessed anatomical knowledge gained from helping doctors to dissect bodies in Germany. Ludwig carried a long-bladed knife and one can well imagine any police officer being extremely excited by having him under lock and key and knowing about his alleged surgical knowledge and his association with East End prostitutes. However, on the night of the double murder Ludwig was still in the hands of the police.

The furore caused by the murders prompted George Bernard Shaw to write a letter to the *Star*. It was his opinion that the murderer was a social reformer whose heinous activities were intended to focus attention on the East End with its slums and poverty. Beaumont also mentions the Vigilance Committee and the fact that one newspaper boldly suggested that members of the Metropolitan Police should shave off their facial hair and dress up as women. Another suggestion was that if the murderer was not escaping the murder scenes via the streets and alleys, then perhaps he was using the sewer system. It was pointed out that the Ripper would need a key to open the street grids and they were extremely heavy.

According to Mr Beaumont's article, the Ripper could have been caught. Shortly after the murder of Liz Stride he met up with Cathy Eddowes and they headed west along Commercial Road and towards the City. As they approached Mitre Square by way of Church Passage, the heavy tread of PC Watkins could be heard as he entered the passage from the square. The Ripper covered Catharine's mouth and pulled her up tight against the wall as Watkins brushed passed them. The author of this article goes on to explain, incorrectly, that a caretaker was sitting at the open door of a warehouse, and although he was looking directly at the spot where the murder took place, he saw nothing because it was too dark.

Infamous Murders, published by Treasure Press in 1985, covered cases such as the Moors Murders, Dr Crippen, Neville Heath, Peter Kurten and the 'East End Slaughters'. The chapter concerning the Ripper names Montague John Druitt as being the most plausible suspect for the East End crimes. The reader is told that evidence existed which indicated that the police and Druitt's own family had some inkling of his involvement in the murders. Apparently, Druitt committed suicide once he discovered he was insane. Unfortunately, some of the facts regarding other aspects of the case are incorrect. According to the writer, Mary Kelly's organs and shreds of flesh were pieced together by a team of surgeons - and *then* the photographers were allowed to move in. Further on we learn that Sir Charles Warren, whose morality was regarded to be as villainous as the Ripper's, had greater faith in bloodhounds than his detective force. The champion bloodhounds, Burgho and Barnaby, proved to be useless when taken to Miller's Court, we are told. Annie Chapman was murdered as viciously as before, but this time there was a difference: two new farthings, along with various other coins and two brass rings, were arranged at her feet in the form of a sacrifice. All in all though, the article itself is a compact and interesting account of the murders and it closes by asking if the murderer could have been a midwife, a mad surgeon or even a mad policeman. The thought that Jack the Ripper may have been a policeman does, I admit, sound ludicrous but this idea has occurred many times before.

The true crime magazine, *Murder Most Foul* (no. 22), shows the sinister figure of the Whitechapel fiend brandishing his knife. One of the headings reads, 'Autumn of Terror - Six Chapters of Evil...'

Half of the magazine is devoted to the Whitechapel crimes and one particular chapter poses the question, 'Was Jack the Ripper a policeman?' A theory was put forward by an enthusiast of the mystery, a man named Bernard Brown. He makes a valid point in saying that a Metropolitan policeman could not have entered Mitre Square (situated within the City of London jurisdiction) without being immediately recognisable by his distinctive uniform. An alternative theory, and one that deserves consideration, looks at the actual murder sites themselves. Bernard Brown wrote:

> The one common denominator associated with all the murder scenes, hitherto overlooked, is the fact that they all occurred in the vicinity of a railway line, in particular an underground station.

Brown set out to prove that the murderer was a member of the Underground Railway Police. His theory would go a long way in explaining how the Ripper was able to avoid the police patrols and members of the Whitechapel Vigilance Committee.

Following the murder of Mary Nichols, Detective Sergeant George Godley and Inspector John Spratling (both from J Division, Bethnal Green) reported that the East London and District Railway stations and embankments had been searched. According to Brown, this cannot have been entirely accurate because the 'entire system lay in tunnels below the surface'. An important aspect of his theory relates to the appearance of the police constables who worked for the Metropolitan and District Railway (formed respectively in 1863 and 1868.) They were practically indistinguishable from the Metropolitan Police apart from the railway company arms on their buttons and helmet plates. However, the essence of the Ripper's ability to escape from the crime scenes undetected lies in the fact that underground railways were steam generated back then, and the 'blowholes' (built beneath the roadway to allow sulphurous fumes to escape) would have provided him with access to the tunnels. So, the killer did not need to enter a public railway station; he could continue his journey home in the fog and steam – practically invisible.

After the murder of Annie Chapman, Brown's railway policeman could have escaped by travelling down Brick Lane to the Shoreditch underground station. It has been suggested that Chapman was murdered for her organs, but Brown is clear on this point:

> Unfortunately this theory was at least 70 years out of date, as after the Anatomy Act of 1832 police were no longer required to be stationed at burial grounds armed with cutlasses against the resurrectionists.

If I could digress for a moment. It was not until 1832 that doctors were allowed to dissect bodies for the purpose of advancing medical science. Some of the bodies used had been donated and many were unclaimed, for example the corpses of paupers from hospitals and workhouses. Because of the demands of medical science there were insufficient numbers of cadavers to meet the requirements of doctors, and with the increasing interest in anatomy and physiology in the seventeenth and eighteenth centuries the trade known as 'body snatching' came into existence. In the 1990s archaeological excavations on development sites has shown clear evidence that they were once eighteenth and nineteenth-century burial grounds for dissected body parts. Obviously, illegal dissections had been performed many years before the Anatomy Act was in place. In 1997 the site of the Newcastle Infirmary was redeveloped for a Millennium Project. The archaeological examinations showed clearly that patients who had died at the infirmary between 1753 and 1845 had been used for dissection purposes. Interestingly, several similar burials were discovered at Christ Church, Spitalfields in graves dating between 1729 and 1859.

Let us return to Mr Brown's theory. His examination of the Jack the Ripper letter, sent to the Central News Agency, showed that it contained a vital clue as to the murderer's identity. The letter refers to the police as being *on the right track* – a cryptic clue, in fact, referring to the railway. There is another clue in a letter sent to the police and posted from Liverpool in the latter part of September. It read:

> Beware I shall be at work on the first and second in the Minories at 12 midnight and I give the authorities a good chance, but there is never a policeman near when I am at work.

Apparently, the letter was an indication to Sir Charles Warren that the Ripper would probably have been caught. The murders had all taken place near a fixed point. Brown refers to Charles Dickens' *Encyclopaedia of London* for 1888/89 which lists the fixed points in the East End. All the murder locations were very close to these fixed points. This knowledge enables one to see how the Ripper could pass from Berner Street to Mitre Square undetected and in less than an hour. He would have used the underground tunnels from St Mary's station on the south side of Whitechapel Road to the Aldgate station in the City. From there to Mitre Square was only a short distance.

What about the 'Juwes' message discovered in Goulston Street? Well, according to the railway policeman theory, the word actually read 'Jayes' (referring to the policemen of J Division), who were also patrolling the Whitechapel Division.

It is clear that Bernard Brown, a researcher and editor of the Metropolitan Police History Society magazine, has intimate knowledge of the London railway systems. The policeman murderer, he says, may have been in danger of being exposed by one or more of the prostitutes for indulging in the temptations of the flesh.

In the September of 1970, *Queen* magazine ran an article on the murders. It was called 'Was Gladstone Jack the Ripper?' and was written by Graham

Norton, author of *Discovering Victorian London*. Many East Enders of the time believed the killer to have been a foreigner. According to Norton, the Ripper wrote letters which are obviously genuine. Not only that, but one of the letters came with a portion of a victim's kidney; it was a 'ginny' kidney like the other one which was still inside the body. Another letter actually gave the date of the next murder. Norton goes on to say that Jack was British all right; in fact the murderer wrote that he was 'society's pillar', therefore he must have been important. Graham Norton discounts Queen Victoria because the police doctors believed the murderer to have possessed considerable strength and the Queen was sixty-nine years old in 1888. At the time of the Ripper's grip on London, the Queen was at Balmoral for most of the duration. We can say, with confidence, she has been exonerated.

William Ewart Gladstone was the only other person to be viewed with the same degree of respect as the Queen and the author of the article says, 'It is on him that the dark shadow of suspicion inevitably falls.'

Gladstone, we are told, had been fascinated by prostitutes for a long time. After he got married he took to the streets and urged the unfortunates to alter their ways and repent. He was keen to 'save' prostitutes, but Norton draws the reader's attention to a curious editorial in *The Times*. It appeared during the period of the murders and the subject matter was Glastone's political record. It read, 'we encounter at every step examples of almost incredible intellectual perversity.'

Gladstone helped to form the Church Penitentiary Association for the Reclamation of Fallen Women and his duties afforded him with the opportunity to talk to young women on the streets and then take them home where his wife could offer them tea and biscuits. He was seen on many occasions prowling around the streets and hiding in doorways and it was thought that even the Queen herself knew of his activities. Gladstone's biographer, Sir Philip Magnus, wrote that his life of grinding toil and prayer were his only means of keeping his demonic energy in check. Though he was seventy-nine years old in 1888, he was still in possession of his faculties and was physically fit. Norton suggests that these aspects of Gladstone's character may have combined to produce a series of legendary murders.

Again, he was cunning and had physical strength; he was interested in prostitution and a little anatomical learning was well within his capacity. He always had a sense of mission. The question is, could something inside him have snapped and did he ultimately become the religious maniac that some believed the Ripper to have been? One thing is certain though: Jack the Ripper is believed to have carried a shiny black bag (the Ripper's obligatory Gladstone bag). William Ewart always carried one – wherever he went.

The swift and merciless way in which the Ripper dispatched his victims has usually been of interest to most authors and enthusiasts of the case. His method of killing and subsequent mutilations were highlighted in a study of the case by William Eckert, M.D., who was Head of the Milton Helpern International Center of Forensic Sciences at Wichita State University in Kansas. He wrote two articles for *The American Journal of Forensic Medicine and Pathology*: 'The Whitechapel Murders - The Case of Jack the Ripper' (1981) - which concerns us here; his other contribution, 'The Ripper Project - Modern Science Solving Mysteries of History', was published in 1989. In his 'abstract' of The Whitechapel Murders he reminds the reader that the case is now a standard by which similar cases have been compared over the past century. The brief overview of the crimes tells us that part of the method used to render the victims helpless included strangulation, because only a few cries were reported by witnesses. Unfortunately, some of his information in Table 1 (about the victims) is incorrect. For example, Mary Kelly was supposedly pregnant at the time of her death and her intestines were draped on the mirror.

Eckert goes on to discuss the murderer's familiarity with the knife. This has led to speculation about the professional experience that might have provided him with such a deadly technique. The killer's apparent knowledge of anatomy could be explained if he was a butcher, hunter, physician or even a veterinarian. It would have been possible, at that period in British history, for many men to be acquainted with the cultural traits of Indians and the Zulu. Indeed, the Zulu wars of 1879 onwards included certain acts of ritual cleansing, like ripping open the enemy's abdomen. William Eckert suggested that cultural traits such as these may have been known to members of the British army. He refers to A M Hamilton's 'The Scientific Detection of Crime' (*Appleton's Journal*, 1876) and other pre-1888 scientific articles relating to the use of the microscope, and postulates (in his summary) that more evidence might have been uncovered at the crime scene with the use of modern techniques. (In this case he uses the term 'modern' meaning techniques that were being developed in the last half of the 19th century.)

At last the answer to the Ripper's true identity was revealed in 1996 when an article called 'Jack the Ripper's Mummy Found' appeared in the *Weekly World News*. The body was discovered along with the remains of two women in a secret chamber below an old bakery undergoing demolition. The corpses of the women are unidentified but they had been stabbed and dissected. Experts speculate that the dry atmosphere, caused by the heat from the ovens, has helped preserve the bodies since the turn of the century. The building used to be the home of a doctor in the late 1800s when five prostitutes were killed in London's East End. The report says that experts possess indisputable evidence that has now solved the mystery. The women found in the chamber were killed in the same vicious way as the Ripper's prostitute victims, and bloody knives were found alongside the mummy by Jeanne Benot, who is a French criminologist and Ripper expert. The vital evidence which proves the body is that of Jack the Ripper is a piece of material from one of the murder scenes. It matches perfectly with material taken from the overcoat found on the corpse. The doctor committed suicide because his guilt became unbearable. Officials believe that he built the secret death chamber so he could lure his victims there. The Ripper's name was Nigel Torme – so now we know!

The headline 'Did Jack the Ripper Kill a Hampshire Schoolboy?' appeared in the *Independent on Sunday* in January 1999. Gavin Maidment, a retired police officer who became senior assistant at Havant Museum, found documents which may connect the Whitechapel killer to the murder of Percy Knight Searle. Searle, who was nine years old, was stabbed to death in Havant in 1888 whilst on an errand for his mother. Mr Maidment discovered papers in the museum. They tell of a magistrate who received a letter bearing a Portsmouth postmark. The letter was received only a few days before the lad was murdered and it was signed, 'Yours, Jack the Ripper'. It indicated that the Ripper was no longer in London and had moved to the south coast. Apparently, the Portsmouth letter was taken seriously at the time, though Gavin Maidment admits it is difficult to discover if the murderer was in some way connected to the area because his identity has never been proven.

The only witness to the killing was an 11-year-old boy named Robert Husband, who stated that he saw a man stab Percy. Robert was charged with the murder after a pocket knife was found at the scene. He was later acquitted at Winchester assizes. The retired police officer believed the Ripper link could be a red herring, but the murderer may have killed outside London as the letter suggests.

As the centenary of the murders was approaching, the author and broadcaster Peter Underwood, FRSA, made his contribution. It was called *Jack the Ripper: One Hundred Years of Mystery* (1987). Underwood has, for many years, been involved with the paranormal and particularly the study of ghosts and haunted places. His addition to the many books about the Whitechapel murders includes a section on ghosts of the Ripper - an aspect that is rarely covered.

It is thought that violent and tragic events may leave an impression on the atmosphere when conditions are just right. When these conditions re-emerge they are witnessed, occasionally, by certain people. In the early 1960s Underwood visited Whitechapel and the sites of the five murders. The murder locations had hardly changed, and the venerable ghost hunter spoke to elderly residents who still had memories of the Ripper's crimes and the ghost stories associated with them.

A gentleman named Mr Thomas actually lived in Hanbury Street in the 1930s and told Underwood about the night he passed Number 29. He heard muffled voices and the sound of a struggle coming from the door leading into the passage. He walked down the passage and peered into the yard where Annie Chapman was brutally killed.

The sounds could still be heard even though the scene was deserted. It transpired that other ghostly sounds had emanated from the yard of Number 29 at various intervals in time. Early one morning in autumn, an elderly resident saw a ghostly couple enter the passage. One of the figures was that of a woman wearing a very long skirt; the man wore a coat and a tall hat with a wide brim.

Elliott O'Donnell, who wrote *Haunted Britain* (1948), and, incidentally, was referred to as 'the champion ghost hunter' by Dan Farson, once told Peter Underwood that Hanbury Street was haunted by screams and the sound of running footsteps for which there was no explanation. He said that reports of the ghostly couple seen entering the passage went back as far as 1888 and continued up until about 1930. O'Donnell said that such apparitions rarely lasted more than fifty years after the event and he believed they occurred in an area where a violent or traumatic event had taken place.

The best known haunting associated with the Ripper murders occurred in Mitre Square where Cathy Eddowes died. It was at this spot (once known as 'Ripper's Corner') that people had reported seeing the ghostly shape of the victim. These witnesses included a doctor and a policeman. The apparition was usually seen in late September and occasionally on the anniversary of the murder itself. The glossy booklet *Haunted London* (1996), by Rupert Matthews, features a short section on the haunting of Durward Street. The sad phantom was that of Polly Nichols whose faintly glowing shape used to startle horses in the days before cars took over.

With this talk about phantoms of the Ripper and blood-curdling screams in the night, one might be tempted into suggesting that a séance be conducted to see if the victims could be contacted and, moreover, to furnish some new clues as to the identity of their killer. This very same idea occurred to Pamela Ball, whose *Jack the Ripper: A Psychic Investigation*, came out in 1998. In order to assess each victim, Ms Ball and her colleagues devised astrological charts so that a general portrait of how the victims would react to their circumstances could be drawn up. A profile of the Ripper was also constructed by looking at the moment of death for each victim. (This was done by considering the positions and movements of the planets.) From the chart readings produced it seems that the murderer was attempting to rid himself of extreme anger; he had a rage against all women but there wasn't necessarily a sexual motive involved. The author goes on to say that the Ripper's motive may have been more to do with ridding the world of *mothers* rather than prostitutes. In the final murder the Ripper mutilated the symbols of motherhood.

Contact with Cathy Eddowes revealed that Cathy could survive anything, so long as she kept faith with those close to her. Ms Ball had the feeling that Eddowes was not a regular prostitute and it seems she was going to meet somebody on the night of her murder (possibly the Ripper). However, she could not sense a 'feeling' of her murderer, only that he was stocky. This session had to be prematurely terminated because she could not get a proper link with Cathy Eddowes, her attacker or indeed the circumstances surrounding the crime.

Incidentally, Pamela Ball was presented with the Maybrick Diary in order to see what, if anything, she could make of it. She concluded that Maybrick was connected with the murders in some way and the diary itself 'is more than probably a transcript of his thoughts and feelings'.

The crime historian Donald Rumbelow possesses a knife thought to have been used by Jack the Ripper during his reign of terror. The knife, originally one of a pair, came into the possession of Dorothy Stroud in 1937; she received them from Hugh Pollard who was sporting editor for *Country Life* back then. Miss Stroud gave one knife to a friend and kept the other one, which eventually got broken. The pieces of the alleged Ripper knife were given to Mr Rumbelow who later discovered that it was a post-mortem knife made in the late nineteenth century. It has a thumb-grip which facilitates upward cutting.

Pamela Ball was offered the knife for examination and had the impression that it had picked up some of the 'myth'. She could not be sure of its past and it did not seem to have a direct link with the Ripper. She states in her book that it might be impossible to establish a connection with the murderer by psychic means until he is positively identified.

Towards the end of her psychic investigation, she was compelled to suggest a theory to help substantiate her findings. The contact sessions with the victims and many of the Ripper suspects (including Kosminski, Ostrog, George Chapman, Joe Barnett, Druitt, Maybrick and Tumblety) indicated an underlying theme of intrigue and suspicion. The Ripper drama may have started with Martha Tabram who had worked in a hospital environment. Apparently, she picked up some information regarding the birth of a boy whose existence had to be kept secret. Ms Ball mentions Sir William Gull, who may have been connected in some way. In any event, Martha knew about the child and this placed her in a precarious position. The parentage of the child may have been a cause for some concern and Pamela Ball's feelings indicate that the Prince of Wales was involved in some way.

As we can see, the mystery of Jack the Ripper has exploded into myriads of what we might call concepts, theories and explanations, major and minor suspects, and all the time new information is coming to light and articles are being written every month (maybe even everyday), which add more intrigue to this awesome legacy.

11

The Mind of Jack the Ripper

What has always seemed to me of paramount interest
is contained not in the word 'who' but in the word 'why'.

Marie Belloc Lowndes

One of the most difficult tasks for me during the writing of this book was in trying to discover not only the exact causes behind the Whitechapel murders but also the nature of the fantasies that permeated the mind of the man responsible. Secondly, I wanted to extend the FBI's profile of the murderer. From a detailed analysis of the mutilations, and after studying various books on serial-killer profiling, I think I have come a little closer to understanding the mind of this seriously disordered person.

Retired FBI agent John Douglas trained himself how to think like a killer and spent most of his career in trying to develop a technique which became known as Behavioural Science. The Ripper murders occurred in 1888. The question is: Can profiling techniques be applied to a case that is so old? I believe the techniques available at this present time can be used to give a fairly accurate picture of the criminal type involved in 1888.

In a high percentage of cases the reasons for mutilation murder go back to a person's childhood, to a time when the giving and receiving of love and affection are extremely important in the making of a normal, well-balanced adult. Men who commit murder do so because of the intensity of inner conflicts; it is these conflicts, formed out of sexual and self-preserving feelings, that are the root cause of the person's problems. Here I am talking about human emotion: love, affection, hate, depression, loneliness and feelings which are sexual in nature. A child who is emotionally and sexually abused turns out, on rare occasions, to be a serial killer. If someone was abused in the same way in say, the year 1850, could we be looking at the emergence of a serial killer? In other words, could a child react emotionally the same way then as a child in 1950? Nobody can answer this question with certainty but I think the answer is yes, because we are dealing with fundamental human feelings.

A murderer like the Ripper is someone who is immensely tormented. It's simply not enough to say Jack the Ripper was a religious maniac who wanted to eliminate prostitutes because they are evil or, for example, the Ripper killed women because he caught venereal disease and it drove him mad. Those murders committed in 1888 were the work of an extremely disturbed person. To understand why he did them we must turn to psychology, and to know what he was like as a person we have to look at psychological profiling.

The most important single factor in the development of a serial killer is the role of fantasy. Later, I will tell you what the Ripper's fantasies were, but to understand his way of thinking one has to consider his motives and the gains he expected from his crimes - a difficult challenge indeed. Serial murder is baffling and disturbing; perhaps we will never be able to fully comprehend the distorted sexual feelings that permeate the psyches of such murderers when they execute their crimes.

Serial killers strike again and again. Their crimes can span months or even years and they continue to kill until they are caught or arrested for another unrelated offence. Sometimes, but not often, they commit suicide. There is always the possibility that the Whitechapel murderer took his own life, and in doing so, took his awful secret to the grave with him.

We must firstly consider what kind of serial killer the Ripper was. There are four different categories. Jack the Ripper comes under the grouping known as 'lust' killer. (This falls under the general heading of hedonistic serial murderer.) Hedonism implies the use of aggression or violence in order to obtain pleasure. This type of murder defies our understanding because the person who kills actually derives sexual gratification from the murder. The murderous thoughts of a lust killer ferment over a long period of time and they go back to childhood days. Such people reach a point in their lives when they are ready to commit a violent act. When a potential victim appears, those murderous thoughts can be put into physical action *if* the circumstances are right. In trying to understand the dark forces within the Ripper's mind we must look at the primary causes. His motive for the crimes is similar to other modern sex killers like Edmund Kemper and Jerry Brudos. There isn't really a lot of difference; only in the way their crimes are carried out and the type of victims they choose.

Generally speaking, the murderer's mind is filled with turbulent emotions which have festered since their early childhood. When these repressed emotions are stirred up, their minds react by becoming frustrated and this is often followed by feelings of violence. The Ripper lived, for many years, with feelings of immense conflict: feelings which emanated from struggling sexual and self-preserving emotions on the one hand, and his external surroundings on the other. There was undoubtedly some kind of inner turmoil eating away at the Ripper for a long time. I should imagine that to some degree he experienced emotional and maybe even sexual abuse as a child. Resentment and anger build up in such circumstances and these feelings are pushed to one side and forgotten about until they become unconscious.

The Ripper had great difficulty in dealing with his anger, like so many other violent criminals. His motive for the crimes was hidden deep within himself - even he was not aware of it. Homicide, in this instance, was triggered by an unconscious motive attached to a forgotten emotion experienced in childhood; an emotion which was sexual in its nature. What happens next is the formation of a deep-seated psychosexual disturbance and this leads to passivity and loss of self-esteem, the outcome of which is hostility. His passivity was then defended by being hostile. It is important to realise that any sexual feelings experienced by the Ripper would not have been connected with the emotions of love and affection. As a child he would become withdrawn from the outside world, trapped in his inner world of turmoil. In his lonely world of withdrawal he had feelings of vengeance and, being unable to come to terms with the hurt he once felt, he began to fantasise about taking revenge. In the case of Jack the Ripper his mother, or even sisters if he had any, might have been the focal point for his hateful feelings. Grotesque fantasies would begin to emerge and nobody would have known about them. Retired FBI agent Robert Ressler, who pioneered psychological profiling, wrote about a murderer who pulled the heads of his sister's dolls when he was a child. In adulthood he beheaded his victims.

With the sexually orientated crimes of the Ripper, sex and violence have become fused together in a way that we cannot understand. The sexually motivated crimes of lust murderers usually start off with violent fantasies: they experience a sexual 'high' by killing somebody. It's not now a case of 'I get turned on when I hurt you,' but, 'I get turned on when I stab you' (or strangle or mutilate). Ressler interviewed many serial murderers in order to create his profiling techniques. All of them experienced irresistible fantasies. They carried out their crimes to make happen in reality what they had visualised over and over in their minds. Retreating into a world of sexually violent daydreaming was their way of controlling *their* world. The abuse they suffered as children is repeated in what eventually becomes distorted fantasy, but this time *they* are dishing out the abuse. Fantasy was the driving force behind Jack the Ripper - he was getting his own back! What I find disturbing and incomprehensible is how the Ripper's thought processes should lead him to such horrendous acts of mutilation, coupled with feelings of sexual satisfaction, control and power.

Serial killers who deal in fantasy are 'sex' murderers: their crimes are sexual homicides. The act of sex itself, be it penetration or any other sex act, does not need to be involved. As Ressler wrote, 'sexual maladjustment is at the heart of all the fantasies'. The lust serial killer receives sexual gratification from his crimes (the 'gains') and he will stop only when suitable victims are not available or when sex ceases to be important. The sexual impulse is the driving force but it does not manifest itself in the way as we perceive it (i.e. wanting to have sex with a partner). Their distorted perception of sex can only be satiated by putting their ritualistic fantasy into action, and that action is pertinent to the killer in question.

Jack the Ripper did not receive pleasure by merely killing his victims, but from the mutilation and displacement of their organs. The crime traits of the Ripper were strangulation, overkill and body mutilation. Firstly, he strangled his victim to render her unconscious. Secondly, he cut the throat very deeply (in two cases it looked as if he had attempted to severe the heads completely). Thirdly, the woman's body suffered mutilation. In three cases bodily organs were actually removed. With each victim there was a strong sexual component present in the murder. Significantly, the killing of the victims was not the main priority; this was only done to facilitate the next step, which was the mutilation and removal of organs. This point must be stressed. *It was not enough for him to engage in the act of murder alone.* The mutilations - crude operations in effect - were of paramount importance.

Like the Whitechapel fiend, lust killers need to have physical contact with their victims, whether it be strangulation or vicious assault with a knife. If organs are taken away they are used as a reminder of the kill when the excitement of the murder dies down, or they may be used in conjunction with masturbation. Jerry Brudos, born in 1939, started off as a shoe fetishist but his fantasies eventually led to murder and mutilation. He cut the foot off one of his victims and fitted it into a high-heeled shoe.

Brudos cut off the breasts of another victim and made plastic moulds of them which he placed on each side of his mantel.

In order to answer the question, 'What was the Ripper like as a person?', we must turn to the FBI's profile of Jack the Ripper, which was included in William Eckert's 'The Ripper Project' and was also aired in a 1988 television documentary entitled *The Secret Identity of Jack the Ripper*, hosted by the actor Peter Ustinov. This documentary featured a panel of expert judges, including Special Agents John Douglas and Roy Hazelwood who were working for the Behavioural Science Unit at that time. Their analysis of the case involved a study of the victimology (i.e. profiles of the victims), the doctor's reports of the mutilations and the crime scenes.

The murdered women were prostitutes who were prone to bouts of heavy drinking. These two factors place them in a high risk group. In other words, they were likely to be the victims of violent crime. As previously mentioned, because of their immoral occupation they were easily accessible. Analysis of the medical reports showed, amongst other factors, the likelihood of some anatomical knowledge being possessed by the murderer due to the removal of body organs. This point has been debated for many years. Did the Ripper possess any anatomical knowledge or surgical skill at all? In his book *Mindhunter* (1996) John Douglas wrote, 'As for the supposed medical knowledge needed for the post-mortem mutilation and dissection, this was really nothing but elementary butchery'. I shall be returning to this aspect of the case a little later.

To continue with the profile. The murderer probably lived or worked close to the first crime scene location, which is generally regarded as being Buck's Row. His possible residence was discussed in Professor David Canter's *Criminal Shadows* (1994). Canter, who is an expert in psychological profiling in this country, made an assumption. It is possible to walk round all the murder locations in a couple of hours. If the Ripper left the area in a horse-drawn cab, why was the farthest distance between two crime scenes still within an easy walk? There were many other places in London's East End where the murderer could have stalked potential victims. The assumption is that the crime scenes were well within walking distance of each other because the killer walked to them from where he lived.

The profile includes the terms 'modus operandi' (MO) and 'signature'. These terms need to be explained. The MO refers to what the person does when he commits the crime and it is dynamic; it is learned behaviour. In the Ripper's case the MO would be his selection of victims, his method of approach and the method of the initial attack. MOs can change as the perpetrator gets better at it. The signature is what he has to do to fulfil himself. In other words, what he hopes to achieve. Jack the Ripper's signature was the mutilation and subsequent extraction of the organs.

Another aspect of the case which was taken into consideration were the letters sent to the police. None of them were thought to have been sent by the Ripper, because serial killers of this type do not have the desire to challenge the police in any way.

You might be asking yourself, what if the Ripper was a woman? It is of course a very remote possibility, but female serial lust killers have never been encountered. I think we can safely say that a man was involved with these murders. The Ripper was of white race because the locations of the crimes were in 'white' areas and such crimes are usually intraracial. Serial lust killers are in their mid to late twenties when they commit their first homicide. However, the Ripper was placed in a later age bracket - 28 to 36 years. The FBI have pointed out that age can be difficult to categorise and consequently they do not eliminate potential suspects if the age does not fit the profile. They thought it highly likely that the Whitechapel murderer would have been interviewed by the police on several occasions. Further points from the FBI's Ripper profile are listed below:

1) The mutilations suggest a mentally disturbed individual who was sexually inadequate.
2) The murderer was single. In fact, he probably never married and did not socialise with women at all.
3) He possessed average intelligence and both Douglas and Hazelwood remarked, on Peter Ustinov's programme, that 'Jack' was lucky rather than clever. (This observation is certainly true when one considers the confined murder locations, particularly Mitre Square and the backyard in Hanbury Street. Having said this, he would have *appeared* to be cool and calm after committing the murders.)
4) The murderer came from a broken home and was raised by a dominant female figure who physically (and possibly sexually) abused him.
5) His fantasies escalated with age, probably starting off with thoughts of cruelty and culminating in images of extreme violence and mutilation.
6) If he worked, it would have been in a menial type of job involving little or no contact with people. He would not be involved in a profession.
7) The Ripper was a loner, withdrawn from society. Also, he was nocturnal.
8) He hated and feared women.

In summing up, Roy Hazelwood said the mutilations were the 'key' to understanding the murderer. There was definitely a sexual motive involved; by displacing his victims' organs he neutered or desexed them and they were no longer anything to be feared. In essence, I would say he was removing their womanhood and making them into mere objects. To Jack the Ripper, women were less than human. There is little doubt that he experienced immense relief when removing the organs, possibly sexual relief. He may have experienced spontaneous orgasm when carrying out the ritual - the fantasy he had developed over many years. It was a moment of triumph for him; he was asserting his rightful position in the world as a human being by making a powerful statement at that particular point in time. By being the perpetrator of these ghastly crimes he was attempting to recover his self-esteem, or gain self-esteem which he never had in the first place.

In profiling the Ripper a difficult question to answer is: Was he an organised or disorganised killer? Certain personality traits vary from one group to the other and personality affects the way they behave. This is an important aspect when it comes to deciphering the crime. Some murderers (not just serial killers) leave a crime scene that exhibits both organised and disorganised characteristics. Such categorisation of an offender often helps the police in an investigation. 'Organised' offenders feel superior to everybody else and they often have many sex partners. They like crowds and are not averse to starting punch-ups in bars or driving cars erratically. 'Disorganised' types are under-achievers. They take jobs involving menial tasks and cannot get along with other people. They do not normally live with members of the opposite sex; if they do, it would probably be with a single parent. These people are seen as rejects.

An organised criminal thinks about the crime he is going to commit. It is not carried out on impulse. Also, they tend to hide the victim's body. They will patrol an area, looking for a particular victim type. He may con his chosen prey by creating a situation whereby he has the victim under his control. For example, he might offer them a lift in his car or offer help to a stranded motorist who catches his eye. I have purposely mentioned this scenario because, obviously, there were no cars in 1888 and so we cannot judge what the Ripper might have done in a modern setting. In Whitechapel at that time, the Ripper's high-risk victims were there in abundance and they already knew the quiet spots where they could take their clients for sex. They also knew the police beats and this fact would have worked in the Ripper's favour. So, when using profiling techniques we have to be aware of the 'times' in which he lived.

With the disorganised killer there is no logic in the way he chooses a victim. It could very well be that the victim is a high risk to the offender because he or she may put up a fierce struggle. Because of the circumstances surrounding the Whitechapel crimes – the mode of transport and availability of prostitutes – it is difficult to say, at this point, whether he was organised or not. But let's continue.

A disorganised killer may leave his weapon at the crime scene whereas the opposite type takes his weapon with him after the crime, which is the case with the Ripper. Also, we know that he left the bodies at the places where the murder was carried out. If a body has been moved and hidden then methodical planning has been involved, but we cannot use this premiss to evaluate the Ripper's criminality. There was nowhere to hide the bodies so he simply left them where they were found.

Mutilation after death and disfigurement of a victim's face is a strong indicator of a disorganised personality type. They kill their victims very quickly, as the Ripper did. This type of criminal will also take away body parts as souvenirs. It rather looks as if Jack the Ripper falls into the disorganised category, yet other factors imply the contrary:

a) He left no weapon or clues at the crime scene. With regard to the knife, it was kept sharp.
b) He evaded capture. Luck was certainly on his side, however.
c) The mutilations increased with each crime. This indicates planning.
d) He conversed with the victims without raising fear or alarm. Mary Kelly even took him back to her own room. Furthermore, he had sense enough to know when and where to attack. All in all he was in a high-risk situation, therefore he must have possessed a certain amount of confidence.

There does seem to have been an organised way of thinking in the Ripper's crimes. It has been written that lust killers are organised because they have rehearsed their crimes through fantasy over a long period of time. However, we ought to be careful when trying to make the distinction with Jack the Ripper, because he displayed both organised and disorganised characteristics. This puts him somewhere in the middle.

For a long time I believed that Aaron Kosminski was responsible for the Ripper murders. As previously stated, he was identified at the Seaside Home in Brighton. The unknown witness had, to quote Anderson's own words, 'a good view of the murderer'. Kosminski was sent to Colney Hatch Lunatic Asylum some two years after the murder of Mary Kelly and he was kept there for about three years. By the April of 1891 he was described as incoherent and from then onwards his mental state rapidly deteriorated. During his stay at Colney Hatch nothing came to light to suggest he had homicidal tendencies and he did not exhibit overt signs of aggression to any other patients or members of staff. The same can be said of him during his remaining years at Leavesden Asylum, where he had been signed in as a harmless imbecile. Many Ripper enthusiasts and authors do not see Kosminski as being a likely suspect, merely by virtue of his condition. A pathetic, wandering Jew scouring the gutters for food could not be the same man who was seen with the prostitutes. In any case, those women would not have entertained such a lowly creature. So, is Kosminski out of the frame once and for all? Maybe not. I spoke to Paul Begg, one of the co-authors of the highly recommended *The Complete Jack the Ripper A to Z* (2010), regarding the suspect Kosminski. He said that his condition in 1891 (when a lay witness said he picked food from the gutters and was dirty) may have been considerably different to his condition in 1888. This is a valid point. A newspaper report in 1998 described Peter Sutcliffe (the Yorkshire Ripper) as being a mere shell. He was quiet and showed no signs of aggression. When violent murderers like Sutcliffe are removed from society they often become morose and harmless; their personalities change.

The present situation is this: there is not enough information available for scrutiny concerning Kosminski's guilt or otherwise, and this holds for all the other suspects who have been investigated over the years. I can only say that Kosminski remains a tantalising possibility.

If we can learn anything at all about Jack the Ripper it is to be found when we look at *exactly* what he did to his victims. There have always been theories suggesting he may have been a doctor, medical student or even a slaughterer. The important question is - did he possess any medical knowledge at all? I believe he did, and this aspect is crucial because it leads us to a better understanding of his fantasies. The answer regarding his supposed medical/anatomical knowledge can be found by considering the mutilations of Catharine Eddowes and Mary Kelly. There was a time when I believed the Ripper had no anatomical knowledge whatsoever, and although I am prepared to say he was not a doctor or medical student, I will go as far as to say this: Jack the Ripper knew exactly what he wanted during the time he spent with his victims and he had a good idea of how to go about it. He knew more about female anatomy than the average East Ender. He possessed *some* anatomical knowledge and may have seen operations being carried out. Cathy Eddowes' left kidney had been removed - and in almost total darkness. The human kidney is embedded in fat and loose connective tissue. Once the intestines have been removed you can get at the kidneys, but they are not visible until you cut away the connective tissue. The Ripper was aware of this and he specifically removed the woman's left kidney. Eddowes' uterus had also been removed (as was Annie Chapman's). The uterus is a hollow organ and normally, in women who are not pregnant, it is three or four inches long and two inches wide. Again, this organ was specifically sought by the murderer. There are sexual implications attached to his interest in the uterus - a further point indicating a sexual motive for the crimes; but what about the kidney? I see this as another trophy. It was something he wanted to take home. Both the uterus and the kidney can be stuffed into a large pocket.

When considering Mary Kelly's mutilations I was struck by two things: heart and breast removal. The only way a human heart can be extracted is by cutting through the diaphragm and entering the ribcage from below. There is the implication of anatomical knowledge here; obviously, the murderer knew how to get at the heart. Furthermore, Dr Bond's report states that Mary Kelly's breasts had been removed by more or less circular incisions. This method of removal is very suggestive because surgeons perform mastectomy by using an elliptical incision. I became utterly convinced that Jack the Ripper possessed some degree of anatomical knowledge and had witnessed breast removal in the operating theatre, otherwise why should he remove the victim's breasts in such a fashion? Again, Mary Kelly's heart was missing, and this points to trophy seeking. The heart is pink and rounded and can be fitted into a pocket.

The butchery of Mary Kelly was appalling and her mutilations echo the Ripper's ultimate fantasy. She was desecrated. Her eyes though, were completely untouched and this is a curious feature. They were open as if they could still 'see'. *You are watching me as I take you apart – totally still, totally under my control and within my power...* Could this have been the thought in the Ripper's mind as he cut piece after piece out of the body and mutilated her beyond recognition, in a state of euphoria?

The fact that Mary's breasts were removed using more or less circular incisions is indicative of some surgical knowledge. But did surgeons operate this way in Victorian times? I put this question to N P Warren, FRCS (editor of *Ripperana*) in a letter I wrote in November 1999. The answer was 'yes'. Surgeons in those days did indeed perform breast amputation (on patients with cancer) by using such an incision. It is, of course, possible for the

Ripper to have picked up this information from a textbook, but it is very specific knowledge and you would probably have to go out of your way to obtain such a book. What is perhaps of greater importance is the fact that in those days ordinary members of the public were sometimes allowed access to viewing areas in the operating theatre.

Here we have a definite medical connotation in the mutilations carried out by this man. If the Ripper was not an assistant in the post-mortem room, then certainly he may have had the opportunity to fuel his grotesque fantasies by merely going to the hospital and watching surgeons performing operations. It would have been an ideal situation for the murderer. He could look down innocently, observing the incisions being made, and nobody would have known about the ecstatic vibrations running through his mind. He could easily have picked up his medical knowledge from his observations. I will even go as far as to say this: somewhere along the line Jack the Ripper saw himself in the role of doctor or surgeon because he copied their techniques, even though his method of organ removal was extremely crude. The Ripper was not intelligent or stable enough to have qualified as a doctor or a surgeon but certain aspects of the mutilations, particularly the way in which Mary Kelly's breasts were removed, have led me to the core of his fantasies.

A peculiar feature of his victims' injuries, to my way of thinking, were the strange markings (cuts) on Catharine Eddowes' face. Small incisions were made to both eyelids, and cuts were made on each cheek which, when peeled up, formed a triangular flap. Also, the tip of the nose had been cut off. Why such delicate knife-work? These incisions were made for a specific reason and the murderer took extra time and care to make them. They meant something to him. The Ripper was making her into a clown or perhaps a doll by altering her appearance. It was his way of making her into a non-person and this is a reflection of his childhood fantasies.

American serial killer Ted Bundy spoke of his female victims as being 'images'; he also referred to them as 'dolls'. Another serial killer, Edmund Kemper, harboured fantasies of sadistic acts of torturing women and brutalising female corpses. He spoke about murdering women to stop them rejecting him as a man. He thought of his victims as dolls and said he was carrying out his fantasies - when in the act of murder - with *living human dolls*. If we can accept this as being true for the Ripper then we are beginning to understand him better than ever before.

Is it not possible, therefore, that a very young Jack the Ripper cut up dolls for his own gratification? This action would be similar to the murderer who went from cutting the heads of his sister's dolls to beheading his victims in later life.

My understanding of the Ripper's mind is this:

'Jack' had sexual fantasies involving mutilation and organ removal. He was interested in certain aspects of surgery as a means of destroying or neutering women, and this would constitute the springboard from which his enraged feelings could be satiated. This man may well have watched operations being performed. He was fixated on female anatomy, particularly sexual organs. With respect to his last victim, his acts of butchery and extensive organ removal were attempts to completely annihilate her; to make her into nothing by taking everything away. During the mutilation of Mary Kelly, the organs that he removed were, in a sense, an integral part of what he was doing. The 'parts' were equally as important as the 'whole' because he did not throw the body parts about the room; they were all kept close to the body. In fact some organs were placed under his victim's head and on the bedside table so as not to obliterate the spectacle of his appalling actions. This was *his* surgical work and he was saying, 'Look what I have done'. His fantasies involving dolls/clowns is clearly reflected in the markings on Cathy Eddowes' face (a clown's face in effect). To him she became a doll. She was no longer human.

Jack the Ripper possessed an unbelievable hatred towards women and I think there is another clue which is pertinent to his status in life. During his reign of terror I think it would have been quite feasible for him to lure a woman back to his home, especially the likes of Nichols and Chapman, who were in need of shelter. In the privacy of his home the Ripper could commit murder, possibly have sex with the corpse and then proceed to mutilate and dismember it. He did not do this, not as far as we know. The reason why this couldn't happen was because he was living with somebody else. He had to kill and mutilate the victim at her preferred location. The Ripper's ultimate desire was to completely destroy a female body and remove whatever he could from within. Unfortunately, he succeeded.

By now you might be wondering who I think Jack the Ripper was. This question cannot be answered with any degree of certainty and with each and every suspect that has come our way there is always something that doesn't quite fit. The one person who exhibits some of the traits assigned to the Ripper and who fits the profile in many ways is Thomas Cutbush. This man has never featured as a strong candidate for the role of the Ripper and he is not as well known as Kosminski, Tumblety or Maybrick, but his lifestyle and disposition make him a suspect who deserves to be scrutinised. In the light of what we know about serial killers today, Thomas Cutbush should be amongst the top suspects - but he isn't! At this point in time he is my *preferred* suspect. He is featured in A P Wolf's *Jack the Myth* (1993), and has, in recent years, come to the attention of serious students of the case, as well as experts.

In his memoranda, Sir Melville Macnaghten wrote about three men - Druitt, Kosminski and Ostrog - who (in his opinion) were more likely to have committed the murders than Cutbush. Details of Michael Ostrog's life show him to have been a charlatan, a thief and a swindler. He was in his mid-fifties at the time of the Whitechapel murders and Macnaghten described him as a mad Russian doctor who carried surgical knives and was cruel to women. Ostrog was described as a homicidal maniac, but his life of deceit and thieving does not, to my mind, make him a strong suspect. Having said this, his whereabouts at the time of the Ripper murders were unknown. Apparently, he was in Paris during the crime period so this takes him out of the frame completely.

Aaron Kosminski has been discussed in some detail already and the crucial information regarding him is missing. It would be unwise to discount him altogether. As for Druitt - well, the medical connections are certainly there but there is nothing of substance to connect him in any way to the murders in Whitechapel; and the same applies to Cutbush. However, when we look at the personality and habits of Cutbush we see a person who had all the requisites that make him a plausible candidate for this series of murders.

Thomas Hayne Cutbush worked in the East End in 1888, canvassing for a business directory. He suddenly abandoned his work and took to roaming the streets late at night. His behaviour became increasingly strange, so much so that on 5 March 1891 he was detained at St Saviour's Workhouse as it was thought he was a lunatic. (Indeed his mother Kate and aunt Clara were so concerned about his mental state they decided to have him examined by a doctor.) Within hours he had escaped from the workhouse. On 7 March he stabbed Florence Grace Johnson in the bottom, and the next day he attempted to stab Isabella Fraser Anderson. Both attacks occurred in Kennington, an area of South London. On 9 March, he was arrested and charged with malicious wounding. Cutbush was judged to be criminally insane and spent the rest of his life in Broadmoor, where he died in 1903.

Superintendent Charles Henry Cutbush was, allegedly, Thomas's uncle and was in charge of Supplies and Pay at Scotland Yard. In 1896, after suffering several years of depression and insomnia, he committed suicide by shooting himself. A P Wolf suggests the possibility of the superintendent's depression being partly due to his nephew's activities.

In Macnaghten's mind it seemed highly improbable for the Ripper to have stopped his crimes in November 1888 and then to 'recommence operations by merely prodding a girl behind some two years and four months afterwards'. In view of this statement it seems unlikely for Cutbush to have been involved in the Whitechapel killings. Wolf also agrees that Macnaghten's statement seems reasonable enough. In his book he describes behaviour changes in other murderers in support of his conviction that a murderer does not necessarily have to go on killing. Wolf suggests the possibility of a conspiracy of silence regarding Cutbush and the Ripper murders. Could it be that Macnaghten was indeed defending not only Thomas Cutbush but also his own police department? It was an embarrassment for a senior officer's nephew to be arrested for attacking women with a knife, but the slightest suggestion that he could have been Jack the Ripper would surely have caused problems for Scotland Yard. I do not intend to go into Wolf's theory in any more detail but I see it as being very plausible. All the relevant information implicating Cutbush with the murders appeared in extensive articles in the *Sun* newspaper for the dates 13 to 19 February 1894.

Wolf had already gathered some material from the aforementioned articles which he used for his book *Jack the Myth*, but I decided to consult them for myself.

Obviously, certain reporters of the day had spent many hours investigating the life of Thomas Cutbush. I made notes including the details which I considered were important for assessing the possibility of this man being the Ripper. Wolf contributed a chapter for *The Mammoth Book of Jack the Ripper*. Cutbush, he wrote, was the only suspect to be named at the actual time of the killings. The files on the Ripper case were officially closed in 1892. Interestingly, the police were still making enquiries into the Ripper murders long after 1888, so they must have believed he was still at large. As we know, Cutbush was arrested in 1891. Putting all of this to one side, let's have a look at the man himself.

The *Sun* article states whatever was written about their suspect could be backed up with documentary proof. Cutbush lived with his mother and aunt in Albert Street, Kennington. He was employed in Whitechapel. Apparently, his parents were separated when he was young and the father had ill-treated the mother. The preamble to the main report refers to the finding of diagrams in Cutbush's rooms. They were drawings of women, mutilated in the same way as the actual Whitechapel victims. This man studied anatomy almost exclusively and he was obsessed with a certain doctor whom he wanted to kill. The report also states that he had seized his mother or aunt by the throat and produced a large knife with the intention of cutting her throat. He was incoherent at times, whilst on other occasions he spoke naturally. Cutbush apparently always entered and left his home by climbing over the back wall.

The newspaper article then goes on to the investigation made by two *Sun* representatives. They visited Broadmoor asylum in an attempt to come face to face with Thomas Hayne Cutbush.

When he was brought into the room, where the Medical Superintendent and representatives were waiting, he kept silent and bared his chest as if ready to be examined. The man's eyes were dull and expressionless; apparently he was in the final stages of lunacy. (At this time Cutbush had spent three years at the asylum.) Without warning, the pathetic creature grabbed his own throat and threw back his head, placing the right hand at the base of his skull. There was no explanation for this irrational display. Cutbush, it was learned, could eat his meals with either his right or his left hand. The *Sun* article mentions this as being another link in the chain of evidence. (The killer was thought to be left-handed.)

There is more interesting information about this man. In 1891 he asked a work associate if he could borrow a pistol in order to shoot a certain doctor, and a legal adviser told a story of how Cutbush wanted him to prosecute a doctor who had been poisoning him. Thomas Cutbush attached unwarranted suspicion to doctors because they were allowed to dispense their own prescriptions.

The articles from the *Sun* newspaper are very long and make for tedious reading in parts. Below, I have summarised the most important points about Cutbush.

1) He could never hold a job down for long. He had a history of violence plus homicidal tendencies.
2) When questioned about his anatomical drawings he said he was studying for the medical profession. (This ties in with my belief that the Ripper was fixated with doctors or surgeons.)
3) Cutbush worked in the East End and therefore knew the area.
4) A police inspector found wet waistcoats and coats stuffed up the chimney in his room. The sleeves of the coats smelled of turpentine.

5) One of his so-called anatomical drawings showed the trunk of a woman with the walls opened up and revealing the intestines.

The fact that Cutbush was arrested for stabbing women in the bottom does not necessarily mean he was incapable of ferocious murder. I shall return to this aspect a little later. His delusions about being poisoned are a significant aspect of his personality because other murderers have suffered from the same disorder. Wolf draws parallels between Cutbush and the serial killer Richard Chase, who was operating in the 1970s and became known as 'The Vampire of Sacramento'. Chase was, amongst other things, obsessed by the idea that he was being poisoned.

There are certain comparisons to be made between Cutbush and a murderer named Robert Napper. In 1993, Samantha Bissett and her young daughter were murdered in their flat in Plumstead, London. After the mother had been killed, her attacker opened her stomach and pulled back the ribcage to reveal the internal organs. Napper, who was twenty-eight at the time, was eventually caught. The police found his notes and diaries, which told of his arguments with other people and about his fears that his food was being doctored. Amongst his belongings detectives found a photocopy of a diagram showing the internal parts of a torso. If Thomas Cutbush was a serial killer, then his delusion about being poisoned is certainly interesting in the light of what we know about Chase and Napper.

The *Sun* also reported an incident which I find extremely interesting. It is worth mentioning that the incident was later confirmed by the aunt in a statement she gave for *Lloyd's Weekly News*. As previously mentioned, in early March 1891 Cutbush's mother and aunt were so concerned about his mental condition that they sought to have him examined by doctors at St Saviour's Infirmary. Initially, he was taken to St Saviour's Workhouse but somehow managed to escape, scantily clad, by climbing a 12ft-high wall. He entered a house close by and stole clothes, a hat and some boots. After midnight he arrived home, had a wash, and changed his clothes. He left home early the following morning. When night came he was in Camden Town where he chanced upon a young man and his lady friend. Cutbush was in an anxious and delusional state, though he was described as quite the gentleman in manner and dress. He rambled on about being wanted on a serious charge: 'You must know that they say I am Jack the Ripper, but I am not, though all their insides are open and their bowels are all out. I am a medical man, you know, but not Jack the Ripper – you must not think I am; but they do and they are after me, and the runners are after me, for they want the £500 which is offered for my capture, and I have only been cutting up girls and laying them out.'

It is also interesting to note that in April 1891 a lengthy article was published in *Lloyd's Weekly News* about the Cutbush case. It gave credence to the notion that a certain section of the police, as well as some journalists, believed Cutbush might have been the Ripper.

Cutbush appeared to be insane in 1891 and was not allowed to plead in court. The instructions of his defence solicitor mentioned that he was Jack the Ripper. Being unable to plead, he was spared the necessity of all defence and did not have to stand in the dock to answer any charges regarding his attack on women - or the Ripper murders.

Is it conceivable that in 1891 his illness had ravaged him so much that he was reduced to merely prodding women in the backside?

In November 2008 the Broadmoor files on Thomas Cutush were made available for public viewing. For me, this was an opportunity to delve deeper into the mind of this strange individual. Did the files contain crucial information that would enable me to solve the perplexing mystery of the Ripper's identity? It was some time before I decided to contact the Berkshire Record Office. The archivist sent me photocopies of the relevant papers. Unfortunately, some of the material was illegible, but there was enough readable information to enable me to shed more light on the man's character.

He was born on 29 June 1866. He was unmarried and belonged to the Church of England. A description of him for April 1891 (when he was admitted from Holloway prison) is contained within the files: age, 26 years (in fact he would have been 24); height, 5 feet 9½ inches; weight, 9 stones 6½ pounds; hair, black; whiskers, black (very short); eyes, dark blue (very sharp); complexion, dark; build, slight; features, thin.

The file dated 21 April gives some interesting information about him. It says, although he was found to be insane upon arraignment, his education is 'good' and his habits 'temperate.' His illness is thought to have been due to over-study. We learn from the files that he was violent and destructive when living with his mother and aunt. There were times when he thought he was being poisoned, and would only accept food from his mother. In 1891 a memorandum was written saying, 'he has been strange for about two years.'

During his time in the asylum he refused meals, and there are definite indications that he thought his food was poisoned. On one particular occasion he struck a fellow inmate a violent blow to the face. This was done without any provocation.

A letter to a certain Mr Gardner describes how a night attendant named Mr Bailey was listening outside Cutbush's window one night. Cutbush was using disgusting and threatening language, and Mr Bailey heard him say that if he had a knife *suitable for the job* (author's emphasis) he would rip up the attendants or anyone else that upset him. On a previous occasion he told an attendant at dinner time that he would stick a knife in any of them if he had to. I find it interesting, and suggestive, in that he used the word 'suitable.' Obviously, he was thinking not about any old knife but one that could do the job efficiently. We can say for certain that he possessed violent thoughts and destructive emotions. On another occasion he received a visit from his mother and aunt. When his mother offered him a kiss he tried to bite her face and then started to swear at them. From this we can infer that he had no capacity for a loving relationship with them, nor, perhaps, with any other female. In the months following this incident his physical condition deteriorated. On 5 July 1903 he died; the cause was given as chronic kidney disease.

In summing up, I would say that Thomas Cutbush was probably suffering from paranoid schizophrenia. He could have been in the Whitechapel area at the time of the murders, with the intent of cutting up women. He was strong, and agile enough to make a fast kill and then exit the scene with rapid speed. In 1888 he would have appeared fairly well-dressed, mild mannered – certainly not the evil-looking villain as portrayed in the newspapers. I believe he was very cunning, and would change his appearance by wearing different types of clothing. If the *Sun* newspaper reports are anything to go by – bearing in mind that the contents of the Broadmoor files substantiate the reports – then the evidence against him, though circumstantial, is compelling. Consider again his interest in medical studies, the mutilation drawings (one of which was produced at his trial), his nocturnal ramblings, his violent nature, and the clothes stuffed up the chimney. All of this, together with the information about his behaviour at Broadmoor, makes this man an extremely important suspect. In my opinion, Thomas Hayne Cutbush is a credible contender for this ghastly series of murders; I would even go as far as to say he is almost perfect for the mantle of Jack the Ripper. If senior officers had any suspicions at all regarding Cutbush and the Ripper crimes, then it seems likely they would wish to prevent the matter from being made public *if* he was related to Superintendent Charles Henry Cutbush. We have to bear in mind that the Macnaghten Memoranda was kept in the Metropolitan Police Files and was not intended to become public knowledge. Remember, Macnaghten wrote about three men, any one of whom would have been more likely to have perpetrated the crimes than Cutbush. There does not appear to be any real concern over the *Sun* newspaper allegations and, in fact, one might say that Macnaghten was de-emphasizing the contents of the report. Was this because he knew more than he was prepared to admit? Whatever the reason, something certainly prompted him to put his thoughts down on paper.

When considering the Ripper's rudimentary surgical and anatomical knowledge – as evinced by the kidney, heart and breast removal – I was struck by the fact that the murder of Poly Nichols was committed close to the London Hospital. This could be more than a coincidence. Serial killers tend to commit their first crime in areas where they feel comfortable: areas where they live, work or visit. I wondered if the murderer could have observed operations being carried out at the hospital in 1888? Well, the archives department at what is now The Royal London Hospital in Whitechapel do not have a register of operations performed at the Hospital for 1888, but they do have the Surgery Beadle's register of operations which were performed in 1894. The total number of operations for that year was 1,777. About one dozen of those operations involved removal of the breast and there were approximately twenty-five kidney operations (although in many cases this did not involve its removal). The Trust Archivist informed me that, in his opinion, it was not unusual for members of the public to view operations taking place in the eighteenth century, though it would have been more unusual for this to take place by the late nineteenth century. In the latter instance admission would probably have been at the discretion of the Surgery Beadle who was, at that time, Josiah Rampley. Unfortunately, the earliest theatre visitors book contained in the London Hospital Archives dates from 1930-1954.

Bearing all of this in mind, there is a good chance that the murderer may have been able to gain access to the operating theatre at the London Hospital in 1888 or before. I feel that there might be some sort of connection between the Ripper and the London Hospital. His elementary anatomical knowledge is the reason why many people believe him to have been a doctor or a surgeon. It is this belief, along with his anonymity, that has transformed the real killer into the almost mythical figure that he has become.

My researches have, I am sure, brought us a little closer to understanding the mind of the man who became known as Jack the Ripper. It is a chilling name and the mystery of his identity will always remain so. If Thomas Cutbush was the murderer then the story ends here. Unfortunately – and maybe even thankfully – I am not in a position to make such a statement. To be perfectly honest, there is a nagging doubt in the back of my mind that of all the suspects mentioned since the execution of the Whitechapel murders up until the present time, the name 'Jack the Ripper' cannot be assigned to any of them.

The murderer's name doesn't really matter now; it's the fascination with the mystery surrounding his identity that counts for most of us.

If we can ever put a name to this mysterious Victorian character, this elusive gaslight fiend, then surely we cannot hope to be enlightened any more than we already are.

The real murderer has long since vanished into the mists of time, along with his hidden violent fantasies. Desperate and alone, he has escaped forever from a world in which he did not belong. He has emerged with his cloak, top hat and Gladstone bag. He is the 'other' Jack the Ripper whom we have created - and we simply cannot afford to lose him. Perhaps the mystery is, after all, better than the truth.

Select Bibliography

Abrahamsen, Dr David, *Murder and Madness: The Secret Life of Jack the Ripper*, Donald I. Fine Inc., 1992

The Murdering Mind, Harper and Row, 1975

Ball, Pamela, *Jack the Ripper: A Psychic Investigation*, Arcturus, 1998

Baring-Gould, W. S., *Sherlock Holmes of Baker Street*, Popular Library, 1963

Barker, Richard, *The Fatal Caress*, New York, Duell, Sloan and Pearce, 1947

Barnard, Allan, [ed.], *The Harlot Killer*, Dodd, Mead and Co., 1953

Beadle, William, *Jack the Ripper: Anatomy of a Myth*, Wat Tyler Books, 1995

Begg, Paul, *Jack the Ripper: The Uncensored Facts*, Robson Books, 1988

Begg, Paul, Fido, Marin, and Skinner, Keith, and Fido, *The Jack the Ripper A* to Z, Headline, 1996

The Jack the Ripper A to Z, John Blake Publishing Ltd, 2010

Bloch, Robert, *The Night of the Ripper*, Robert Hale, 1986

Booth, Martin, *The Doctor, the Detective and Arthur Conan Doyle*, Hodder and Stroughton, 1997

Canter, Professor David, *Criminal Shadows*, Harper Collins, 1994

Caputi, Jane, *The Age of Sex Crime*, Women's Press Ltd., 1988

Casper, Susan and Dozois, Gardner, [ed.], *Jack the Ripper*, Futura, 1988

Cornwell, Patricia, *Portrait of a Killer: Jack the Ripper Case Close*, Little, Brown,2002

Dibdin, Michael, *The Last Sherlock Holmes Story*, Sphere Books, 1980

Douglas, John and Olshaker, Mark, *Mindhunter*, William Heinemann, 1996

Evans, Stewart P, and Gainey, Paul, *The Lodger: The Arrest and Escape of Jack the Ripper*, Century, 1995

Evans, Stewart P, and Skinner Keith, *The Ultimate Jack the Ripper Sourcebook*, Constable & Robinson Ltd., 2000

Farson, Daniel, *Jack the Ripper*, Sphere Books, 1973

Feldman, Paul, *Jack the Ripper: The Final Chapter*, Virgin Books, 1997

Fido, Martin, *The Crimes, Detection and Death of Jack the Ripper*, Weidenfeld and Nicholson, 1987

Green, Richard Lancelyn, *The Uncollected Sherlock Holmes*, (compilation), Penguin, 1983

Halstead, Dr Dennis Gratwick, *Doctor in the Nineties*, Johnson, 1959

Harris, Melvin, *The True Face of Jack the Ripper*, Michael O'Mara, 1994

Harrison, Shirley, *The Diary of Jack the Ripper*, Smith Gryphon, 1993

Hinton, Bob, *From Hell… The Jack the Ripper Mystery*, Old Bakehouse Publications, 1998

Hirschfeld, Dr Magnus, *Sexual Anomalies and Perversions*, second edition, Encyclopedic Press, 1952

Holmes, Robert M, and Holmes, Stephen T, *Serial Murder*, Sage Publications, 1998

Hutchinson, Philip, *The Jack the Ripper Location Photographs*, Amberley Publishing Plc., 2009

Knight, Stephen, *Jack the Ripper: The Final Solution*, Harrap and Co., 1976

London, Jack, *People of the Abyss*, Journeyman Press, 1992

Lowndes, Marie Belloc, *The Lodger*, New English Library, 1966

Marriott, Trevor, *Jack the Ripper: The 21st Century Investigation*, John Blake Publishing Ltd., 2007

Matters, Leonard, *The Mystery of Jack the Ripper*, Hutchinson, 1929

McCormick, Donald, *The Identity of Jack the Ripper*, Arrow Books, 1971

Mitchelson, Austin, *The Baker Street Irregular: The Unauthorised Biography of Sherlock Holmes*, Ian Henry, 1944

Norris, Joel, *Serial Killers*, Senate, 1997

Odell, Robin, *Jack the Ripper in Fact and Fiction*, Mayflower, 1966

O'Donnell, Kevin, *The Jack the Ripper Whitechapel Murders*, Ten Bells Publishing, 1997

Palmer, Scott, *Jack the Ripper: A Reference Guide*, Scarecrow Press, 1995

Parry, Michael, [ed.], *Jack the Knife*, Mayflower Books, 1975

Queen, Ellery, *A Study In Terror*, Lancer Books, New York, 1966

Ressler, Robert K., *Whoever Fights Monsters*, Pocket Books, 1993

Rumbelow, Donald, *The Complete Jack the Ripper,* W. H. Allen, 1975

Sinclair, Robert, *East London*, Robert Hale, 1950

Smith, Terrence Lore, *Yours Truly, From Hell,* Grafton Books, 1988

Smyth, Frank, *Cause of Death: The Story of Forensic Science,* Orbis, 1980

Steinbrunner, Chris, and Michaels, Norman, *The Films of Sherlock Holmes*, Carol Publishing, 1991

Stewart, William, *Jack the Ripper: A New Theory,* Quality Press, 1939

Sugden, Philip, *The Complete History of Jack the Ripper,* Robinson, 1994

Thomson, Sir Basil, *The Story of Scotland Yard,* Grayson and Grayson, 1935

Trow, M. J., *Jack the Ripper: Quest for a Killer*, Wharncliffe True Crime, 2009

Tully, James, *The Secret of Prisoner 1167: Was This Man Jack the Ripper?,* Robinson, 1997

Turnbull, Peter, *The Killer Who Never Was,* Clark Lawrence Publishers, 1996

Underwood, Peter, *Jack the Ripper: One Hundred Years of Mystery,* Javelin, 1988

West, Pamela, *Yours Truly, Jack the Ripper,* Dell Publishing, 1987

West, Paul, *The Women of Whitechapel and Jack the Ripper,* Random House, 1991

Wilding, John, *Jack the Ripper Revealed*, Constable, 1993

Wilson, Colin, and Seaman, Donald, *The Serial Killers,* Virgin, 1991

Wolf, A. P., *Jack the Myth,* Robert Hale, 1993

Woodhall, Edwin T., *Jack the Ripper or When London Walked in Terror,* Mellifont Press Ltd., 1937

Other Sources

'The Hunt for Jack the Ripper' (from the memoirs of ex-Chief Inspector Walter Dew), facsimile edition, n.d.

Robinson, Tom, 'The Whitechapel Horrors', Daisy Bank Publishing, Circa 1920s, facsimile edition, n.d.

'The Whitechapel Atrocities: Arrest of a Newspaper Reporter', Woodford Fawcett and Co., 1888, facsimile edition, n.d.

The American Journal of Forensic Medicine and Pathology, 1981

British Archaeology, no. 48, October 1999

The Independent On Sunday, 31 January 1999

Infamous Murderers, Treasure Press, 1985

Murder Most Foul, no. 22, October 1996

Ripperana, Quarterly journal, editor, N. P. Warren, FRCS, October 1996

'Was Gladstone Jack the Ripper?' article by Graham Norton, *Queen* magazine, September 1970

Weekly World News, July 1996

The Fifty Most Amazing Crimes of the Last 100 Years, Odhams (London), 1936

Archer, Rodney and Jones, Powell, *The Harlots Curse*, London, Preston Editions, 1990

Pemberton, Ron and De Marne, Denis, *Jack the Ripper – A Musical Play*, Samuel French, 1976

The *Sun*, London 13, 14, 15, 16, 17, 18 and 19 February 1894